SUPER HOROSCOPE
LEO
2007
JULY 21 – AUGUST 21

BERKLEY BOOKS, NEW YORK

THE BERKLEY PUBLISHING GROUP
Published by the Penguin Group
Penguin Group (USA) Inc.
375 Hudson Street, New York, New York 10014, USA
Penguin Group (Canada), 90 Eglinton Avenue East, Suite 700, Toronto, Ontario M4P 2Y3, Canada
(a division of Pearson Penguin Canada Inc.)
Penguin Books Ltd., 80 Strand, London WC2R 0RL, England
Penguin Group Ireland, 25 St. Stephen's Green, Dublin 2, Ireland (a division of Penguin Books Ltd.)
Penguin Group (Australia), 250 Camberwell Road, Camberwell, Victoria 3124, Australia
(a division of Pearson Australia Group Pty. Ltd.)
Penguin Books India Pvt. Ltd., 11 Community Centre, Panchsheel Park, New Delhi—110 017, India
Penguin Group (NZ), Cnr. Airborne and Rosedale Roads, Albany, Auckland 1310, New Zealand
(a division of Pearson New Zealand Ltd.)
Penguin Books (South Africa) (Pty.) Ltd., 24 Sturdee Avenue, Rosebank, Johannesburg 2196,
South Africa

Penguin Books Ltd., Registered Offices: 80 Strand, London WC2R 0RL, England

2007 SUPER HOROSCOPE LEO

The publishers regret that they cannot answer individual letters requesting personal horoscope information.

Copyright © 1974, 1978, 1979, 1980, 1981, 1982 by Grosset & Dunlap, Inc.

Copyright © 1983, 1984 by Charter Communications, Inc.

Copyright © 1985, 1986, 1987, 1988, 1989, 1990, 1991, 1992, 1993, 1994, 1995, 1996, 1997, 1998, 1999, 2000, 2001, 2002, 2003, 2004, 2005, 2006 by The Berkley Publishing Group.

Cover design by Steven Ferlauto.

All rights reserved.
No part of this book may be reproduced, scanned, or distributed in any printed or electronic form without permission. Please do not participate in or encourage piracy of copyrighted materials in violation of the author's rights. Purchase only authorized editions.
BERKLEY is a registered trademark of Penguin Group (USA) Inc.
The "B" design is a trademark belonging to Penguin Group (USA) Inc.

PRINTING HISTORY
Berkley trade paperback edition / July 2006

Berkley trade paperback ISBN: 0-425-20931-8

Library of Congress Cataloging-in-Publication Data

ISSN: 1535-8968

PRINTED IN THE UNITED STATES OF AMERICA

10 9 8 7 6 5 4 3 2 1

CONTENTS

THE CUSP-BORN LEO 4
   The Cusps of Leo 5
THE ASCENDANT: LEO RISING 6
   Rising Signs for Leo 8
THE PLACE OF ASTROLOGY IN TODAY'S WORLD 10
   Astrology and Relationships 10
   The Challenge of Love 11
   Astrology and Science 12
   Know Thyself—Why? 14
WHAT IS A HOROSCOPE? 16
   The Zodiac 16
   The Sun Sign and the Cusp 17
   The Rising Sign and the Zodiacal Houses 17
   The Planets in the Houses 20
   How To Use These Predictions 21
HISTORY OF ASTROLOGY 22
ASTROLOGICAL BRIDGE TO THE 21st CENTURY 28
THE SIGNS OF THE ZODIAC 31
   Dominant Characteristics 31
   Sun Sign Personalities 56
   Key Words 58
   The Elements and Qualities of the Signs 59
THE PLANETS OF THE SOLAR SYSTEM 67
   The Planets and the Signs They Rule 67
   Characteristics of the Planets 68
THE MOON IN EACH SIGN 78
MOON TABLES 85
   Time Conversions 85
   Moon Sign Dates for 2007 86
   Moon Phases for 2007 90
   Fishing Guide for 2007 90
   Planting Guide for 2007 91
   Moon's Influence Over Plants 91
   Moon's Influence Over Health and Daily Affairs 92
LEO 93
   Character Analysis 94
   Love and Marriage 100
LEO LUCKY NUMBERS FOR 2007 128
LEO YEARLY FORECAST FOR 2007 129
LEO DAILY FORECAST FOR 2007 133
   November and December Daily Forecasts for 2006 231

THE CUSP-BORN LEO

Are you *really* a Leo? If your birthday falls during the fourth week of July, at the beginning of Leo, will you still retain the traits of Cancer, the sign of the Zodiac before Leo? And what if you were born late in August—are you more Virgo than Leo? Many people born at the edge, or cusp, of a sign have difficulty determining exactly what sign they are. If you are one of these people, here's how you can figure it out, once and for all.

Consult the cusp table on the facing page, then locate the year of your birth. The table will tell you the precise days on which the Sun entered and left your sign for the year of your birth. In that way you can determine if you are a true Leo—or whether you are a Cancer or Virgo—according to the variations in cusp dates from year to year (see also page 17).

If you were born at the beginning or end of Leo, yours is a lifetime reflecting a process of subtle transformation. Your life on Earth will symbolize a significant change in consciousness, for you are either about to enter a whole new way of living or are leaving one behind.

If you are a Leo, born during the fourth week of July, you may want to read the horoscope book for Cancer as well as Leo. Cancer holds the keys to many of your secret uncertainties and deep-rooted problems, and your secret needs and wishes. You are the spirit of independence and creativity, or want to be. Yet through Cancer you reveal your deep, but often hidden, need to have strong ties. You may be trying to leave dependencies behind, yet you find yourself drawn again and again to the past or to family responsibilities.

You reflect the birth of a new sign, a ripe, whole person, fully able to tap and realize all your potentials for love and creativity.

If you were born after the third week of August, you may want to read the horoscope book for Virgo as well, for through Virgo you learn to put all your talents as a lover or creator to work. Your love for life is infectious, and your zest and sunny disposition are an inspiration to everyone around you. You are capable of seriousness, discipline, and great diligence.

You are a lover—ardent, passionate, and determined that love will not elude you. Though you may try to avoid it, you will find yourself in work, health, or duty situations that demand less emotion and more mind. You are not afraid of taking a gamble and are reluctant to give up your love of enjoyment for work or studies. You can blend professionalism and propriety in perfect amounts. You are the natural mixture of creativity and discipline, able to feel and to analyze. You symbolize the warmth and fullness of a late summer day, a natural ripeness and maturity that is mellow and comfortable to be near.

THE CUSPS OF LEO

DATES SUN ENTERS LEO (LEAVES CANCER)

July 23 every year from 1900 to 2010, except for the following:

		July 22				
1928	1953	1968	1981	1992	2001	2010
32	56	69	84	93	2002	
36	57	72	85	94	2004	
40	60	73	86	96	2005	
44	61	76	88	97	2006	
48	64	77	89	98	2008	
52	65	80	90	2000	2009	

DATES SUN LEAVES LEO (ENTERS VIRGO)

August 23 every year from 1900 to 2010, except for the following:

August 22				August 24	
1960	1980	1992	2001	1903	1919
64	84	93	2004	07	23
68	88	96	2005	11	27
72	89	97	2008	15	
76		2000	2009		

THE ASCENDANT: LEO RISING

Could you be a "double" Leo? That is, could you have Leo as your Rising sign as well as your Sun sign? The tables on pages 8–9 will tell you Leos what your Rising sign happens to be. Just find the hour of your birth, then find the day of your birth, and you will see which sign of the Zodiac is your Ascendant, as the Rising sign is called. The Ascendant is called that because it is the sign rising on the eastern horizon at the time of your birth. For a more detailed discussion of the Rising sign and the twelve houses of the Zodiac, see pages 17–20.

The Ascendant, or Rising sign, is placed on the 1st house in a horoscope, of which there are twelve houses. The 1st house represents your response to the environment—your unique response. Call it identity, personality, ego, self-image, facade, come-on, body-mind-spirit—whatever term best conveys to you the meaning of the you that acts and reacts in the world. It is a you that is always changing, discovering a new you. Your identity started with birth and early environment, over which you had little conscious control, and continues to experience, to adjust, to express itself. The 1st house also represents how others see you. Has anyone ever guessed your sign to be your Rising sign? People may respond to that personality, that facade, that body type governed by your Rising sign.

Your Ascendant, or Rising sign, modifies your basic Sun sign personality, and it affects the way you act out the daily predictions for your Sun sign. If your Rising sign indeed is Leo, what follows is a description of its effect on your horoscope. If your Rising sign is not Leo, but some other sign of the Zodiac, you may wish to read the horoscope book for that sign as well.

With Leo on the Ascendant, that is, in the 1st house, the planet that rules Leo is therefore in the 1st house. That planet is the Sun. Here it may give you a special robustness—in appearance, in health, in spirit, in action—that you can count on long after your normal energy reserves have dried up. On the negative side, the Sun here may give you an overdose of pride or insolence. Such pride could make you quick to resent or retaliate when reason instead should be the response.

Leo in the 1st house accentuates every Leo trait, for the Rising sign has a strong influence in your horoscope. A flair for the dramatic will be especially evident in the fabric of your life. You like managing people and events as long as you can play center stage, or at least weave a powerful character part, for much of the time. You could create intrigue if it provides an opportunity for you to take a leading role. However much you like pulling strings, though, your frank and generous disposition rises above petty disputes. You abhor superficial alliances or cliques of any sort.

There may also be drama in your personal appearance and in your possessions and surroundings. You have been known to adorn yourself and your environment as much, maybe sometimes more, for the effect it will create as for the comfort it will give you and others. Your appearance itself, whether natural or affected, may well run to the true Leo type: high coloring, proud head, bold stance. You can use physical gestures as signals to people—to lure, to persuade, to threaten. And because love, especially to be loved, is a fundament of your ego, your body language acts instinctively to attract people to you.

Your search for identity will never be a solitary, introspective one. Public appreciation and power are important to you. You need constant interaction with and approval from people. You are likely to find the most satisfying ties with groups whose goals are humanitarian and ideological, whether the groups are social or political or educational. But before you do, you may discover in youth and early adulthood many facets of yourself through creations that are not so tightly bound to an organized group. And it is imperative for you to create—a work of art, a child, an intrigue, a love affair, a partnership, a principle.

Your need for people may reflect an inner insecurity. That self-image, which you experience as constantly changing, may not be actualized until you see it mirrored in people's responses; a positive one reinforces your natural enthusiasm, a negative one may induce self-pity. Your need for creation may also be tied to the building of an ego. You seek success, and are very likely to get your lion's share of it in your lifetime, through what you do, not through what you are. For what you do allows you to know and then to be who you are. You expect your creations and your things to bestow honor upon you; they are not merely natural or spontaneous expressions.

Above all, love and loyalty are the key words through which you with Leo Rising seek to root yourself in your environment. Love and loyalty motivate your simplest act, your grandest attempt. They, too, can be the cause of pain and loss. You are happiest when you love and are loved in return.

RISING SIGNS FOR LEO

Hour of Birth*	Day of Birth		
	July 22–27	July 28–August 1	August 2–6
Midnight	Taurus	Taurus	Gemini
1 AM	Gemini	Gemini	Gemini
2 AM	Gemini	Gemini	Cancer
3 AM	Cancer	Cancer	Cancer
4 AM	Cancer	Cancer	Cancer
5 AM	Leo	Leo	Leo
6 AM	Leo	Leo	Leo
7 AM	Leo	Leo; Virgo 8/1	Virgo
8 AM	Virgo	Virgo	Virgo
9 AM	Virgo	Virgo	Virgo
10 AM	Libra	Libra	Libra
11 AM	Libra	Libra	Libra
Noon	Libra	Libra; Scorpio 7/30	Scorpio
1 PM	Scorpio	Scorpio	Scorpio
2 PM	Scorpio	Scorpio	Scorpio
3 PM	Sagittarius	Sagittarius	Sagittarius
4 PM	Sagittarius	Sagittarius	Sagittarius
5 PM	Sagittarius	Capricorn	Capricorn
6 PM	Capricorn	Capricorn	Capricorn
7 PM	Capricorn; Aquarius 7/26	Aquarius	Aquarius
8 PM	Aquarius	Aquarius	Aquarius; Pisces 8/3
9 PM	Pisces	Pisces	Pisces
10 PM	Aries	Aries	Aries
11 PM	Aries; Taurus 7/26	Taurus	Taurus

*Hour of birth given here is for Standard Time in any time zone. If your hour of birth was recorded in Daylight Saving Time, subtract one hour from it and consult that hour in the table above. For example, if you were born at 6 AM D.S.T., see 5 AM above.

	Day of Birth		
Hour of Birth*	**August 7–11**	**August 12–17**	**August 18–24**
Midnight	Gemini	Gemini	Gemini
1 AM	Gemini	Gemini	Cancer
2 AM	Cancer	Cancer	Cancer
3 AM	Cancer	Cancer	Cancer; Leo 8/22
4 AM	Leo	Leo	Leo
5 AM	Leo	Leo	Leo
6 AM	Leo	Leo; Virgo 8/16	Virgo
7 AM	Virgo	Virgo	Virgo
8 AM	Virgo	Virgo	Virgo; Libra 8/22
9 AM	Libra	Libra	Libra
10 AM	Libra	Libra	Libra
11 AM	Libra	Libra; Scorpio 8/14	Scorpio
Noon	Scorpio	Scorpio	Scorpio
1 PM	Scorpio	Scorpio	Scorpio; Sagittarius 8/22
2 PM	Sagittarius	Sagittarius	Sagittarius
3 PM	Sagittarius	Sagittarius	Sagittarius
4 PM	Sagittarius	Capricorn	Capricorn
5 PM	Capricorn	Capricorn	Capricorn
6 PM	Capricorn	Aquarius	Aquarius
7 PM	Aquarius	Aquarius	Pisces
8 PM	Pisces	Pisces	Pisces; Aries 8/21
9 PM	Aries	Aries	Aries
10 PM	Aries; Taurus 8/11	Taurus	Taurus
11 PM	Taurus	Taurus	Gemini

*See note on facing page.

THE PLACE OF ASTROLOGY IN TODAY'S WORLD

Does astrology have a place in the fast-moving, ultra-scientific world we live in today? Can it be justified in a sophisticated society whose outriders are already preparing to step off the moon into the deep space of the planets themselves? Or is it just a hangover of ancient superstition, a psychological dummy for neurotics and dreamers of every historical age?

These are the kind of questions that any inquiring person can be expected to ask when they approach a subject like astrology which goes beyond, but never excludes, the materialistic side of life.

The simple, single answer is that astrology works. It works for many millions of people in the western world alone. In the United States there are 10 million followers and in Europe, an estimated 25 million. America has more than 4000 practicing astrologers, Europe nearly three times as many. Even down-under Australia has its hundreds of thousands of adherents. In the eastern countries, astrology has enormous followings, again, because it has been proved to work. In India, for example, brides and grooms for centuries have been chosen on the basis of their astrological compatibility.

Astrology today is more vital than ever before, more practicable because all over the world the media devotes much space and time to it, more valid because science itself is confirming the precepts of astrological knowledge with every new exciting step. The ordinary person who daily applies astrology intelligently does not have to wonder whether it is true nor believe in it blindly. He can see it working for himself. And, if he can use it—and this book is designed to help the reader to do just that—he can make living a far richer experience, and become a more developed personality and a better person.

Astrology and Relationships

Astrology is the science of relationships. It is not just a study of planetary influences on man and his environment. It is the study of man himself.

We are at the center of our personal universe, of all our relationships. And our happiness or sadness depends on how we act, how we relate to the people and things that surround us. The emotions that we generate have a distinct effect—for better or worse—on the world around us. Our friends and our enemies will confirm this. Just look in the mirror the next time you are angry. In other words, each of us is a kind of sun or planet or star radiating our feelings on the environment around us. Our influence on our personal universe, whether loving, helpful, or destructive, varies with our changing moods, expressed through our individual character.

Our personal "radiations" are potent in the way they affect our moods and our ability to control them. But we usually are able to throw off our emotion in some sort of action—we have a good cry, walk it off, or tell someone our troubles—before it can build up too far and make us physically ill. Astrology helps us to understand the universal forces working on us, and through this understanding, we can become more properly adjusted to our surroundings so that we find ourselves coping where others may flounder.

The Challenge of Love

The challenge of love lies in recognizing the difference between infatuation, emotion, sex, and, sometimes, the intentional deceit of the other person. Mankind, with its record of broken marriages, despair, and disillusionment, is obviously not very good at making these distinctions.

Can astrology help?

Yes. In the same way that advance knowledge can usually help in any human situation. And there is probably no situation as human, as poignant, as pathetic and universal, as the failure of man's love.

Love, of course, is not just between man and woman. It involves love of children, parents, home, and friends. But the big problems usually involve the choice of partner.

Astrology has established degrees of compatibility that exist between people born under the various signs of the Zodiac. Because people are individuals, there are numerous variations and modifications. So the astrologer, when approached on mate and marriage matters, makes allowances for them. But the fact remains that some groups of people are suited for each other and some are not, and astrology has expressed this in terms of characteristics we all can study and use as a personal guide.

No matter how much enjoyment and pleasure we find in the different aspects of each other's character, if it is not an overall compatibility, the chances of our finding fulfillment or enduring happiness in each other are pretty hopeless. And astrology can help us to find someone compatible.

Astrology and Science

Closely related to our emotions is the "other side" of our personal universe, our physical welfare. Our body, of course, is largely influenced by things around us over which we have very little control. The phone rings, we hear it. The train runs late. We snag our stocking or cut our face shaving. Our body is under a constant bombardment of events that influence our daily lives to varying degrees.

The question that arises from all this is, what makes each of us act so that we have to involve other people and keep the ball of activity and evolution rolling? This is the question that both science and astrology are involved with. The scientists have attacked it from different angles: anthropology, the study of human evolution as body, mind and response to environment; anatomy, the study of bodily structure; psychology, the science of the human mind; and so on. These studies have produced very impressive classifications and valuable information, but because the approach to the problem is fragmented, so is the result. They remain "branches" of science. Science generally studies effects. It keeps turning up wonderful answers but no lasting solutions. Astrology, on the other hand, approaches the question from the broader viewpoint. Astrology began its inquiry with the totality of human experience and saw it as an effect. It then looked to find the cause, or at least the prime movers, and during thousands of years of observation of man and his *universal* environment came up with the extraordinary principle of planetary influence—or astrology, which, from the Greek, means the science of the stars.

Modern science, as we shall see, has confirmed much of astrology's foundations—most of it unintentionally, some of it reluctantly, but still, indisputably.

It is not difficult to imagine that there must be a connection between outer space and Earth. Even today, scientists are not too sure how our Earth was created, but it is generally agreed that it is only a tiny part of the universe. And as a part of the universe, people on Earth see and feel the influence of heavenly bodies in almost every aspect of our existence. There is no doubt that the Sun has the greatest influence on life on this planet. Without it there would be no life, for without it there would be no warmth, no division into day and night, no cycles of time or season at all. This is clear and easy to see. The influence of the Moon, on the other hand, is more subtle, though no less definite.

There are many ways in which the influence of the Moon manifests itself here on Earth, both on human and animal life. It is a well-known fact, for instance, that the large movements of water on our planet—that is the ebb and flow of the tides—are caused by the Moon's gravitational pull. Since this is so, it follows that these water movements do not occur only in the oceans, but that all bodies of water are affected, even down to the tiniest puddle.

The human body, too, which consists of about 70 percent water, falls within the scope of this lunar influence. For example the menstrual cycle of most women corresponds to the 28-day lunar month; the period of pregnancy in humans is 273 days, or equal to nine lunar months. Similarly, many illnesses reach a crisis at the change of the Moon, and statistics in many countries have shown that the crime rate is highest at the time of the Full Moon. Even human sexual desire has been associated with the phases of the Moon. But it is in the movement of the tides that we get the clearest demonstration of planetary influence, which leads to the irresistible correspondence between the so-called metaphysical and the physical.

Tide tables are prepared years in advance by calculating the future positions of the Moon. Science has known for a long time that the Moon is the main cause of tidal action. But only in the last few years has it begun to realize the possible extent of this influence on mankind. To begin with, the ocean tides do not rise and fall as we might imagine from our personal observations of them. The Moon as it orbits around Earth sets up a circular wave of attraction which pulls the oceans of the world after it, broadly in an east to west direction. This influence is like a phantom wave crest, a loop of power stretching from pole to pole which passes over and around the Earth like an invisible shadow. It travels with equal effect across the land masses and, as scientists were recently amazed to observe, caused oysters placed in the dark in the middle of the United States where there is no sea to open their shells to receive the nonexistent tide. If the land-locked oysters react to this invisible signal, what effect does it have on us who not so long ago in evolutionary time came out of the sea and still have its salt in our blood and sweat?

Less well known is the fact that the Moon is also the primary force behind the circulation of blood in human beings and animals, and the movement of sap in trees and plants. Agriculturists have established that the Moon has a distinct influence on crops, which explains why for centuries people have planted according to Moon cycles. The habits of many animals, too, are directed by the movement of the Moon. Migratory birds, for instance, depart only at or near the time of the Full Moon. And certain sea creatures, eels in particular, move only in accordance with certain phases of the Moon.

Know Thyself—Why?

In today's fast-changing world, everyone still longs to know what the future holds. It is the one thing that everyone has in common: rich and poor, famous and infamous, all are deeply concerned about tomorrow.

But the key to the future, as every historian knows, lies in the past. This is as true of individual people as it is of nations. You cannot understand your future without first understanding your past, which is simply another way of saying that you must first of all know yourself.

The motto "know thyself" seems obvious enough nowadays, but it was originally put forward as the foundation of wisdom by the ancient Greek philosophers. It was then adopted by the "mystery religions" of the ancient Middle East, Greece, Rome, and is still used in all genuine schools of mind training or mystical discipline, both in those of the East, based on yoga, and those of the West. So it is universally accepted now, and has been through the ages.

But how do you go about discovering what sort of person you are? The first step is usually classification into some sort of system of types. Astrology did this long before the birth of Christ. Psychology has also done it. So has modern medicine, in its way.

One system classifies people according to the source of the impulses they respond to most readily: the muscles, leading to direct bodily action; the digestive organs, resulting in emotion; or the brain and nerves, giving rise to thinking. Another such system says that character is determined by the endocrine glands, and gives us such labels as "pituitary," "thyroid," and "hyperthyroid" types. These different systems are neither contradictory nor mutually exclusive. In fact, they are very often different ways of saying the same thing.

Very popular, useful classifications were devised by Carl Jung, the eminent disciple of Freud. Jung observed among the different faculties of the mind, four which have a predominant influence on character. These four faculties exist in all of us without exception, but not in perfect balance. So when we say, for instance, that someone is a "thinking type," it means that in any situation he or she tries to be rational. Emotion, which may be the opposite of thinking, will be his or her weakest function. This thinking type can be sensible and reasonable, or calculating and unsympathetic. The emotional type, on the other hand, can often be recognized by exaggerated language—everything is either marvelous or terrible—and in extreme cases they even invent dramas and quarrels out of nothing just to make life more interesting.

The other two faculties are intuition and physical sensation. The sensation type does not only care for food and drink, nice clothes and furniture; he or she is also interested in all forms of physical experience. Many scientists are sensation types as are athletes and nature-lovers. Like sensation, intuition is a form of perception and we all possess it. But it works through that part of the mind which is not under conscious control—consequently it sees meanings and connections which are not obvious to thought or emotion. Inventors and original thinkers are always intuitive, but so, too, are superstitious people who see meanings where none exist.

Thus, sensation tells us what is going on in the world, feeling (that is, emotion) tells us how important it is to ourselves, thinking enables us to interpret it and work out what we should do about it, and intuition tells us what it means to ourselves and others. All four faculties are essential, and all are present in every one of us. But some people are guided chiefly by one, others by another. In addition, Jung also observed a division of the human personality into the extrovert and the introvert, which cuts across these four types.

A disadvantage of all these systems of classification is that one cannot tell very easily where to place oneself. Some people are reluctant to admit that they act to please their emotions. So they deceive themselves for years by trying to belong to whichever type they think is the "best." Of course, there is no best; each has its faults and each has its good points.

The advantage of the signs of the Zodiac is that they simplify classification. Not only that, but your date of birth is personal—

it is unarguably yours. What better way to know yourself than by going back as far as possible to the very moment of your birth? And this is precisely what your horoscope is all about, as we shall see in the next section.

WHAT IS A HOROSCOPE?

If you had been able to take a picture of the skies at the moment of your birth, that photograph would be your horoscope. Lacking such a snapshot, it is still possible to recreate the picture—and this is at the basis of the astrologer's art. In other words, your horoscope is a representation of the skies with the planets in the exact positions they occupied at the time you were born.

The year of birth tells an astrologer the positions of the distant, slow-moving planets Jupiter, Saturn, Uranus, Neptune, and Pluto. The month of birth indicates the Sun sign, or birth sign as it is commonly called, as well as indicating the positions of the rapidly moving planets Venus, Mercury, and Mars. The day and time of birth will locate the position of our Moon. And the moment—the exact hour and minute—of birth determines the houses through what is called the Ascendant, or Rising sign.

With this information the astrologer consults various tables to calculate the specific positions of the Sun, Moon, and other planets relative to your birthplace at the moment you were born. Then he or she locates them by means of the Zodiac.

The Zodiac

The Zodiac is a band of stars (constellations) in the skies, centered on the Sun's apparent path around the Earth, and is divided into twelve equal segments, or signs. What we are actually dividing up is the Earth's path around the Sun. But from our point of view here on Earth, it seems as if the Sun is making a great circle around our planet in the sky, so we say it is the Sun's apparent path. This twelvefold division, the Zodiac, is a reference system for the astrologer. At any given moment the planets—and in astrology both the Sun and Moon are considered to be planets—can all be located at a specific point along this path.

Now where in all this are you, the subject of the horoscope? Your character is largely determined by the sign the Sun is in. So that is where the astrologer looks first in your horoscope, at your Sun sign.

The Sun Sign and the Cusp

There are twelve signs in the Zodiac, and the Sun spends approximately one month in each sign. But because of the motion of the Earth around the Sun—the Sun's apparent motion—the dates when the Sun enters and leaves each sign may change from year to year. Some people born near the cusp, or edge, of a sign have difficulty determining which is their Sun sign. But in this book a Table of Cusps is provided for the years 1900 to 2010 (page 5) so you can find out what your true Sun sign is.

Here are the twelve signs of the Zodiac, their ancient zodiacal symbol, and the dates when the Sun enters and leaves each sign for the year 2007. Remember, these dates may change from year to year.

ARIES	Ram	March 20–April 20
TAURUS	Bull	April 20–May 21
GEMINI	Twins	May 21–June 21
CANCER	Crab	June 21–July 23
LEO	Lion	July 23–August 23
VIRGO	Virgin	August 23–September 23
LIBRA	Scales	September 23–October 23
SCORPIO	Scorpion	October 23–November 22
SAGITTARIUS	Archer	November 22–December 22
CAPRICORN	Sea Goat	December 22–January 20
AQUARIUS	Water Bearer	January 20–February 18
PISCES	Fish	February 18–March 20

It is possible to draw significant conclusions and make meaningful predictions based simply on the Sun sign of a person. There are many people who have been amazed at the accuracy of the description of their own character based only on the Sun sign. But an astrologer needs more information than just your Sun sign to interpret the photograph that is your horoscope.

The Rising Sign and the Zodiacal Houses

An astrologer needs the exact time and place of your birth in order to construct and interpret your horoscope. The illustration on the next page shows the flat chart, or natural wheel, an astrologer uses. Note the inner circle of the wheel labeled 1 through 12. These 12 divisions are known as the houses of the Zodiac.

18 / WHAT IS A HOROSCOPE?

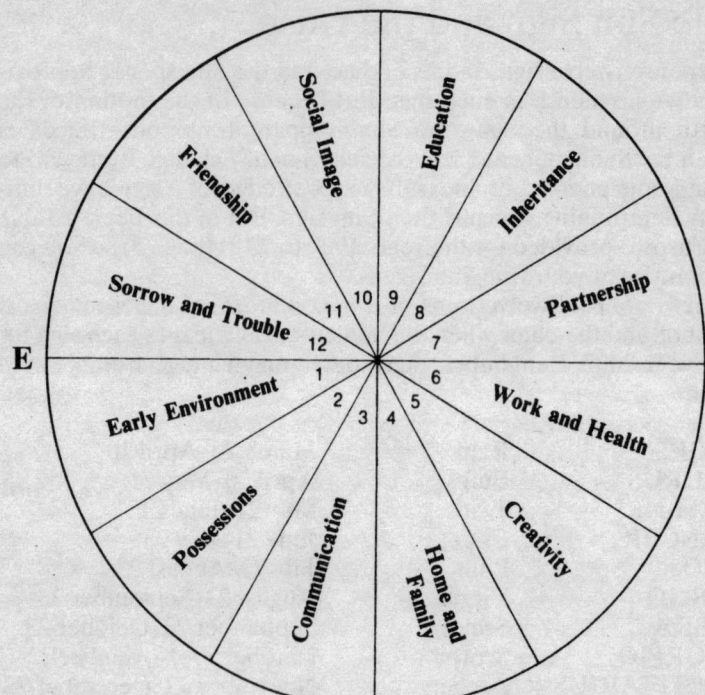

The 1st house always starts from the position marked E, which corresponds to the eastern horizon. The rest of the houses 2 through 12 follow around in a "counterclockwise" direction. The point where each house starts is known as a cusp, or edge.

The cusp, or edge, of the 1st house (point E) is where an astrologer would place your Rising sign, the Ascendant. And, as already noted, the exact time of your birth determines your Rising sign. Let's see how this works.

As the Earth rotates on its axis once every 24 hours, each one of the twelve signs of the Zodiac appears to be "rising" on the horizon, with a new one appearing about every 2 hours. Actually it is the turning of the Earth that exposes each sign to view, but in our astrological work we are discussing apparent motion. This Rising sign marks the Ascendant, and it colors the whole orientation of a horoscope. It indicates the sign governing the 1st house of the chart, and will thus determine which signs will govern all the other houses.

To visualize this idea, imagine two color wheels with twelve divisions superimposed upon each other. For just as the Zodiac is divided into twelve constellations that we identify as the signs, another twelvefold division is used to denote the houses. Now imagine one wheel (the signs) moving slowly while the other wheel (the houses) remains still. This analogy may help you see how the signs keep shifting the "color" of the houses as the Rising sign continues to change every two hours. To simplify things, a Table of Rising Signs has been provided (pages 8–9) for your specific Sun sign.

Once your Rising sign has been placed on the cusp of the 1st house, the signs that govern the rest of the 11 houses can be placed on the chart. In any individual's horoscope the signs do not necessarily correspond with the houses. For example, it could be that a sign covers part of two adjacent houses. It is the interpretation of such variations in an individual's horoscope that marks the professional astrologer.

But to gain a workable understanding of astrology, it is not necessary to go into great detail. In fact, we just need a description of the houses and their meanings, as is shown in the illustration above and in the table below.

THE 12 HOUSES OF THE ZODIAC

1st	Individuality, body appearance, general outlook on life	Personality house
2nd	Finance, possessions, ethical principles, gain or loss	Money house
3rd	Relatives, communication, short journeys, writing, education	Relatives house
4th	Family and home, parental ties, land and property, security	Home house
5th	Pleasure, children, creativity, entertainment, risk	Pleasure house
6th	Health, harvest, hygiene, work and service, employees	Health house
7th	Marriage and divorce, the law, partnerships and alliances	Marriage house
8th	Inheritance, secret deals, sex, death, regeneration	Inheritance house
9th	Travel, sports, study, philosophy Ω house	Travel house
10th	Career, social standing, success and honor	Business house
11th	Friendship, social life, hopes and wishes	Friends house
12th	Troubles, illness, secret enemies, hidden agendas	Trouble house

The Planets in the Houses

An astrologer, knowing the exact time and place of your birth, will use tables of planetary motion in order to locate the planets in your horoscope chart. He or she will determine which planet or planets are in which sign and in which house. It is not uncommon, in an individual's horoscope, for there to be two or more planets in the same sign and in the same house.

The characteristics of the planets modify the influence of the Sun according to their natures and strengths.

Sun: Source of life. Basic temperament according to the Sun sign. The conscious will. Human potential.
Moon: Emotions. Moods. Customs. Habits. Changeable. Adaptive. Nurturing.
Mercury: Communication. Intellect. Reasoning power. Curiosity. Short travels.
Venus: Love. Delight. Charm. Harmony. Balance. Art. Beautiful possessions.
Mars: Energy. Initiative. War. Anger. Adventure. Courage. Daring. Impulse.
Jupiter: Luck. Optimism. Generous. Expansive. Opportunities. Protection.
Saturn: Pessimism. Privation. Obstacles. Delay. Hard work. Research. Lasting rewards after long struggle.
Uranus: Fashion. Electricity. Revolution. Independence. Freedom. Sudden changes. Modern science.
Neptune: Sensationalism. Theater. Dreams. Inspiration. Illusion. Deception.
Pluto: Creation and destruction. Total transformation. Lust for power. Strong obsessions.

Superimpose the characteristics of the planets on the functions of the house in which they appear. Express the result through the character of the Sun sign, and you will get the basic idea.

Of course, many other considerations have been taken into account in producing the carefully worked out predictions in this book: the aspects of the planets to each other; their strength according to position and sign; whether they are in a house of exaltation or decline; whether they are natural enemies or not; whether a planet occupies its own sign; the position of a planet in relation to its own house or sign; whether the sign is male or female; whether the sign is a fire, earth, water, or air sign. These are only a few of the colors on the astrologer's pallet which he or she must mix with the inspiration of the artist and the accuracy of the mathematician.

How To Use These Predictions

A person reading the predictions in this book should understand that they are produced from the daily position of the planets for a group of people and are not, of course, individually specialized. To get the full benefit of them our readers should relate the predictions to their own character and circumstances, coordinate them, and draw their own conclusions from them.

If you are a serious observer of your own life, you should find a definite pattern emerging that will be a helpful and reliable guide.

The point is that we always retain our free will. The stars indicate certain directional tendencies but we are not compelled to follow. We can do or not do, and wisdom must make the choice.

We all have our good and bad days. Sometimes they extend into cycles of weeks. It is therefore advisable to study daily predictions in a span ranging from the day before to several days ahead.

Daily predictions should be taken very generally. The word "difficult" does not necessarily indicate a whole day of obstruction or inconvenience. It is a warning to you to be cautious. Your caution will often see you around the difficulty before you are involved. This is the correct use of astrology.

In another section (pages 78–84), detailed information is given about the influence of the Moon as it passes through each of the twelve signs of the Zodiac. There are instructions on how to use the Moon Tables (pages 85–92), which provide Moon Sign Dates throughout the year as well as the Moon's role in health and daily affairs. This information should be used in conjunction with the daily forecasts to give a fuller picture of the astrological trends.

HISTORY OF ASTROLOGY

The origins of astrology have been lost far back in history, but we do know that reference is made to it as far back as the first written records of the human race. It is not hard to see why. Even in primitive times, people must have looked for an explanation for the various happenings in their lives. They must have wanted to know why people were different from one another. And in their search they turned to the regular movements of the Sun, Moon, and stars to see if they could provide an answer.

It is interesting to note that as soon as man learned to use his tools in any type of design, or his mind in any kind of calculation, he turned his attention to the heavens. Ancient cave dwellings reveal dim crescents and circles representative of the Sun and Moon, rulers of day and night. Mesopotamia and the civilization of Chaldea, in itself the foundation of those of Babylonia and Assyria, show a complete picture of astronomical observation and well-developed astrological interpretation.

Humanity has a natural instinct for order. The study of anthropology reveals that primitive people—even as far back as prehistoric times—were striving to achieve a certain order in their lives. They tried to organize the apparent chaos of the universe. They had the desire to attach meaning to things. This demand for order has persisted throughout the history of man. So that observing the regularity of the heavenly bodies made it logical that primitive peoples should turn heavenward in their search for an understanding of the world in which they found themselves so random and alone.

And they did find a significance in the movements of the stars. Shepherds tending their flocks, for instance, observed that when the cluster of stars now known as the constellation Aries was in sight, it was the time of fertility and they associated it with the Ram. And they noticed that the growth of plants and plant life corresponded with different phases of the Moon, so that certain times were favorable for the planting of crops, and other times were not. In this way, there grew up a tradition of seasons and causes connected with the passage of the Sun through the twelve signs of the Zodiac.

Astrology was valued so highly that the king was kept informed of the daily and monthly changes in the heavenly bodies, and the results of astrological studies regarding events of the future. Head astrologers were clearly men of great rank and position, and the office was said to be a hereditary one.

Omens were taken, not only from eclipses and conjunctions of the Moon or Sun with one of the planets, but also from storms and earthquakes. In the eastern civilizations, particularly, the reverence inspired by astrology appears to have remained unbroken since the very earliest days. In ancient China, astrology, astronomy, and religion went hand in hand. The astrologer, who was also an astronomer, was part of the official government service and had his own corner in the Imperial Palace. The duties of the Imperial astrologer, whose office was one of the most important in the land, were clearly defined, as this extract from early records shows:

> This exalted gentleman must concern himself with the stars in the heavens, keeping a record of the changes and movements of the Planets, the Sun and the Moon, in order to examine the movements of the terrestrial world with the object of prognosticating good and bad fortune. He divides the territories of the nine regions of the empire in accordance with their dependence on particular celestial bodies. All the fiefs and principalities are connected with the stars and from this their prosperity or misfortune should be ascertained. He makes prognostications according to the twelve years of the Jupiter cycle of good and evil of the terrestrial world. From the colors of the five kinds of clouds, he determines the coming of floods or droughts, abundance or famine. From the twelve winds, he draws conclusions about the state of harmony of heaven and earth, and takes note of good and bad signs that result from their accord or disaccord. In general, he concerns himself with five kinds of phenomena so as to warn the Emperor to come to the aid of the government and to allow for variations in the ceremonies according to their circumstances.

The Chinese were also keen observers of the fixed stars, giving them such unusual names as Ghost Vehicle, Sun of Imperial Concubine, Imperial Prince, Pivot of Heaven, Twinkling Brilliance, Weaving Girl. But, great astrologers though they may have been, the Chinese lacked one aspect of mathematics that the Greeks applied to astrology—deductive geometry. Deductive geometry was the basis of much classical astrology in and after the time of the Greeks, and this explains the different methods of prognostication used in the East and West.

Down through the ages the astrologer's art has depended, not so much on the uncovering of new facts, though this is important, as on the interpretation of the facts already known. This is the essence of the astrologer's skill.

But why should the signs of the Zodiac have any effect at all on the formation of human character? It is easy to see why people thought they did, and even now we constantly use astrological expressions in our everyday speech. The thoughts of "lucky star," "ill-fated," "star-crossed," "mooning around," are interwoven into the very structure of our language.

Wherever the concept of the Zodiac is understood and used, it could well appear to have an influence on the human character. Does this mean, then, that the human race, in whose civilization the idea of the twelve signs of the Zodiac has long been embedded, is divided into only twelve types? Can we honestly believe that it is really as simple as that? If so, there must be pretty wide ranges of variation within each type. And if, to explain the variation, we call in heredity and environment, experiences in early childhood, the thyroid and other glands, and also the four functions of the mind together with extroversion and introversion, then one begins to wonder if the original classification was worth making at all. No sensible person believes that his favorite system explains everything. But even so, he will not find the system much use at all if it does not even save him the trouble of bothering with the others.

In the same way, if we were to put every person under only one sign of the Zodiac, the system becomes too rigid and unlike life. Besides, it was never intended to be used like that. It may be convenient to have only twelve types, but we know that in practice there is every possible gradation between aggressiveness and timidity, or between conscientiousness and laziness. How, then, do we account for this?

A person born under any given Sun sign can be mainly influenced by one or two of the other signs that appear in their individual horoscope. For instance, famous persons born under the sign of Gemini include Henry VIII, whom nothing and no one could have induced to abdicate, and Edward VIII, who did just that. Obviously, then, the sign Gemini does not fully explain the complete character of either of them.

Again, under the opposite sign, Sagittarius, were both Stalin, who was totally consumed with the notion of power, and Charles V, who freely gave up an empire because he preferred to go into a monastery. And we find under Scorpio many uncompromising characters such as Luther, de Gaulle, Indira Gandhi, and Montgomery, but also Petain, a successful commander whose name later became synonymous with collaboration.

A single sign is therefore obviously inadequate to explain the differences between people; it can only explain resemblances, such as the combativeness of the Scorpio group, or the far-reaching devotion of Charles V and Stalin to their respective ideals—the Christian heaven and the Communist utopia.

But very few people have only one sign in their horoscope chart.

In addition to the month of birth, the day and, even more, the hour to the nearest minute if possible, ought to be considered. Without this, it is impossible to have an actual horoscope, for the word horoscope literally means "a consideration of the hour."

The month of birth tells you only which sign of the Zodiac was occupied by the Sun. The day and hour tell you what sign was occupied by the Moon. And the minute tells you which sign was rising on the eastern horizon. This is called the Ascendant, and, as some astrologers believe, it is supposed to be the most important thing in the whole horoscope.

The Sun is said to signify one's heart, that is to say, one's deepest desires and inmost nature. This is quite different from the Moon, which signifies one's superficial way of behaving. When the ancient Romans referred to the Emperor Augustus as a Capricorn, they meant that he had the Moon in Capricorn. Or, to take another example, a modern astrologer would call Disraeli a Scorpion because he had Scorpio Rising, but most people would call him Sagittarius because he had the Sun there. The Romans would have called him Leo because his Moon was in Leo.

So if one does not seem to fit one's birth month, it is always worthwhile reading the other signs, for one may have been born at a time when any of them were rising or occupied by the Moon. It also seems to be the case that the influence of the Sun develops as life goes on, so that the month of birth is easier to guess in people over the age of forty. The young are supposed to be influenced mainly by their Ascendant, the Rising sign, which characterizes the body and physical personality as a whole.

It is nonsense to assume that all people born at a certain time will exhibit the same characteristics, or that they will even behave in the same manner. It is quite obvious that, from the very moment of its birth, a child is subject to the effects of its environment, and that this in turn will influence its character and heritage to a decisive extent. Also to be taken into account are education and economic conditions, which play a very important part in the formation of one's character as well.

People have, in general, certain character traits and qualities which, according to their environment, develop in either a positive or a negative manner. Therefore, selfishness (inherent selfishness, that is) might emerge as unselfishness; kindness and consideration as cruelty and lack of consideration toward others. In the same way, a naturally constructive person may, through frustration, become destructive, and so on. The latent characteristics with which people are born can, therefore, through environment and good or bad training, become something that would appear to be its opposite, and so give the lie to the astrologer's description of their character.

But this is not the case. The true character is still there, but it is buried deep beneath these external superficialities.

Careful study of the character traits of various signs of the Zodiac are of immeasurable help, and can render beneficial service to the intelligent person. Undoubtedly, the reader will already have discovered that, while he is able to get on very well with some people, he just "cannot stand" others. The causes sometimes seem inexplicable. At times there is intense dislike, at other times immediate sympathy. And there is, too, the phenomenon of love at first sight, which is also apparently inexplicable. People appear to be either sympathetic or unsympathetic toward each other for no apparent reason.

Now if we look at this in the light of the Zodiac, we find that people born under different signs are either compatible or incompatible with each other. In other words, there are good and bad interrelating factors among the various signs. This does not, of course, mean that humanity can be divided into groups of hostile camps. It would be quite wrong to be hostile or indifferent toward people who happen to be born under an incompatible sign. There is no reason why everybody should not, or cannot, learn to control and adjust their feelings and actions, especially after they are aware of the positive qualities of other people by studying their character analyses, among other things.

Every person born under a certain sign has both positive and negative qualities, which are developed more or less according to our free will. Nobody is entirely good or entirely bad, and it is up to each of us to learn to control ourselves on the one hand and at the same time to endeavor to learn about ourselves and others.

It cannot be emphasized often enough that it is free will that determines whether we will make really good use of our talents and abilities. Using our free will, we can either overcome our failings or allow them to rule us. Our free will enables us to exert sufficient willpower to control our failings so that they do not harm ourselves or others.

Astrology can reveal our inclinations and tendencies. Astrology can tell us about ourselves so that we are able to use our free will to overcome our shortcomings. In this way astrology helps us do our best to become needed and valuable members of society as well as helpmates to our family and our friends. Astrology also can save us a great deal of unhappiness and remorse.

Yet it may seem absurd that an ancient philosophy could be a prop to modern men and women. But below the materialistic surface of modern life, there are hidden streams of feeling and thought. Symbology is reappearing as a study worthy of the scholar; the psychosomatic factor in illness has passed from the writings of the crank to those of the specialist; spiritual healing in all its forms is no longer a pious hope but an accepted phenomenon. And it is into this context that we consider astrology, in the sense that it is an analysis of human types.

Astrology and medicine had a long journey together, and only parted company a couple of centuries ago. There still remain in medical language such astrological terms as "saturnine," "choleric," and "mercurial," used in the diagnosis of physical tendencies. The herbalist, for long the handyman of the medical profession, has been dominated by astrology since the days of the Greeks. Certain herbs traditionally respond to certain planetary influences, and diseases must therefore be treated to ensure harmony between the medicine and the disease.

But the stars are expected to foretell and not only to diagnose.

Astrological forecasting has been remarkably accurate, but often it is wide of the mark. The brave person who cares to predict world events takes dangerous chances. Individual forecasting is less clear cut; it can be a help or a disillusionment. Then we come to the nagging question: if it is possible to foreknow, is it right to foretell? This is a point of ethics on which it is hard to pronounce judgment. The doctor faces the same dilemma if he finds that symptoms of a mortal disease are present in his patient and that he can only prognosticate a steady decline. How much to tell an individual in a crisis is a problem that has perplexed many distinguished scholars. Honest and conscientious astrologers in this modern world, where so many people are seeking guidance, face the same problem.

Five hundred years ago it was customary to call in a learned man who was an astrologer who was probably also a doctor and a philosopher. By his knowledge of astrology, his study of planetary influences, he felt himself qualified to guide those in distress. The world has moved forward at a fantastic rate since then, and yet people are still uncertain of themselves. At first sight it seems fantastic in the light of modern thinking that they turn to the most ancient of all studies, and get someone to calculate a horoscope for them. But is it really so fantastic if you take a second look? For astrology is concerned with tomorrow, with survival. And in a world such as ours, tomorrow and survival are the keywords for the twenty-first century.

ASTROLOGICAL BRIDGE TO THE 21st CENTURY

Themes connecting past, present, and future are in play as the first decade reveals hidden paths and personal hints for achieving your potential. Make the most of the messages from the planets.

With the dawning of the twenty-first century look first to Jupiter, the planet of good fortune. Each new yearly Jupiter cycle follows the natural progression of the Zodiac. First is Jupiter in Aries and in Taurus through spring 2000, next Jupiter is in Gemini to summer 2001, then in Cancer to midsummer 2002, in Leo to late summer 2003, in Virgo to early autumn 2004, in Libra to midautumn 2005, and so on through Jupiter in Pisces through June 2010. The beneficent planet Jupiter promotes your professional and educational goals while urging informed choice and deliberation, providing a rich medium for creativity. Planet Jupiter's influence is protective, the generous helper that comes to the rescue just in the nick of time. And while safeguarding good luck, Jupiter can turn unusual risks into achievable aims.

In order to take advantage of luck and opportunity, to gain wisdom from experience, to persevere against adversity, look to beautiful planet Saturn. Saturn, planet of reason and responsibility, began a new cycle in earthy Taurus at the turn of the century. Saturn in Taurus until spring 2001 inspires industry and affection, blends practicality and imagination, all the while inviting caution and care. Saturn in Taurus lends beauty, order, and structure to your life. Then Saturn is in Gemini, the sign of mind and communication, until June 2003. Saturn in Gemini gives a lively intellectual capacity, so the limits of creativity can be stretched and boundaries broken. Saturn in Gemini holds the promise of fruitful endeavor through sustained study, learning, and application. Saturn in Cancer from early June 2003 to mid-July 2005 poses issues of long-term security versus immediate gratification. Rely on deliberation and choice to make sense out of diversity and change. Saturn in Cancer can be a revealing cycle, leading to the desired outcomes of growth and maturity. Saturn in Leo from mid-July 2005 to early September 2007 can be a test of boldness versus caution. Here every challenge must be met with benevolent authority, matched by a caring and generous outlook. Saturn in Virgo early September 2007 into October 2009 sharpens and deepens the mind, conferring precise writing and teaching skills. Saturn in Virgo presents chances to excel, to accomplish a great deal, and to gain prominence through good words and good works.

Uranus, planet of innovation and surprise, started an important new cycle in January of 1996. At that time Uranus entered its natural home in airy Aquarius. Uranus in Aquarius into the year 2003 has a profound effect on your personality and the lens through which you see the world. A basic change in the way you project yourself is just one impact of Uranus in Aquarius. More significantly, a whole new consciousness is evolving. Winds of change blowing your way emphasize movement and freedom. Uranus in Aquarius poses involvement in the larger community beyond self, family, friends, lovers, associates. Radical ideas and progressive thought signal a journey of liberation. As the new century begins, follow Uranus on the path of humanitarianism. A new Uranus cycle begins March 2003 when Uranus visits Pisces, briefly revisits Aquarius, then returns late in 2003 to Pisces where it will stay into May 2010. Uranus in Pisces, a strongly intuitive force, urges work and service for the good of humankind to make the world a better place for all people.

Neptune, planet of vision and mystery, is enjoying a long cycle that excites creativity and imaginative thinking. Neptune is in airy Aquarius from November 1998 to February of 2012. Neptune in Aquarius, the sign of the Water Bearer, represents two sides of the coin of wisdom: inspiration and reason. Here Neptune stirs powerful currents bearing a rich and varied harvest, the fertile breeding ground for idealistic aims and practical considerations. Neptune's fine intuition tunes in to your dreams, your imagination, your spirituality. You can never turn your back on the mysteries of life. Uranus and Neptune, the planets of enlightenment and idealism, give you glimpses into the future, letting you peek through secret doorways into the twenty-first century.

Pluto, planet of beginnings and endings, began a new cycle of growth and learning late in 1995. Pluto entered fiery Sagittarius and remains there into the year 2008. Pluto in Sagittarius during its long stay over twelve years can create significant change. The great power of Pluto in Sagittarius is already starting its transformation of your character and lifestyle. Pluto in Sagittarius takes you on a new journey of exploration and learning. The awakening you experience on intellectual and artistic levels heralds a new cycle of growth. Uncompromising Pluto, seeker of truth, challenges your identity, persona, and self-expression. Uncovering the real you, Pluto holds the key to understanding and meaningful communication. Pluto in Sagittarius can be the guiding light illuminating the first decade of the twenty-first century. Good luck is riding on the waves of change.

THE SIGNS OF THE ZODIAC

Dominant Characteristics

Aries: March 21–April 20

The Positive Side of Aries

The Aries has many positive points to his character. People born under this first sign of the Zodiac are often quite strong and enthusiastic. On the whole, they are forward-looking people who are not easily discouraged by temporary setbacks. They know what they want out of life and they go out after it. Their personalities are strong. Others are usually quite impressed by the Ram's way of doing things. Quite often they are sources of inspiration for others traveling the same route. Aries men and women have a special zest for life that can be contagious; for others, they are a fine example of how life should be lived.

The Aries person usually has a quick and active mind. He is imaginative and inventive. He enjoys keeping busy and active. He generally gets along well with all kinds of people. He is interested in mankind, as a whole. He likes to be challenged. Some would say he thrives on opposition, for it is when he is set against that he often does his best. Getting over or around obstacles is a challenge he generally enjoys. All in all, Aries is quite positive and young-thinking. He likes to keep abreast of new things that are happening in the world. Aries are often fond of speed. They like things to be done quickly, and this sometimes aggravates their slower colleagues and associates.

The Aries man or woman always seems to remain young. Their whole approach to life is youthful and optimistic. They never say die, no matter what the odds. They may have an occasional setback, but it is not long before they are back on their feet again.

The Negative Side of Aries

Everybody has his less positive qualities—and Aries is no exception. Sometimes the Aries man or woman is not very tactful in communicating with others; in his hurry to get things done he is apt to be a little callous or inconsiderate. Sensitive people are likely to find him somewhat sharp-tongued in some situations. Often in his eagerness to get the show on the road, he misses the mark altogether and cannot achieve his aims.

At times Aries can be too impulsive. He can occasionally be stubborn and refuse to listen to reason. If things do not move quickly enough to suit the Aries man or woman, he or she is apt to become rather nervous or irritable. The uncultivated Aries is not unfamiliar with moments of doubt and fear. He is capable of being destructive if he does not get his way. He can overcome some of his emotional problems by steadily trying to express himself as he really is, but this requires effort.

Taurus: April 21–May 20

The Positive Side of Taurus

The Taurus person is known for his ability to concentrate and for his tenacity. These are perhaps his strongest qualities. The Taurus man or woman generally has very little trouble in getting along with others; it's his nature to be helpful toward people in need. He can always be depended on by his friends, especially those in trouble.

Taurus generally achieves what he wants through his ability to persevere. He never leaves anything unfinished but works on something until it has been completed. People can usually take him at his word; he is honest and forthright in most of his dealings. The Taurus person has a good chance to make a success of his life because of his many positive qualities. The Taurus who aims high seldom falls short of his mark. He learns well by experience. He is thorough and does not believe in shortcuts of any kind. The Bull's thoroughness pays off in the end, for through his deliberateness he learns how to rely on himself and what he has learned. The Taurus person tries to get along with others, as a rule. He is not overly critical and likes people to be themselves. He is a tolerant person and enjoys peace and harmony—especially in his home life.

Taurus is usually cautious in all that he does. He is not a person

who believes in taking unnecessary risks. Before adopting any one line of action, he will weigh all of the pros and cons. The Taurus person is steadfast. Once his mind is made up it seldom changes. The person born under this sign usually is a good family person—reliable and loving.

The Negative Side of Taurus

Sometimes the Taurus man or woman is a bit too stubborn. He won't listen to other points of view if his mind is set on something. To others, this can be quite annoying. Taurus also does not like to be told what to do. He becomes rather angry if others think him not too bright. He does not like to be told he is wrong, even when he is. He dislikes being contradicted.

Some people who are born under this sign are very suspicious of others—even of those persons close to them. They find it difficult to trust people fully. They are often afraid of being deceived or taken advantage of. The Bull often finds it difficult to forget or forgive. His love of material things sometimes makes him rather avaricious and petty.

Gemini: May 21–June 20

The Positive Side of Gemini

The person born under this sign of the Heavenly Twins is usually quite bright and quick-witted. Some of them are capable of doing many different things. The Gemini person very often has many different interests. He keeps an open mind and is always anxious to learn new things.

Gemini is often an analytical person. He is a person who enjoys making use of his intellect. He is governed more by his mind than by his emotions. He is a person who is not confined to one view; he can often understand both sides to a problem or question. He knows how to reason, how to make rapid decisions if need be.

He is an adaptable person and can make himself at home almost anywhere. There are all kinds of situations he can adapt to. He is a person who seldom doubts himself; he is sure of his talents and his ability to think and reason. Gemini is generally most satisfied when he is in a situation where he can make use of his intellect. Never

short of imagination, he often has strong talents for invention. He is rather a modern person when it comes to life; Gemini almost always moves along with the times—perhaps that is why he remains so youthful throughout most of his life.

Literature and art appeal to the person born under this sign. Creativity in almost any form will interest and intrigue the Gemini man or woman.

The Gemini is often quite charming. A good talker, he often is the center of attraction at any gathering. People find it easy to like a person born under this sign because he can appear easygoing and usually has a good sense of humor.

The Negative Side of Gemini

Sometimes the Gemini person tries to do too many things at one time—and as a result, winds up finishing nothing. Some Twins are easily distracted and find it rather difficult to concentrate on one thing for too long a time. Sometimes they give in to trifling fancies and find it rather boring to become too serious about any one thing. Some of them are never dependable, no matter what they promise.

Although the Gemini man or woman often appears to be well-versed on many subjects, this is sometimes just a veneer. His knowledge may be only superficial, but because he speaks so well he gives people the impression of erudition. Some Geminis are sharp-tongued and inconsiderate; they think only of themselves and their own pleasure.

Cancer: June 21–July 20

The Positive Side of Cancer

The Moon Child's most positive point is his understanding nature. On the whole, he is a loving and sympathetic person. He would never go out of his way to hurt anyone. The Cancer man or woman is often very kind and tender; they give what they can to others. They hate to see others suffering and will do what they can to help someone in less fortunate circumstances than themselves. They are often very concerned about the world. Their interest in people generally goes beyond that of just their own families and close friends; they have a deep sense of community and respect humanitarian values. The Moon Child means what he says, as a rule; he is honest about his feelings.

The Cancer man or woman is a person who knows the art of patience. When something seems difficult, he is willing to wait until the situation becomes manageable again. He is a person who knows how to bide his time. Cancer knows how to concentrate on one thing at a time. When he has made his mind up he generally sticks with what he does, seeing it through to the end.

Cancer is a person who loves his home. He enjoys being surrounded by familiar things and the people he loves. Of all the signs, Cancer is the most maternal. Even the men born under this sign often have a motherly or protective quality about them. They like to take care of people in their family—to see that they are well loved and well provided for. They are usually loyal and faithful. Family ties mean a lot to the Cancer man or woman. Parents and in-laws are respected and loved. Young Cancer responds very well to adults who show faith in him. The Moon Child has a strong sense of tradition. He is very sensitive to the moods of others.

The Negative Side of Cancer

Sometimes Cancer finds it rather hard to face life. It becomes too much for him. He can be a little timid and retiring, when things don't go too well. When unfortunate things happen, he is apt to just shrug and say, "Whatever will be will be." He can be fatalistic to a fault. The uncultivated Cancer is a bit lazy. He doesn't have very much ambition. Anything that seems a bit difficult he'll gladly leave to others. He may be lacking in initiative. Too sensitive, when he feels he's been injured, he'll crawl back into his shell and nurse his imaginary wounds. The immature Moon Child often is given to crying when the smallest thing goes wrong.

Some Cancers find it difficult to enjoy themselves in environments outside their homes. They make heavy demands on others, and need to be constantly reassured that they are loved. Lacking such reassurance, they may resort to sulking in silence.

Leo: July 21–August 21

The Positive Side of Leo

Often Leos make good leaders. They seem to be good organizers and administrators. Usually they are quite popular with others. Whatever group it is that they belong to, the Leo man or woman is almost sure to be or become the leader. Loyalty, one of the Lion's noblest traits, enables him or her to maintain this leadership position.

Leo is generous most of the time. It is his best characteristic. He or she likes to give gifts and presents. In making others happy, the Leo person becomes happy himself. He likes to splurge when spending money on others. In some instances it may seem that the Lion's generosity knows no boundaries. A hospitable person, the Leo man or woman is very fond of welcoming people to his house and entertaining them. He is never short of company.

Leo has plenty of energy and drive. He enjoys working toward some specific goal. When he applies himself correctly, he gets what he wants most often. The Leo person is almost never unsure of himself. He has plenty of confidence and aplomb. He is a person who is direct in almost everything he does. He has a quick mind and can make a decision in a very short time.

He usually sets a good example for others because of his ambitious manner and positive ways. He knows how to stick to something once he's started. Although Leo may be good at making a joke, he is not superficial or glib. He is a loving person, kind and thoughtful.

There is generally nothing small or petty about the Leo man or woman. He does what he can for those who are deserving. He is a person others can rely upon at all times. He means what he says. An honest person, generally speaking, he is a friend who is valued and sought out.

The Negative Side of Leo

Leo, however, does have his faults. At times, he can be just a bit too arrogant. He thinks that no one deserves a leadership position except him. Only he is capable of doing things well. His opinion of himself is often much too high. Because of his conceit, he is

sometimes rather unpopular with a good many people. Some Leos are too materialistic; they can only think in terms of money and profit.

Some Leos enjoy lording it over others—at home or at their place of business. What is more, they feel they have the right to. Egocentric to an impossible degree, this sort of Leo cares little about how others think or feel. He can be rude and cutting.

Virgo: August 22–September 22

The Positive Side of Virgo

The person born under the sign of Virgo is generally a busy person. He knows how to arrange and organize things. He is a good planner. Above all, he is practical and is not afraid of hard work.

Often called the sign of the Harvester, Virgo knows how to attain what he desires. He sticks with something until it is finished. He never shirks his duties, and can always be depended upon. The Virgo person can be thoroughly trusted at all times.

The man or woman born under this sign tries to do everything to perfection. He doesn't believe in doing anything halfway. He always aims for the top. He is the sort of a person who is always learning and constantly striving to better himself—not because he wants more money or glory, but because it gives him a feeling of accomplishment.

The Virgo man or woman is a very observant person. He is sensitive to how others feel, and can see things below the surface of a situation. He usually puts this talent to constructive use.

It is not difficult for the Virgo to be open and earnest. He believes in putting his cards on the table. He is never secretive or underhanded. He's as good as his word. The Virgo person is generally plainspoken and down to earth. He has no trouble in expressing himself.

The Virgo person likes to keep up to date on new developments in his particular field. Well-informed, generally, he sometimes has a keen interest in the arts or literature. What he knows, he knows well. His ability to use his critical faculties is well-developed and sometimes startles others because of its accuracy.

Virgos adhere to a moderate way of life; they avoid excesses. Virgo is a responsible person and enjoys being of service.

The Negative Side of Virgo

Sometimes a Virgo person is too critical. He thinks that only he can do something the way it should be done. Whatever anyone else does is inferior. He can be rather annoying in the way he quibbles over insignificant details. In telling others how things should be done, he can be rather tactless and mean.

Some Virgos seem rather emotionless and cool. They feel emotional involvement is beneath them. They are sometimes too tidy, too neat. With money they can be rather miserly. Some Virgos try to force their opinions and ideas on others.

Libra: September 23–October 22

The Positive Side of Libra

Libras love harmony. It is one of their most outstanding character traits. They are interested in achieving balance; they admire beauty and grace in things as well as in people. Generally speaking, they are kind and considerate people. Libras are usually very sympathetic. They go out of their way not to hurt another person's feelings. They are outgoing and do what they can to help those in need.

People born under the sign of Libra almost always make good friends. They are loyal and amiable. They enjoy the company of others. Many of them are rather moderate in their views; they believe in keeping an open mind, however, and weighing both sides of an issue fairly before making a decision.

Alert and intelligent, Libra, often known as the Lawgiver, is always fair-minded and tries to put himself in the position of the other person. They are against injustice; quite often they take up for the underdog. In most of their social dealings, they try to be tactful and kind. They dislike discord and bickering, and most Libras strive for peace and harmony in all their relationships.

The Libra man or woman has a keen sense of beauty. They appreciate handsome furnishings and clothes. Many of them are artistically inclined. Their taste is usually impeccable. They know how to use color. Their homes are almost always attractively arranged and inviting. They enjoy entertaining people and see to it that their guests always feel at home and welcome.

Libra gets along with almost everyone. He is well-liked and socially much in demand.

The Negative Side of Libra

Some people born under this sign tend to be rather insincere. So eager are they to achieve harmony in all relationships that they will even go so far as to lie. Many of them are escapists. They find facing the truth an ordeal and prefer living in a world of make-believe.

In a serious argument, some Libras give in rather easily even when they know they are right. Arguing, even about something they believe in, is too unsettling for some of them.

Libras sometimes care too much for material things. They enjoy possessions and luxuries. Some are vain and tend to be jealous.

Scorpio: October 23–November 22

The Positive Side of Scorpio

The Scorpio man or woman generally knows what he or she wants out of life. He is a determined person. He sees something through to the end. Scorpio is quite sincere, and seldom says anything he doesn't mean. When he sets a goal for himself he tries to go about achieving it in a very direct way.

The Scorpion is brave and courageous. They are not afraid of hard work. Obstacles do not frighten them. They forge ahead until they achieve what they set out for. The Scorpio man or woman has a strong will.

Although Scorpio may seem rather fixed and determined, inside he is often quite tender and loving. He can care very much for others. He believes in sincerity in all relationships. His feelings about someone tend to last; they are profound and not superficial.

The Scorpio person is someone who adheres to his principles no matter what happens. He will not be deterred from a path he believes to be right.

Because of his many positive strengths, the Scorpion can often achieve happiness for himself and for those that he loves.

He is a constructive person by nature. He often has a deep understanding of people and of life, in general. He is perceptive and unafraid. Obstacles often seem to spur him on. He is a positive person who enjoys winning. He has many strengths and resources; challenge of any sort often brings out the best in him.

The Negative Side of Scorpio

The Scorpio person is sometimes hypersensitive. Often he imagines injury when there is none. He feels that others do not bother to recognize him for his true worth. Sometimes he is given to excessive boasting in order to compensate for what he feels is neglect.

Scorpio can be proud, arrogant, and competitive. They can be sly when they put their minds to it and they enjoy outwitting persons or institutions noted for their cleverness.

Their tactics for getting what they want are sometimes devious and ruthless. They don't care too much about what others may think. If they feel others have done them an injustice, they will do their best to seek revenge. The Scorpion often has a sudden, violent temper; and this person's interest in sex is sometimes quite unbalanced or excessive.

Sagittarius: November 23–December 20

The Positive Side of Sagittarius

People born under this sign are honest and forthright. Their approach to life is earnest and open. Sagittarius is often quite adult in his way of seeing things. They are broad-minded and tolerant people. When dealing with others the person born under the sign of the Archer is almost always open and forthright. He doesn't believe in deceit or pretension. His standards are high. People who associate with Sagittarius generally admire and respect his tolerant viewpoint.

The Archer trusts others easily and expects them to trust him. He is never suspicious or envious and almost always thinks well of others. People always enjoy his company because he is so friendly and easygoing. The Sagittarius man or woman is often good-humored. He can always be depended upon by his friends, family, and co-workers.

The person born under this sign of the Zodiac likes a good joke every now and then. Sagittarius is eager for fun and laughs, which makes him very popular with others.

A lively person, he enjoys sports and outdoor life. The Archer is fond of animals. Intelligent and interesting, he can begin an ani-

mated conversation with ease. He likes exchanging ideas and discussing various views.

He is not selfish or proud. If someone proposes an idea or plan that is better than his, he will immediately adopt it. Imaginative yet practical, he knows how to put ideas into practice.

The Archer enjoys sport and games, and it doesn't matter if he wins or loses. He is a forgiving person, and never sulks over something that has not worked out in his favor.

He is seldom critical, and is almost always generous.

The Negative Side of Sagittarius

Some Sagittarius are restless. They take foolish risks and seldom learn from the mistakes they make. They don't have heads for money and are often mismanaging their finances. Some of them devote much of their time to gambling.

Some are too outspoken and tactless, always putting their feet in their mouths. They hurt others carelessly by being honest at the wrong time. Sometimes they make promises which they don't keep. They don't stick close enough to their plans and go from one failure to another. They are undisciplined and waste a lot of energy.

Capricorn: December 21–January 19

The Positive Side of Capricorn

The person born under the sign of Capricorn, known variously as the Mountain Goat or Sea Goat, is usually very stable and patient. He sticks to whatever tasks he has and sees them through. He can always be relied upon and he is not averse to work.

An honest person, Capricorn is generally serious about whatever he does. He does not take his duties lightly. He is a practical person and believes in keeping his feet on the ground.

Quite often the person born under this sign is ambitious and knows how to get what he wants out of life. The Goat forges ahead and never gives up his goal. When he is determined about something, he almost always wins. He is a good worker—a hard worker. Although things may not come easy to him, he will not complain, but continue working until his chores are finished.

He is usually good at business matters and knows the value of money. He is not a spendthrift and knows how to put something away for a rainy day; he dislikes waste and unnecessary loss.

Capricorn knows how to make use of his self-control. He can apply himself to almost anything once he puts his mind to it. His ability to concentrate sometimes astounds others. He is diligent and does well when involved in detail work.

The Capricorn man or woman is charitable, generally speaking, and will do what is possible to help others less fortunate. As a friend, he is loyal and trustworthy. He never shirks his duties or responsibilities. He is self-reliant and never expects too much of the other fellow. He does what he can on his own. If someone does him a good turn, then he will do his best to return the favor.

The Negative Side of Capricorn

Like everyone, Capricorn, too, has faults. At times, the Goat can be overcritical of others. He expects others to live up to his own high standards. He thinks highly of himself and tends to look down on others.

His interest in material things may be exaggerated. The Capricorn man or woman thinks too much about getting on in the world and having something to show for it. He may even be a little greedy.

He sometimes thinks he knows what's best for everyone. He is too bossy. He is always trying to organize and correct others. He may be a little narrow in his thinking.

Aquarius: January 20–February 18

The Positive Side of Aquarius

The Aquarius man or woman is usually very honest and forthright. These are his two greatest qualities. His standards for himself are generally very high. He can always be relied upon by others. His word is his bond.

Aquarius is perhaps the most tolerant of all the Zodiac personalities. He respects other people's beliefs and feels that everyone is entitled to his own approach to life.

He would never do anything to injure another's feelings. He is never unkind or cruel. Always considerate of others, the Water

Bearer is always willing to help a person in need. He feels a very strong tie between himself and all the other members of mankind.

The person born under this sign, called the Water Bearer, is almost always an individualist. He does not believe in teaming up with the masses, but prefers going his own way. His ideas about life and mankind are often quite advanced. There is a saying to the effect that the average Aquarius is fifty years ahead of his time.

Aquarius is community-minded. The problems of the world concern him greatly. He is interested in helping others no matter what part of the globe they live in. He is truly a humanitarian sort. He likes to be of service to others.

Giving, considerate, and without prejudice, Aquarius have no trouble getting along with others.

The Negative Side of Aquarius

Aquarius may be too much of a dreamer. He makes plans but seldom carries them out. He is rather unrealistic. His imagination has a tendency to run away with him. Because many of his plans are impractical, he is always in some sort of a dither.

Others may not approve of him at all times because of his unconventional behavior. He may be a bit eccentric. Sometimes he is so busy with his own thoughts that he loses touch with the realities of existence.

Some Aquarius feel they are more clever and intelligent than others. They seldom admit to their own faults, even when they are quite apparent. Some become rather fanatic in their views. Their criticism of others is sometimes destructive and negative.

Pisces: February 19–March 20

The Positive Side of Pisces

Known as the sign of the Fishes, Pisces has a sympathetic nature. Kindly, he is often dedicated in the way he goes about helping others. The sick and the troubled often turn to him for advice and assistance. Possessing keen intuition, Pisces can easily understand people's deepest problems.

He is very broad-minded and does not criticize others for their faults. He knows how to accept people for what they are. On the whole, he is a trustworthy and earnest person. He is loyal to his friends and will do what he can to help them in time of need. Generous and good-natured, he is a lover of peace; he is often willing to help others solve their differences. People who have taken a wrong turn in life often interest him and he will do what he can to persuade them to rehabilitate themselves.

He has a strong intuitive sense and most of the time he knows how to make it work for him. Pisces is unusually perceptive and often knows what is bothering someone before that person, himself, is aware of it. The Pisces man or woman is an idealistic person, basically, and is interested in making the world a better place in which to live. Pisces believes that everyone should help each other. He is willing to do more than his share in order to achieve cooperation with others.

The person born under this sign often is talented in music or art. He is a receptive person; he is able to take the ups and downs of life with philosophic calm.

The Negative Side of Pisces

Some Pisces are often depressed; their outlook on life is rather glum. They may feel that they have been given a bad deal in life and that others are always taking unfair advantage of them. Pisces sometimes feel that the world is a cold and cruel place. The Fishes can be easily discouraged. The Pisces man or woman may even withdraw from the harshness of reality into a secret shell of his own where he dreams and idles away a good deal of his time.

Pisces can be lazy. He lets things happen without giving the least bit of resistance. He drifts along, whether on the high road or on the low. He can be lacking in willpower.

Some Pisces people seek escape through drugs or alcohol. When temptation comes along they find it hard to resist. In matters of sex, they can be rather permissive.

Sun Sign Personalities

ARIES: Hans Christian Andersen, Pearl Bailey, Marlon Brando, Wernher Von Braun, Charlie Chaplin, Joan Crawford, Da Vinci, Bette Davis, Doris Day, W.C. Fields, Alec Guinness, Adolf Hitler, William Holden, Thomas Jefferson, Nikita Khrushchev, Elton John, Arturo Toscanini, J.P. Morgan, Paul Robeson, Gloria Steinem, Sarah Vaughn, Vincent van Gogh, Tennessee Williams

TAURUS: Fred Astaire, Charlotte Brontë, Carol Burnett, Irving Berlin, Bing Crosby, Salvador Dali, Tchaikovsky, Queen Elizabeth II, Duke Ellington, Ella Fitzgerald, Henry Fonda, Sigmund Freud, Orson Welles, Joe Louis, Lenin, Karl Marx, Golda Meir, Eva Peron, Bertrand Russell, Shakespeare, Kate Smith, Benjamin Spock, Barbra Streisand, Shirley Temple, Harry Truman

GEMINI: Ruth Benedict, Josephine Baker, Rachel Carson, Carlos Chavez, Walt Whitman, Bob Dylan, Ralph Waldo Emerson, Judy Garland, Paul Gauguin, Allen Ginsberg, Benny Goodman, Bob Hope, Burl Ives, John F. Kennedy, Peggy Lee, Marilyn Monroe, Joe Namath, Cole Porter, Laurence Olivier, Harriet Beecher Stowe, Queen Victoria, John Wayne, Frank Lloyd Wright

CANCER: "Dear Abby," Lizzie Borden, David Brinkley, Yul Brynner, Pearl Buck, Marc Chagall, Princess Diana, Babe Didrikson, Mary Baker Eddy, Henry VIII, John Glenn, Ernest Hemingway, Lena Horne, Oscar Hammerstein, Helen Keller, Ann Landers, George Orwell, Nancy Reagan, Rembrandt, Richard Rodgers, Ginger Rogers, Rubens, Jean-Paul Sartre, O.J. Simpson

LEO: Neil Armstrong, James Baldwin, Lucille Ball, Emily Brontë, Wilt Chamberlain, Julia Child, William J. Clinton, Cecil B. De Mille, Ogden Nash, Amelia Earhart, Edna Ferber, Arthur Goldberg, Alfred Hitchcock, Mick Jagger, George Meany, Annie Oakley, George Bernard Shaw, Napoleon, Jacqueline Onassis, Henry Ford, Francis Scott Key, Andy Warhol, Mae West, Orville Wright

VIRGO: Ingrid Bergman, Warren Burger, Maurice Chevalier, Agatha Christie, Sean Connery, Lafayette, Peter Falk, Greta Garbo, Althea Gibson, Arthur Godfrey, Goethe, Buddy Hackett, Michael Jackson, Lyndon Johnson, D.H. Lawrence, Sophia Loren, Grandma Moses, Arnold Palmer, Queen Elizabeth I, Walter Reuther, Peter Sellers, Lily Tomlin, George Wallace

SIGNS OF THE ZODIAC / 57

LIBRA: Brigitte Bardot, Art Buchwald, Truman Capote, Dwight D. Eisenhower, William Faulkner, F. Scott Fitzgerald, Gandhi, George Gershwin, Micky Mantle, Helen Hayes, Vladimir Horowitz, Doris Lessing, Martina Navratalova, Eugene O'Neill, Luciano Pavarotti, Emily Post, Eleanor Roosevelt, Bruce Springsteen, Margaret Thatcher, Gore Vidal, Barbara Walters, Oscar Wilde

SCORPIO: Vivien Leigh, Richard Burton, Art Carney, Johnny Carson, Billy Graham, Grace Kelly, Walter Cronkite, Marie Curie, Charles de Gaulle, Linda Evans, Indira Gandhi, Theodore Roosevelt, Rock Hudson, Katherine Hepburn, Robert F. Kennedy, Billie Jean King, Martin Luther, Georgia O'Keeffe, Pablo Picasso, Jonas Salk, Alan Shepard, Robert Louis Stevenson

SAGITTARIUS: Jane Austen, Louisa May Alcott, Woody Allen, Beethoven, Willy Brandt, Mary Martin, William F. Buckley, Maria Callas, Winston Churchill, Noel Coward, Emily Dickinson, Walt Disney, Benjamin Disraeli, James Doolittle, Kirk Douglas, Chet Huntley, Jane Fonda, Chris Evert Lloyd, Margaret Mead, Charles Schulz, John Milton, Frank Sinatra, Steven Spielberg

CAPRICORN: Muhammad Ali, Isaac Asimov, Pablo Casals, Dizzy Dean, Marlene Dietrich, James Farmer, Ava Gardner, Barry Goldwater, Cary Grant, J. Edgar Hoover, Howard Hughes, Joan of Arc, Gypsy Rose Lee, Martin Luther King, Jr., Rudyard Kipling, Mao Tse-tung, Richard Nixon, Gamal Nasser, Louis Pasteur, Albert Schweitzer, Stalin, Benjamin Franklin, Elvis Presley

AQUARIUS: Marian Anderson, Susan B. Anthony, Jack Benny, John Barrymore, Mikhail Baryshnikov, Charles Darwin, Charles Dickens, Thomas Edison, Clark Gable, Jascha Heifetz, Abraham Lincoln, Yehudi Menuhin, Mozart, Jack Nicklaus, Ronald Reagan, Jackie Robinson, Norman Rockwell, Franklin D. Roosevelt, Gertrude Stein, Charles Lindbergh, Margaret Truman

PISCES: Edward Albee, Harry Belafonte, Alexander Graham Bell, Chopin, Adelle Davis, Albert Einstein, Golda Meir, Jackie Gleason, Winslow Homer, Edward M. Kennedy, Victor Hugo, Mike Mansfield, Michelangelo, Edna St. Vincent Millay, Liza Minelli, John Steinbeck, Linus Pauling, Ravel, Renoir, Diana Ross, William Shirer, Elizabeth Taylor, George Washington

The Signs and Their Key Words

		POSITIVE	NEGATIVE
ARIES	self	courage, initiative, pioneer instinct	brash rudeness, selfish impetuosity
TAURUS	money	endurance, loyalty, wealth	obstinacy, gluttony
GEMINI	mind	versatility	capriciousness, unreliability
CANCER	family	sympathy, homing instinct	clannishness, childishness
LEO	children	love, authority, integrity	egotism, force
VIRGO	work	purity, industry, analysis	faultfinding, cynicism
LIBRA	marriage	harmony, justice	vacillation, superficiality
SCORPIO	sex	survival, regeneration	vengeance, discord
SAGITTARIUS	travel	optimism, higher learning	lawlessness
CAPRICORN	career	depth	narrowness, gloom
AQUARIUS	friends	human fellowship, genius	perverse unpredictability
PISCES	confinement	spiritual love, universality	diffusion, escapism

The Elements and Qualities of The Signs

Every sign has both an *element* and a *quality* associated with it. The element indicates the basic makeup of the sign, and the quality describes the kind of activity associated with each.

Element	Sign	Quality	Sign
FIRE	ARIES LEO SAGITTARIUS	CARDINAL	ARIES LIBRA CANCER CAPRICORN
EARTH	TAURUS VIRGO CAPRICORN	FIXED	TAURUS LEO SCORPIO AQUARIUS
AIR	GEMINI LIBRA AQUARIUS		
WATER	CANCER SCORPIO PISCES	MUTABLE	GEMINI VIRGO SAGITTARIUS PISCES

Signs can be grouped together according to their element and quality. Signs of the same element share many basic traits in common. They tend to form stable configurations and ultimately harmonious relationships. Signs of the same quality are often less harmonious, but they share many dynamic potentials for growth as well as profound fulfillment.

Further discussion of each of these sign groupings is provided on the following pages.

The Fire Signs

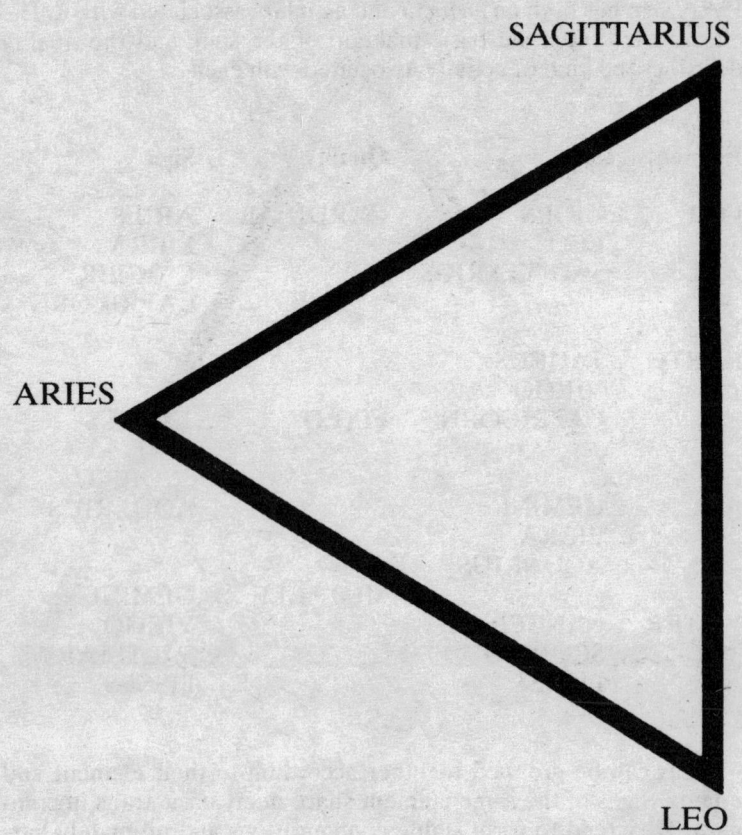

This is the fire group. On the whole these are emotional, volatile types, quick to anger, quick to forgive. They are adventurous, powerful people and act as a source of inspiration for everyone. They spark into action with immediate exuberant impulses. They are intelligent, self-involved, creative, and idealistic. They all share a certain vibrancy and glow that outwardly reflects an inner flame and passion for living.

The Earth Signs

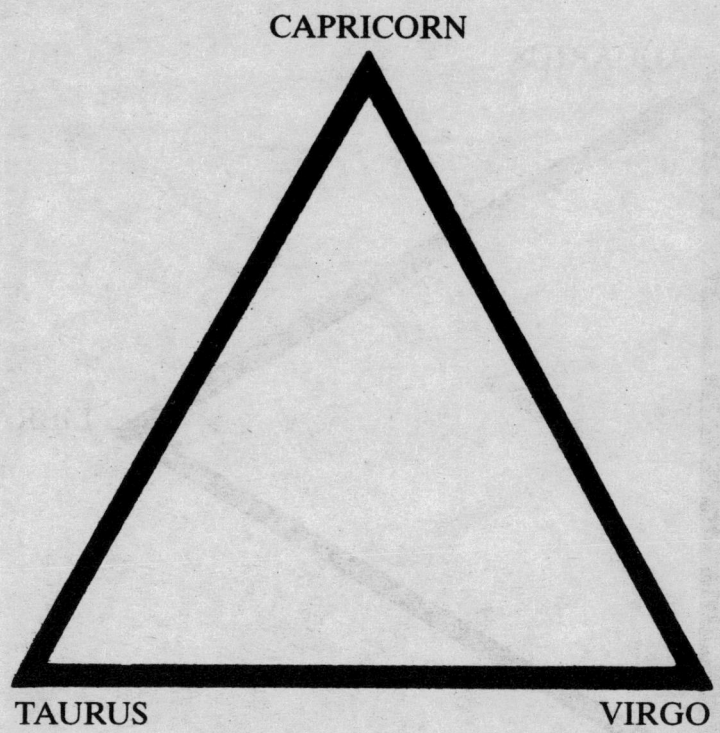

This is the earth group. They are in constant touch with the material world and tend to be conservative. Although they are all capable of spartan self-discipline, they are earthy, sensual people who are stimulated by the tangible, elegant, and luxurious. The thread of their lives is always practical, but they do fantasize and are often attracted to dark, mysterious, emotional people. They are like great cliffs overhanging the sea, forever married to the ocean but always resisting erosion from the dark, emotional forces that thunder at their feet.

The Air Signs

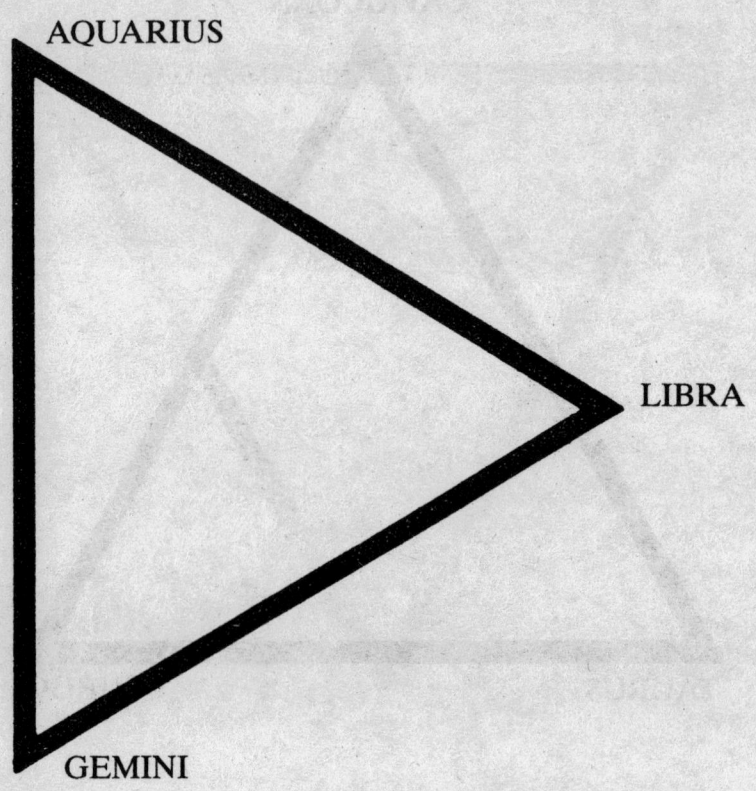

This is the air group. They are light, mental creatures desirous of contact, communication, and relationship. They are involved with people and the forming of ties on many levels. Original thinkers, they are the bearers of human news. Their language is their sense of word, color, style, and beauty. They provide an atmosphere suitable and pleasant for living. They add change and versatility to the scene, and it is through them that we can explore new territory of human intelligence and experience.

The Water Signs

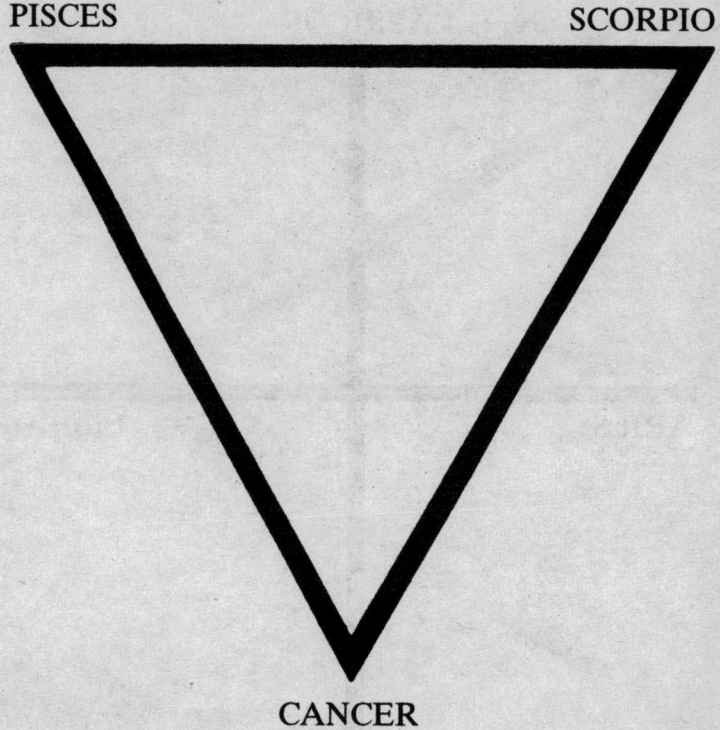

This is the water group. Through the water people, we are all joined together on emotional, nonverbal levels. They are silent, mysterious types whose magic hypnotizes even the most determined realist. They have uncanny perceptions about people and are as rich as the oceans when it comes to feeling, emotion, or imagination. They are sensitive, mystical creatures with memories that go back beyond time. Through water, life is sustained. These people have the potential for the depths of darkness or the heights of mysticism and art.

The Cardinal Signs

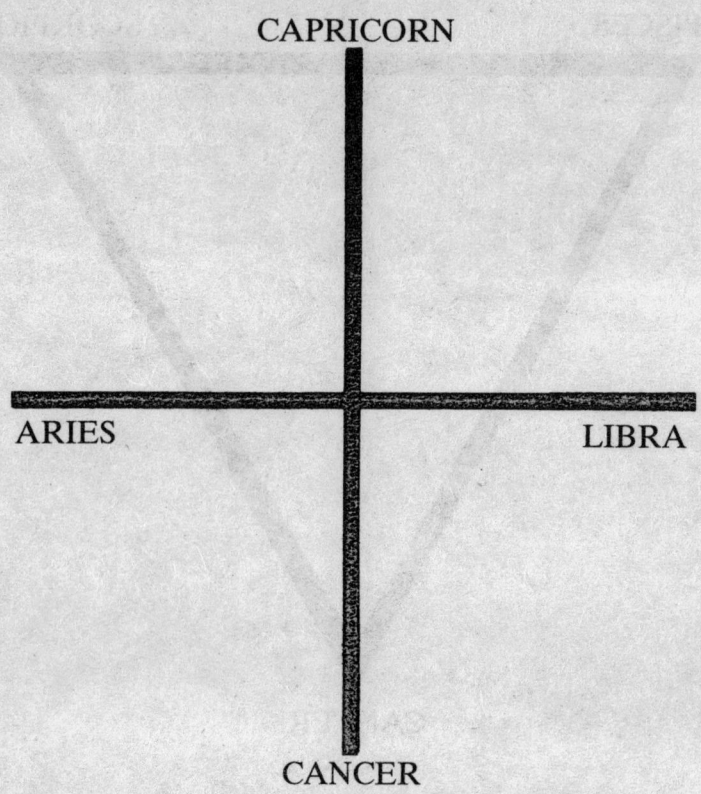

Put together, this is a clear-cut picture of dynamism, activity, tremendous stress, and remarkable achievement. These people know the meaning of great change since their lives are often characterized by significant crises and major successes. This combination is like a simultaneous storm of summer, fall, winter, and spring. The danger is chaotic diffusion of energy; the potential is irrepressible growth and victory.

The Fixed Signs

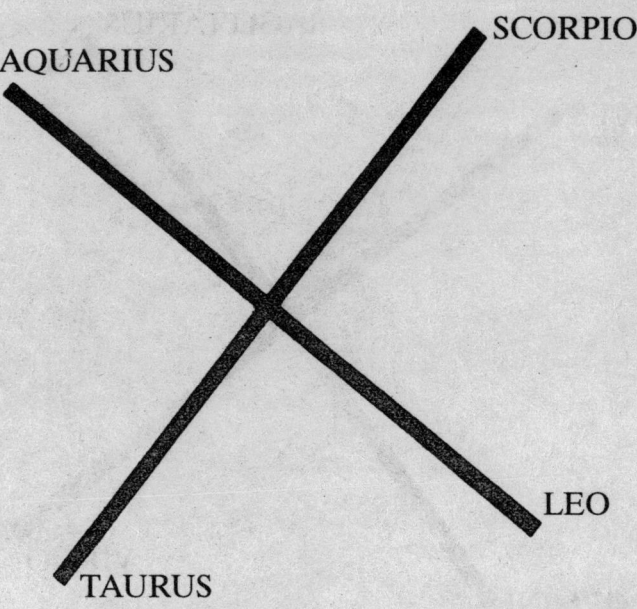

Fixed signs are always establishing themselves in a given place or area of experience. Like explorers who arrive and plant a flag, these people claim a position from which they do not enjoy being deposed. They are staunch, stalwart, upright, trusty, honorable people, although their obstinacy is well-known. Their contribution is fixity, and they are the angels who support our visible world.

The Mutable Signs

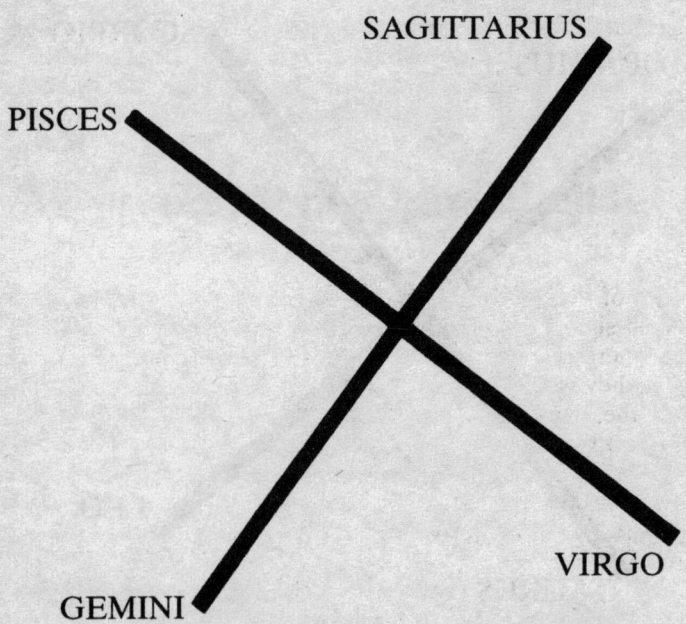

Mutable people are versatile, sensitive, intelligent, nervous, and deeply curious about life. They are the translators of all energy. They often carry out or complete tasks initiated by others. Combinations of these signs have highly developed minds; they are imaginative and jumpy and think and talk a lot. At worst their lives are a Tower of Babel. At best they are adaptable and ready creatures who can assimilate one kind of experience and enjoy it while anticipating coming changes.

THE PLANETS OF THE SOLAR SYSTEM

This section describes the planets of the solar system. In astrology, both the Sun and the Moon are considered to be planets. Because of the Moon's influence in our day-to-day lives, the Moon is described in a separate section following this one.

The Planets and the Signs They Rule

The signs of the Zodiac are linked to the planets in the following way. Each sign is governed or ruled by one or more planets. No matter where the planets are located in the sky at any given moment, they still rule their respective signs, and when they travel through the signs they rule, they have special dignity and their effects are stronger.

Following is a list of the planets and the signs they rule. After looking at the list, read the definitions of the planets and see if you can determine how the planet ruling *your* Sun sign has affected your life.

SIGNS	RULING PLANETS
Aries	Mars, Pluto
Taurus	Venus
Gemini	Mercury
Cancer	Moon
Leo	Sun
Virgo	Mercury
Libra	Venus
Scorpio	Mars, Pluto
Sagittarius	Jupiter
Capricorn	Saturn
Aquarius	Saturn, Uranus
Pisces	Jupiter, Neptune

Characteristics of the Planets

The following pages give the meaning and characteristics of the planets of the solar system. They all travel around the Sun at different speeds and different distances. Taken with the Sun, they all distribute individual intelligence and ability throughout the entire chart.

The planets modify the influence of the Sun in a chart according to their own particular natures, strengths, and positions. Their positions must be calculated for each year and day, and their function and expression in a horoscope will change as they move from one area of the Zodiac to another.

We start with a description of the sun.

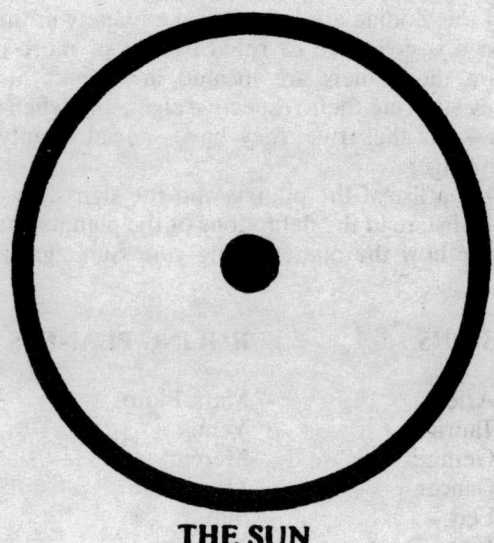

THE SUN

SUN

This is the center of existence. Around this flaming sphere all the planets revolve in endless orbits. Our star is constantly sending out its beams of light and energy without which no life on Earth would be possible. In astrology it symbolizes everything we are trying to become, the center around which all of our activity in life will always revolve. It is the symbol of our basic nature and describes the natural and constant thread that runs through everything that we do from birth to death on this planet.

To early astrologers, the Sun seemed to be another planet because it crossed the heavens every day, just like the rest of the bodies in the sky.

It is the only star near enough to be seen well—it is, in fact, a dwarf star. Approximately 860,000 miles in diameter, it is about ten times as wide as the giant planet Jupiter. The next nearest star is nearly 300,000 times as far away, and if the Sun were located as far away as most of the bright stars, it would be too faint to be seen without a telescope.

Everything in the horoscope ultimately revolves around this singular body. Although other forces may be prominent in the charts of some individuals, still the Sun is the total nucleus of being and symbolizes the complete potential of every human being alive. It is vitality and the life force. Your whole essence comes from the position of the Sun.

You are always trying to express the Sun according to its position by house and sign. Possibility for all development is found in the Sun, and it marks the fundamental character of your personal radiations all around you.

It is the symbol of strength, vigor, wisdom, dignity, ardor, and generosity, and the ability for a person to function as a mature individual. It is also a creative force in society. It is consciousness of the gift of life.

The underdeveloped solar nature is arrogant, pushy, undependable, and proud, and is constantly using force.

MERCURY

Mercury is the planet closest to the Sun. It races around our star, gathering information and translating it to the rest of the system. Mercury represents your capacity to understand the desires of your own will and to translate those desires into action.

In other words it is the planet of mind and the power of communication. Through Mercury we develop an ability to think, write, speak, and observe—to become aware of the world around us. It colors our attitudes and vision of the world, as well as our capacity to communicate our inner responses to the outside world. Some people who have serious disabilities in their power of verbal communication have often wrongly been described as people lacking intelligence.

Although this planet (and its position in the horoscope) indicates your power to communicate your thoughts and perceptions to the world, intelligence is something deeper. Intelligence is distributed throughout all the planets. It is the relationship of the planets to each other that truly describes what we call intelligence. Mercury rules speaking, language, mathematics, draft and design, students, messengers, young people, offices, teachers, and any pursuits where the mind of man has wings.

VENUS

Venus is beauty. It symbolizes the harmony and radiance of a rare and elusive quality: beauty itself. It is refinement and delicacy, softness and charm. In astrology it indicates grace, balance, and the aesthetic sense. Where Venus is we see beauty, a gentle drawing in of energy and the need for satisfaction and completion. It is a special touch that finishes off rough edges. It is sensitivity, and affection, and it is always the place for that other elusive phenomenon: love. Venus describes our sense of what is beautiful and loving. Poorly developed, it is vulgar, tasteless, and self-indulgent. But its ideal is the flame of spiritual love—Aphrodite, goddess of love, and the sweetness and power of personal beauty.

MARS

Mars is raw, crude energy. The planet next to Earth but outward from the Sun is a fiery red sphere that charges through the horoscope with force and fury. It represents the way you reach out for new adventure and new experience. It is energy and drive, initiative, courage, and daring. It is the power to start something and see it through. It can be thoughtless, cruel and wild, angry and hostile, causing cuts, burns, scalds, and wounds. It can stab its way through a chart, or it can be the symbol of healthy spirited adventure, well-channeled constructive power to begin and keep up the drive. If you have trouble starting things, if you lack the get-up-and-go to start the ball rolling, if you lack aggressiveness and self-confidence, chances are there's another planet influencing your Mars. Mars rules soldiers, butchers, surgeons, salesmen—any field that requires daring, bold skill, operational technique, or self-promotion.

JUPITER

This is the largest planet of the solar system. Scientists have recently learned that Jupiter reflects more light than it receives from the Sun. In a sense it is like a star itself. In astrology it rules good luck and good cheer, health, wealth, optimism, happiness, success, and joy. It is the symbol of opportunity and always opens the way for new possibilities in your life. It rules exuberance, enthusiasm, wisdom, knowledge, generosity, and all forms of expansion in general. It rules actors, statesmen, clerics, professional people, religion, publishing, and the distribution of many people over large areas.

Sometimes Jupiter makes you think you deserve everything, and you become sloppy, wasteful, careless and rude, prodigal and lawless, in the illusion that nothing can ever go wrong. Then there is the danger of overconfidence, exaggeration, undependability, and overindulgence.

Jupiter is the minimization of limitation and the emphasis on spirituality and potential. It is the thirst for knowledge and higher learning.

SATURN

Saturn circles our system in dark splendor with its mysterious rings, forcing us to be awakened to whatever we have neglected in the past. It will present real puzzles and problems to be solved, causing delays, obstacles, and hindrances. By doing so, Saturn stirs our own sensitivity to those areas where we are laziest.

Here we must patiently develop *method*, and only through painstaking effort can our ends be achieved. It brings order to a horoscope and imposes reason just where we are feeling least reasonable. By creating limitations and boundary, Saturn shows the consequences of being human and demands that we accept the changing cycles inevitable in human life. Saturn rules time, old age, and sobriety. It can bring depression, gloom, jealousy, and greed, or serious acceptance of responsibilities out of which success will develop. With Saturn there is nothing to do but face facts. It rules laborers, stones, granite, rocks, and crystals of all kinds.

THE OUTER PLANETS: URANUS, NEPTUNE, PLUTO

Uranus, Neptune, Pluto are the outer planets. They liberate human beings from cultural conditioning, and in that sense are the lawbreakers. In early times it was thought that Saturn was the last planet of the system—the outer limit beyond which we could never go. The discovery of the next three planets ushered in new phases of human history, revolution, and technology.

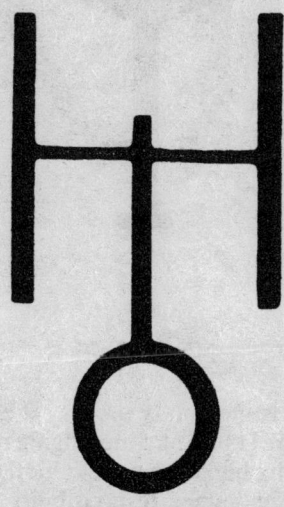

URANUS

Uranus rules unexpected change, upheaval, revolution. It is the symbol of total independence and asserts the freedom of an individual from all restriction and restraint. It is a breakthrough planet and indicates talent, originality, and genius in a horoscope. It usually causes last-minute reversals and changes of plan, unwanted separations, accidents, catastrophes, and eccentric behavior. It can add irrational rebelliousness and perverse bohemianism to a personality or a streak of unaffected brilliance in science and art. It rules technology, aviation, and all forms of electrical and electronic advancement. It governs great leaps forward and topsy-turvy situations, and *always* turns things around at the last minute. Its effects are difficult to predict, since it rules sudden last-minute decisions and events that come like lightning out of the blue.

NEPTUNE

Neptune dissolves existing reality the way the sea erodes the cliffs beside it. Its effects are subtle like the ringing of a buoy's bell in the fog. It suggests a reality higher than definition can usually describe. It awakens a sense of higher responsibility often causing guilt, worry, anxieties, or delusions. Neptune is associated with all forms of escape and can make things seem a certain way so convincingly that you are absolutely sure of something that eventually turns out to be quite different.

It is the planet of illusion and therefore governs the invisible realms that lie beyond our ordinary minds, beyond our simple factual ability to prove what is "real." Treachery, deceit, disillusionment, and disappointment are linked to Neptune. It describes a vague reality that promises eternity and the divine, yet in a manner so complex that we cannot really fathom it at all. At its worst Neptune is a cheap intoxicant; at its best it is the poetry, music, and inspiration of the higher planes of spiritual love. It has dominion over movies, photographs, and much of the arts.

PLUTO

Pluto lies at the outpost of our system and therefore rules finality in a horoscope—the final closing of chapters in your life, the passing of major milestones and points of development from which there is no return. It is a final wipeout, a closeout, an evacuation. It is a distant, subtle but powerful catalyst in all transformations that occur. It creates, destroys, then recreates. Sometimes Pluto starts its influence with a minor event or insignificant incident that might even go unnoticed. Slowly but surely, little by little, everything changes, until at last there has been a total transformation in the area of your life where Pluto has been operating. It rules mass thinking and the trends that society first rejects, then adopts, and finally outgrows.

Pluto rules the dead and the underworld—all the powerful forces of creation and destruction that go on all the time beneath, around, and above us. It can bring a lust for power with strong obsessions.

It is the planet that rules the metamorphosis of the caterpillar into a butterfly, for it symbolizes the capacity to change totally and forever a person's lifestyle, way of thought, and behavior.

THE MOON IN EACH SIGN

The Moon is the nearest planet to the Earth. It exerts more observable influence on us from day to day than any other planet. The effect is very personal, very intimate, and if we are not aware of how it works it can make us quite unstable in our ideas. And the annoying thing is that at these times we often see our own instability but can do nothing about it. A knowledge of what can be expected may help considerably. We can then be prepared to stand strong against the Moon's negative influences and use its positive ones to help us to get ahead. Who has not heard of going with the tide?

The Moon reflects, has no light of its own. It reflects the Sun—the life giver—in the form of vital movement. The Moon controls the tides, the blood rhythm, the movement of sap in trees and plants. Its nature is inconstancy and change so it signifies our moods, our superficial behavior—walking, talking, and especially thinking. Being a true reflector of other forces, the Moon is cold, watery like the surface of a still lake, brilliant and scintillating at times, but easily ruffled and disturbed by the winds of change.

The Moon takes about $27\frac{1}{3}$ days to make a complete transit of the Zodiac. It spends just over $2\frac{1}{4}$ days in each sign. During that time it reflects the qualities, energies, and characteristics of the sign and, to a degree, the planet which rules the sign. When the Moon in its transit occupies a sign incompatible with our own birth sign, we can expect to feel a vague uneasiness, perhaps a touch of irritableness. We should not be discouraged nor let the feeling get us down, or, worse still, allow ourselves to take the discomfort out on others. Try to remember that the Moon has to change signs within 55 hours and, provided you are not physically ill, your mood will probably change with it. It is amazing how frequently depression lifts with the shift in the Moon's position. And, of course, when the Moon is transiting a sign compatible or sympathetic to yours, you will probably feel some sort of stimulation or just be plain happy to be alive.

In the horoscope, the Moon is such a powerful indicator that competent astrologers often use the sign it occupied at birth as the birth sign of the person. This is done particularly when the Sun is on the cusp, or edge, of two signs. Most experienced astrologers, however, coordinate both Sun and Moon signs by reading and confirming from one to the other and secure a far more accurate and personalized analysis.

For these reasons, the Moon tables which follow this section (see pages 86–92) are of great importance to the individual. They show the days and the exact times the Moon will enter each sign of the Zodiac for the year. Remember, you have to adjust the indicated times to local time. The corrections, already calculated for most of the main cities, are at the beginning of the tables. What follows now is a guide to the influences that will be reflected to the Earth by the Moon while it transits each of the twelve signs. The influence is at its peak about 26 hours after the Moon enters a sign. As you read the daily forecast, check the Moon sign for any given day and glance back at this guide.

MOON IN ARIES
This is a time for action, for reaching out beyond the usual self-imposed limitations and faint-hearted cautions. If you have plans in your head or on your desk, put them into practice. New ventures, applications, new jobs, new starts of any kind—all have a good chance of success. This is the period when original and dynamic impulses are being reflected onto Earth. Such energies are extremely vital and favor the pursuit of pleasure and adventure in practically every form. Sick people should feel an improvement. Those who are well will probably find themselves exuding confidence and optimism. People fond of physical exercise should find their bodies growing with tone and well-being. Boldness, strength, determination should characterize most of your activities with a readiness to face up to old challenges. Yesterday's problems may seem petty and exaggerated—so deal with them. Strike out alone. Self-reliance will attract others to you. This is a good time for making friends. Business and marriage partners are more likely to be impressed with the man and woman of action. Opposition will be overcome or thrown aside with much less effort than usual. CAUTION: Be dominant but not domineering.

MOON IN TAURUS
The spontaneous, action-packed person of yesterday gives way to the cautious, diligent, hardworking "thinker." In this period ideas will probably be concentrated on ways of improving finances. A great deal of time may be spent figuring out and going over

schemes and plans. It is the right time to be careful with detail. People will find themselves working longer than usual at their desks. Or devoting more time to serious thought about the future. A strong desire to put order into business and financial arrangements may cause extra work. Loved ones may complain of being neglected and may fail to appreciate that your efforts are for their ultimate benefit. Your desire for system may extend to criticism of arrangements in the home and lead to minor upsets. Health may be affected through overwork. Try to secure a reasonable amount of rest and relaxation, although the tendency will be to "keep going" despite good advice. Work done conscientiously in this period should result in a solid contribution to your future security. CAUTION: Try not to be as serious with people as the work you are engaged in.

MOON IN GEMINI
The humdrum of routine and too much work should suddenly end. You are likely to find yourself in an expansive, quicksilver world of change and self-expression. Urges to write, to paint, to experience the freedom of some sort of artistic outpouring, may be very strong. Take full advantage of them. You may find yourself finishing something you began and put aside long ago. Or embarking on something new which could easily be prompted by a chance meeting, a new acquaintance, or even an advertisement. There may be a yearning for a change of scenery, the feeling to visit another country (not too far away), or at least to get away for a few days. This may result in short, quick journeys. Or, if you are planning a single visit, there may be some unexpected changes or detours on the way. Familiar activities will seem to give little satisfaction unless they contain a fresh element of excitement or expectation. The inclination will be toward untried pursuits, particularly those that allow you to express your inner nature. The accent is on new faces, new places. CAUTION: Do not be too quick to commit yourself emotionally.

MOON IN CANCER
Feelings of uncertainty and vague insecurity are likely to cause problems while the Moon is in Cancer. Thoughts may turn frequently to the warmth of the home and the comfort of loved ones. Nostalgic impulses could cause you to bring out old photographs and letters and reflect on the days when your life seemed to be much more rewarding and less demanding. The love and understanding of parents and family may be important, and, if it is not forthcoming, you may have to fight against bouts of self-pity. The cordiality of friends and the thought of good times with them that are sure to be repeated will help to restore you to a happier frame

of mind. The desire to be alone may follow minor setbacks or rebuffs at this time, but solitude is unlikely to help. Better to get on the telephone or visit someone. This period often causes peculiar dreams and upsurges of imaginative thinking which can be helpful to authors of occult and mystical works. Preoccupation with the personal world of simple human needs can overshadow any material strivings. CAUTION: Do not spend too much time thinking—seek the company of loved ones or close friends.

MOON IN LEO
New horizons of exciting and rather extravagant activity open up. This is the time for exhilarating entertainment, glamorous and lavish parties, and expensive shopping sprees. Any merrymaking that relies upon your generosity as a host has every chance of being a spectacular success. You should find yourself right in the center of the fun, either as the life of the party or simply as a person whom happy people like to be with. Romance thrives in this heady atmosphere and friendships are likely to explode unexpectedly into serious attachments. Children and younger people should be attracted to you and you may find yourself organizing a picnic or a visit to a fun-fair, the movies, or the beach. The sunny company and vitality of youthful companions should help you to find some unsuspected energy. In career, you could find an opening for promotion or advancement. This should be the time to make a direct approach. The period favors those engaged in original research. CAUTION: Bask in popularity, not in flattery.

MOON IN VIRGO
Off comes the party cap and out steps the busy, practical worker. He wants to get his personal affairs straight, to rearrange them, if necessary, for more efficiency, so he will have more time for more work. He clears up his correspondence, pays outstanding bills, makes numerous phone calls. He is likely to make inquiries, or sign up for some new insurance and put money into gilt-edged investment. Thoughts probably revolve around the need for future security—to tie up loose ends and clear the decks. There may be a tendency to be "finicky," to interfere in the routine of others, particularly friends and family members. The motive may be a genuine desire to help with suggestions for updating or streamlining their affairs, but these will probably not be welcomed. Sympathy may be felt for less fortunate sections of the community and a flurry of some sort of voluntary service is likely. This may be accompanied by strong feelings of responsibility on several fronts and health may suffer from extra efforts made. CAUTION: Everyone may not want your help or advice.

MOON IN LIBRA
These are days of harmony and agreement and you should find yourself at peace with most others. Relationships tend to be smooth and sweet-flowing. Friends may become closer and bonds deepen in mutual understanding. Hopes will be shared. Progress by cooperation could be the secret of success in every sphere. In business, established partnerships may flourish and new ones get off to a good start. Acquaintances could discover similar interests that lead to congenial discussions and rewarding exchanges of some sort. Love, as a unifying force, reaches its optimum. Marriage partners should find accord. Those who wed at this time face the prospect of a happy union. Cooperation and tolerance are felt to be stronger than dissension and impatience. The argumentative are not quite so loud in their bellowings, nor as inflexible in their attitudes. In the home, there should be a greater recognition of the other point of view and a readiness to put the wishes of the group before selfish insistence. This is a favorable time to join an art group. CAUTION: Do not be too independent—let others help you if they want to.

MOON IN SCORPIO
Driving impulses to make money and to economize are likely to cause upsets all around. No area of expenditure is likely to be spared the ax, including the household budget. This is a time when the desire to cut down on extravagance can become near fanatical. Care must be exercised to try to keep the aim in reasonable perspective. Others may not feel the same urgent need to save and may retaliate. There is a danger that possessions of sentimental value will be sold to realize cash for investment. Buying and selling of stock for quick profit is also likely. The attention turns to organizing, reorganizing, tidying up at home and at work. Neglected jobs could suddenly be done with great bursts of energy. The desire for solitude may intervene. Self-searching thoughts could disturb. The sense of invisible and mysterious energies in play could cause some excitability. The reassurance of loves ones may help. CAUTION: Be kind to the people you love.

MOON IN SAGITTARIUS
These are days when you are likely to be stirred and elevated by discussions and reflections of a religious and philosophical nature. Ideas of faraway places may cause unusual response and excitement. A decision may be made to visit someone overseas, perhaps a person whose influence was important to your earlier character development. There could be a strong resolution to get away from

present intellectual patterns, to learn new subjects, and to meet more interesting people. The superficial may be rejected in all its forms. An impatience with old ideas and unimaginative contacts could lead to a change of companions and interests. There may be an upsurge of religious feeling and metaphysical inquiry. Even a new insight into the significance of astrology and other occult studies is likely under the curious stimulus of the Moon in Sagittarius. Physically, you may express this need for fundamental change by spending more time outdoors: sports, gardening, long walks appeal. CAUTION: Try to channel any restlessness into worthwhile study.

MOON IN CAPRICORN
Life in these hours may seem to pivot around the importance of gaining prestige and honor in the career, as well as maintaining a spotless reputation. Ambitious urges may be excessive and could be accompanied by quite acquisitive drives for money. Effort should be directed along strictly ethical lines where there is no possibility of reproach or scandal. All endeavors are likely to be characterized by great earnestness, and an air of authority and purpose which should impress those who are looking for leadership or reliability. The desire to conform to accepted standards may extend to sharp criticism of family members. Frivolity and unconventional actions are unlikely to amuse while the Moon is in Capricorn. Moderation and seriousness are the orders of the day. Achievement and recognition in this period could come through community work or organizing for the benefit of some amateur group. CAUTION: Dignity and esteem are not always self-awarded.

MOON IN AQUARIUS
Moon in Aquarius is in the second last sign of the Zodiac where ideas can become disturbingly fine and subtle. The result is often a mental "no-man's land" where imagination cannot be trusted with the same certitude as other times. The dangers for the individual are the extremes of optimism and pessimism. Unless the imagination is held in check, situations are likely to be misread, and rosy conclusions drawn where they do not exist. Consequences for the unwary can be costly in career and business. Best to think twice and not speak or act until you think again. Pessimism can be a cruel self-inflicted penalty for delusion at this time. Between the two extremes are strange areas of self-deception which, for example, can make the selfish person think he is actually being generous. Eerie dreams which resemble the reality and even seem to continue into the waking state are also possible. CAUTION: Look for the fact and not just for the image in your mind.

MOON IN PISCES

Everything seems to come to the surface now. Memory may be crystal clear, throwing up long-forgotten information which could be valuable in the career or business. Flashes of clairvoyance and intuition are possible along with sudden realizations of one's own nature, which may be used for self-improvement. A talent, never before suspected, may be discovered. Qualities not evident before in friends and marriage partners are likely to be noticed. As this is a period in which the truth seems to emerge, the discovery of false characteristics is likely to lead to disenchantment or a shift in attachments. However, when qualities are accepted, it should lead to happiness and deeper feeling. Surprise solutions could bob up for old problems. There may be a public announcement of the solving of a crime or mystery. People with secrets may find someone has "guessed" correctly. The secrets of the soul or the inner self also tend to reveal themselves. Religious and philosophical groups may make some interesting discoveries. CAUTION: Not a time for activities that depend on secrecy.

NOTE: When you read your daily forecasts, use the Moon Sign Dates that are provided in the following section of Moon Tables. Then you may want to glance back here for the Moon's influence in a given sign.

MOON TABLES

CORRECTION FOR NEW YORK TIME, FIVE HOURS WEST OF GREENWICH

Atlanta, Boston, Detroit, Miami, Washington, Montreal,
    Ottawa, Quebec, Bogota, Havana, Lima, Santiago ... Same time
Chicago, New Orleans, Houston, Winnipeg, Churchill,
    Mexico City .... Deduct 1 hour
Albuquerque, Denver, Phoenix, El Paso, Edmonton,
    Helena .... Deduct 2 hours
Los Angeles, San Francisco, Reno, Portland,
    Seattle, Vancouver .... Deduct 3 hours
Honolulu, Anchorage, Fairbanks, Kodiak .... Deduct 5 hours
Nome, Samoa, Tonga, Midway .... Deduct 6 hours
Halifax, Bermuda, San Juan, Caracas, La Paz,
    Barbados .... Add 1 hour
St. John's, Brasilia, Rio de Janeiro, Sao Paulo,
    Buenos Aires, Montevideo .... Add 2 hours
Azores, Cape Verde Islands .... Add 3 hours
Canary Islands, Madeira, Reykjavik .... Add 4 hours
London, Paris, Amsterdam, Madrid, Lisbon,
    Gibraltar, Belfast, Raba .... Add 5 hours
Frankfurt, Rome, Oslo, Stockholm, Prague,
    Belgrade .... Add 6 hours
Bucharest, Beirut, Tel Aviv, Athens, Istanbul, Cairo,
    Alexandria, Cape Town, Johannesburg .... Add 7 hours
Moscow, Leningrad, Baghdad, Dhahran,
    Addis Ababa, Nairobi, Teheran, Zanzibar .... Add 8 hours
Bombay, Calcutta, Sri Lanka .... Add $10^{1}/_{2}$
Hong Kong, Shanghai, Manila, Peking, Perth ...... Add 13 hours
Tokyo, Okinawa, Darwin, Pusan .... Add 14 hours
Sydney, Melbourne, Port Moresby, Guam .... Add 15 hours
Auckland, Wellington, Suva, Wake .... Add 17 hours

2007 MOON SIGN DATES—
NEW YORK TIME

JANUARY		FEBRUARY		MARCH	
Day Moon Enters		**Day Moon Enters**		**Day Moon Enters**	
1. Gemini		1. Leo	12:16 am	1. Leo	
2. Cancer	10:15 am	2. Leo		2. Virgo	4:33 pm
3. Cancer		3. Virgo	9:35 am	3. Virgo	
4. Leo	5:15 pm	4. Virgo		4. Virgo	
5. Leo		5. Libra	9:16 pm	5. Libra	4:26 am
6. Leo		6. Libra		6. Libra	
7. Virgo	1:19 am	7. Libra		7. Scorp.	5:18 pm
8. Virgo		8. Scorp.	10:11 am	8. Scorp.	
9. Libra	1:16 pm	9. Scorp.		9. Scorp.	
10. Libra		10. Sagitt.	10:02 pm	10. Sagitt.	5:36 am
11. Libra		11. Sagitt.		11. Sagitt.	
12. Scorp.	2:09 am	12. Sagitt.		12. Capric.	3:36 pm
13. Scorp.		13. Capric.	6:43 am	13. Capric.	
14. Sagitt.	1:12 pm	14. Capric.		14. Aquar.	9:53 pm
15. Sagitt.		15. Aquar.	11:36 am	15. Aquar.	
16. Capric.	8:50 pm	16. Aquar.		16. Aquar.	
17. Capric.		17. Pisces	1:31 pm	17. Pisces	12:31 am
18. Capric.		18. Pisces		18. Pisces	
19. Aquar.	1:17 am	19. Aries	2:07 pm	19. Aries	12:43 am
20. Aquar.		20. Aries		20. Aries	
21. Pisces	3:49 am	21. Taurus	3:04 pm	21. Taurus	12:16 am
22. Pisces		22. Taurus		22. Taurus	
23. Aries	5:53 am	23. Gemini	5:43 pm	23. Gemini	1:07 am
24. Aries		24. Gemini		24. Gemini	
25. Taurus	8:30 am	25. Cancer	10:49 pm	25. Cancer	4:50 am
26. Taurus		26. Cancer		26. Cancer	
27. Gemini	12:11 pm	27. Cancer		27. Leo	12:05 pm
28. Gemini		28. Leo	6:31 am	28. Leo	
29. Cancer	5:17 pm			29. Virgo	10:28 pm
30. Cancer				30. Virgo	
31. Cancer				31. Virgo	

Daylight saving time to be considered where applicable.

2007 MOON SIGN DATES— NEW YORK TIME

APRIL
Day Moon Enters
1. Libra   10:44 am
2. Libra
3. Scorp.   11:37 pm
4. Scorp.
5. Scorp.
6. Sagitt.   11:58 am
7. Sagitt.
8. Capric.   10:37 pm
9. Capric.
10. Capric.
11. Aquar.   6:24 am
12. Aquar.
13. Pisces   10:40 am
14. Pisces
15. Aries   11:48 am
16. Aries
17. Taurus   11:12 am
18. Taurus
19. Gemini   10:52 am
20. Gemini
21. Cancer   12:51 pm
22. Cancer
23. Leo   6:39 pm
24. Leo
25. Leo
26. Virgo   4:25 am
27. Virgo
28. Libra   4:46 pm
29. Libra
30. Libra

MAY
Day Moon Enters
1. Scorp.   5:42 am
2. Scorp.
3. Sagitt.   5:49 pm
4. Sagitt.
5. Sagitt.
6. Capric.   4:22 am
7. Capric.
8. Aquar.   12:49 pm
9. Aquar.
10. Pisces   6:33 pm
11. Pisces
12. Aries   9:20 pm
13. Aries
14. Taurus   9:49 pm
15. Taurus
16. Gemini   9:35 pm
17. Gemini
18. Cancer   10:39 pm
19. Cancer
20. Cancer
21. Leo   2:58 am
22. Leo
23. Virgo   11:27 am
24. Virgo
25. Libra   11:17 pm
26. Libra
27. Libra
28. Scorp.   12:12 pm
29. Scorp.
30. Scorp.
31. Sagitt. 12:06 am

JUNE
Day Moon Enters
1. Sagitt.
2. Capric.   10:10 am
3. Capric.
4. Aquar.   6:16 pm
5. Aquar.
6. Aquar.
7. Pisces   12:25 am
8. Pisces
9. Aries   4:27 am
10. Aries
11. Taurus   6:30 am
12. Taurus
13. Gemini   7:25 am
14. Gemini
15. Cancer   8:46 am
16. Cancer
17. Leo   12:26 pm
18. Leo
19. Virgo   7:47 pm
20. Virgo
21. Virgo
22. Libra   5:45 am
23. Libra
24. Scorp.   7:26 pm
25. Scorp.
26. Scorp.
27. Sagitt. 7:25 am
28. Sagitt.
29. Capric. 5:06 pm
30. Capric.

Daylight saving time to be considered where applicable.

2007 MOON SIGN DATES— NEW YORK TIME

JULY
Day Moon Enters
1. Capric.
2. Aquar.   12:25 am
3. Aquar.
4. Pisces   5:53 am
5. Pisces
6. Aries   9:58 am
7. Aries
8. Taurus   12:55 pm
9. Taurus
10. Gemini   3:11 pm
11. Gemini
12. Cancer   5:40 pm
13. Cancer
14. Leo   9:44 pm
15. Leo
16. Leo
17. Virgo   4:40 am
18. Virgo
19. Libra   2:54 pm
20. Libra
21. Libra
22. Scorp.   3:19 am
23. Scorp.
24. Sagitt.   3:31 pm
25. Sagitt.
26. Sagitt.
27. Capric.   1:22 am
28. Capric.
29. Aquar.   8:15 am
30. Aquar.
31. Pisces   12:42 pm

AUGUST
Day Moon Enters
1. Pisces
2. Aries   3:44 pm
3. Aries
4. Taurus   6:17 pm
5. Taurus
6. Gemini   9:02 pm
7. Gemini
8. Gemini
9. Cancer   12:37 am
10. Cancer
11. Leo   5:43 am
12. Leo
13. Virgo   1:04 pm
14. Virgo
15. Libra   11:05 pm
16. Libra
17. Libra
18. Scorp.   11:14 am
19. Scorp.
20. Sagitt.   11:45 pm
21. Sagitt.
22. Sagitt.
23. Carpic.   10:21 am
24. Capric.
25. Aquar.   5:36 pm
26. Aquar.
27. Pisces   9:35 pm
28. Pisces
29. Aries   11:26 pm
30. Aries
31. Aries

SEPTEMBER
Day Moon Enters
1. Taurus   12:36 am
2. Taurus
3. Gemini   2:31 am
4. Gemini
5. Cancer   6:09 am
6. Cancer
7. Leo   12:00 pm
8. Leo
9. Virgo   8:11 pm
10. Virgo
11. Virgo
12. Libra   6:32 am
13. Libra
14. Scorp.   6:38 pm
15. Scorp.
16. Scorp.
17. Sagitt.   7:22 am
18. Sagitt.
19. Capric.   6:53 pm
20. Capric.
21. Capric.
22. Aquar.   3:19 am
23. Aquar.
24. Pisces   7:56 am
25. Pisces
26. Aries   9:24 am
27. Aries
28. Taurus   9:18 am
29. Taurus
30. Gemini   9:35 am

Daylight saving time to be considered where applicable.

2007 MOON SIGN DATES
NEW YORK TIME

OCTOBER		NOVEMBER		DECEMBER	
Day Moon Enters		Day Moon Enters		Day Moon Enters	
1. Gemini		1. Leo		1. Virgo	
2. Cancer	11:58 am	2. Leo		2. Virgo	
3. Cancer		3. Virgo	7:46 am	3. Libra	1:02 am
4. Leo	5:26 pm	4. Virgo		4. Libra	
5. Leo		5. Libra	6:48 pm	5. Scorp.	1:32 pm
6. Leo		6. Libra		6. Scorp.	
7. Virgo	2:04 am	7. Libra		7. Scorp.	
8. Virgo		8. Scorp.	7:19 am	8. Sagitt.	2:12 am
9. Libra	12:59 pm	9. Scorp.		9. Sagitt.	
10. Libra		10. Sagitt.	8:00 pm	10. Capric.	1:52 pm
11. Libra		11. Sagitt.		11. Capric.	
12. Scorp.	1:14 am	12. Sagitt.		12. Capric.	
13. Scorp.		13. Capric.	8:02 am	13. Aquar.	12:02 am
14. Sagitt.	1:59 pm	14. Capric.		14. Aquar.	
15. Sagitt.		15. Aquar.	6:31 pm	15. Pisces	8:16 am
16. Sagitt.		16. Aqaur.		16. Pisces	
17. Capric.	2:04 am	17. Aquar.		17. Aries	1:54 pm
18. Capric.		18. Pisces	2:16 am	18. Aries	
19. Aquar.	11:52 am	19. Pisces		19. Taurus	4:39 pm
20. Aquar.		20. Aries	6:25 am	20. Taurus	
21. Pisces	6:03 pm	21. Aries		21. Gemini	5:15 pm
22. Pisces		22. Taurus	7:20 am	22. Gemini	
23. Aries	8:25 pm	23. Taurus		23. Cancer	5:19 pm
24. Aries		24. Gemini	6:30 am	24. Cancer	
25. Taurus	8:06 pm	25. Gemini		25. Leo	6:53 pm
26. Taurus		26. Cancer	6:08 am	26. Leo	
27. Gemini	7:12 pm	27. Cancer		27. Virgo	11:45 pm
28. Gemini		28. Leo	8:24 am	28. Virgo	
29. Cancer	7:51 pm	29. Leo		29. Virgo	
30. Cancer		30. Virgo	2:45 pm	30. Libra	8:38 am
31. Leo	11:49 pm			31. Libra	

Daylight saving time to be considered where applicable.

2007 PHASES OF THE MOON—
NEW YORK TIME

New Moon	First Quarter	Full Moon	Last Quarter
Dec. 20 ('06)	Dec. 27 ('06)	Jan. 3	Jan. 11
Jan. 18	Jan. 25	Feb. 2	Feb. 10
Feb. 17	Feb. 24	March 3	March 11
March 18	March 25	April 2	April 10
April 17	April 24	May 2	May 9
May 16	May 23	May 31	June 8
June 14	June 22	June 30	July 7
July 14	July 22	July 29	August 5
August 12	August 20	August 28	Sept. 3
Sept. 11	Sept. 19	Sept. 26	Oct. 3
Oct. 11	Oct. 19	Oct. 26	Nov. 1
Nov. 9	Nov. 17	Nov. 24	Dec. 1
Dec. 9	Dec. 17	Dec. 23	Dec. 31

Each phase of the Moon lasts approximately seven to eight days, during which the Moon's shape gradually changes as it comes out of one phase and goes into the next.

There will be a solar eclipse during the New Moon phase on March 18 and September 11.

There will be a lunar eclipse during the Full Moon phase on March 3 and August 28.

2007 FISHING GUIDE

	Good	Best
January	1-5-6-19-25	2-3-4-11-30-31
February	1-2-3-4-17-24-28	16-26-27
March	1-2-3-4-11-18-30-31	5-6-25-26
April	17-24-29	2-3-4-5-9-29-30
May	4-5-10-24-31	1-2-15-29-30
June	1-2-14-28-29	3-4-8-23-26-30
July	2-3-7-27-29-30-31	13-23-28
August	2-12-20-26-27-30-31	1-5-24-28-29
September	4-11-22-23-26-27-28	20-24-25-29
October	18-24-25-28-29	3-10-22-26-27
November	2-17-21-22-24-25	9-23-26-27
December	1-10-17-21-22-23-26-27	24-25-31

2007 PLANTING GUIDE

	Aboveground Crops	Root Crops
January	3-21-22-26-30-31	3-10-11-12-13-17-18
February	18-22-23-26-27	6-7-8-9-14
March	21-22-25-26	5-6-7-8-9-13-14-18
April	1-18-22-23-29-30	2-3-4-5-9-10-14
May	1-19-20-26-27-28-29-30	1-2-11-12-15-16
June	15-16-22-23-24-25-26	3-4-7-8-11-12-30
July	20-21-22-23-28	3-4-9-13-14
August	16-17-18-19-24-25	1-5-6-10-28-29
September	12-13-14-15-16-20-21-25	2-5-6-29
October	12-13-18-22-23	3-10-26-27-30-31
November	14-15-18-19-22-23	7-8-9-26-27
December	11-12-16-20	4-5-6-7-24-25-30

	Pruning	Weeds and Pests
January	3-12-13	6-7-8-15-16
February	9-10	2-3-4-11-16
March	8-17-18	4-10-11-15-16
April	4-5-14	7-8-12-16
May	2-11-12	4-5-9-13-14
June	7-8	5-6-9-10-14
July	4-5-13-14	2-3-7-11-12-30
August	10-29	3-7-8-12-30-31
September	5-6	3-4-8-9-10-11-27
October	2-3-30-31	1-5-6-7-8-28-29
November	9-26-27	1-2-3-4-25-29-30
December	6-7-24-25	1-2-9-26-27-28-29

MOON'S INFLUENCE OVER PLANTS

Centuries ago it was established that seeds planted when the Moon is in signs and phases called Fruitful will produce more growth than seeds planted when the Moon is in a Barren sign.
Fruitful Signs: Taurus, Cancer, Libra, Scorpio, Capricorn, Pisces
Barren Signs: Aries, Gemini, Leo, Virgo, Sagittarius, Aquarius
Dry Signs: Aries, Gemini, Sagittarius, Aquarius

Activity	Moon In
Mow lawn, trim plants	**Fruitful sign:** 1st & 2nd quarter
Plant flowers	**Fruitful sign:** 2nd quarter; best in Cancer and Libra
Prune	**Fruitful sign:** 3rd & 4th quarter
Destroy pests; spray	**Barren sign:** 4th quarter
Harvest potatoes, root crops	**Dry sign:** 3rd & 4th quarter; Taurus, Leo, and Aquarius

MOON'S INFLUENCE OVER YOUR HEALTH

ARIES	Head, brain, face, upper jaw
TAURUS	Throat, neck, lower jaw
GEMINI	Hands, arms, lungs, shoulders, nervous system
CANCER	Esophagus, stomach, breasts, womb, liver
LEO	Heart, spine
VIRGO	Intestines, liver
LIBRA	Kidneys, lower back
SCORPIO	Sex and eliminative organs
SAGITTARIUS	Hips, thighs, liver
CAPRICORN	Skin, bones, teeth, knees
AQUARIUS	Circulatory system, lower legs
PISCES	Feet, tone of being

Try to avoid work being done on that part of the body when the Moon is in the sign governing that part.

MOON'S INFLUENCE OVER DAILY AFFAIRS

The Moon makes a complete transit of the Zodiac every 27 days 7 hours and 43 minutes. In making this transit the Moon forms different aspects with the planets and consequently has favorable or unfavorable bearings on affairs and events for persons according to the sign of the Zodiac under which they were born.

When the Moon is in conjunction with the Sun it is called a New Moon; when the Moon and Sun are in opposition it is called a Full Moon. From New Moon to Full Moon, first and second quarter—which takes about two weeks—the Moon is increasing or waxing. From Full Moon to New Moon, third and fourth quarter, the Moon is decreasing or waning.

Activity	Moon In
Business: buying and selling new, requiring public support	Sagittarius, Aries, Gemini, Virgo 1st and 2nd quarter
meant to be kept quiet	3rd and 4th quarter
Investigation	3rd and 4th quarter
Signing documents	1st & 2nd quarter, Cancer, Scorpio, Pisces
Advertising	2nd quarter, Sagittarius
Journeys and trips	1st & 2nd quarter, Gemini, Virgo
Renting offices, etc.	Taurus, Leo, Scorpio, Aquarius
Painting of house/apartment	3rd & 4th quarter, Taurus, Scorpio, Aquarius
Decorating	Gemini, Libra, Aquarius
Buying clothes and accessories	Taurus, Virgo
Beauty salon or barber shop visit	1st & 2nd quarter, Taurus, Leo, Libra, Scorpio, Aquarius
Weddings	1st & 2nd quarter

Leo

LEO

Character Analysis

The person born under the sign of Leo usually knows how to handle a position of authority well. Others have a deep respect for the decisions he makes. The Leo man or woman generally has something aristocratic about him that commands respect. The person born under this fifth sign of the Zodiac generally knows how to stand on his own two feet. He is independent in many things that he does. He knows how to direct his energies so that he will be able to achieve his ends. He seldom wastes time; he is to the point. In love matters, the Leo is quite passionate. He doesn't stint when it comes to romance and is capable of deep emotions. The Leo is a stable person; he has the ability to see things through to the end without wavering on his standpoint.

Leo people are quite generous in all that they do. They give themselves fully to every situation. To others they often appear quite lordly; they are often at the helm of organizations, running things.

The Leo person does not believe in being petty or small. Quite often he goes out of his way to make others happy. He would never stoop to doing anything which he felt was beneath his dignity. He has a deep feeling of self-respect. He would never treat others badly. He is kindhearted, sometimes to a fault. Although he does his best not to hurt others, he is apt to have his moments of irritation when he feels that it is better to speak outright than to give a false impression of his attitudes.

Leo people generally learn to shoulder certain responsibilities at an early age. They have an understanding of life that others sometimes never attain. They do not shy away from conflict or troubles. They believe in dealing with opposition directly. They are quite active in their approach to problems. Life, to them, should be attacked with zest and vigor. There is nothing lazy or retiring about a person born under this sign. He is outgoing, often fond of strenuous sports, keenly interested in having a good time. Everything about his attitudes is likely to be king-sized.

When the Leo man or woman knows what he wants in life, he goes out after it. He is not a person who gives up easily. He perseveres until he wins. He is not interested in occupying a position where he has to be told what to do. He is too independent for that sort of thing. He wants to be the person who runs things and he seems almost naturally suited for an authoritative position. His bearing is that of someone who expects others to listen to him when he speaks. He is a forceful person; he knows how to command respect. He is seldom unsure of himself, but when he is, he sees to it that others do not notice. He is quite clever at organizing things. He is a person who likes order. He knows how to channel his creative talents in such a way that the results of whatever he does are always constructive and original. Leadership positions bring out the best in a person born under this sign.

The Leo person is generally quite tolerant and open-minded. He believes in live-and-let-live as long as the other person does not infringe on what he believes to be his natural rights. In most things, he is fair. He believes in being frank and open. On the whole, the Leo person is active and high-strung. If something irritates him or runs against his grain, he will let it be known. He can be short-tempered if the occasion calls for it.

He is a person who believes in sticking to his principles. He is not interested in making compromises—especially if he feels that his standpoint is the correct one. He can become angry if opposed. But, all in all, his bad temper does not last for a long time. He is the kind of person who does not hold grudges.

The Leo person often has a flair for acting. Some of the best actors in the world have been people born under the sign of the Lion. Their dramatic talents are often considerable. Even as children Leo people have a strong understanding of drama. There is also something poetic about them. They can be quite romantic at times. They have a deep love and appreciation of beauty. They are fond of display and have a love of luxury that often startles modest people.

On the whole, Lion or Lioness is a proud person. His head is easily turned by a compliment. The cultivated Leo, however, knows how to take flattery in his stride. Others may try to get around him by flattering him. They generally succeed with the weaker Leos, for they are quite caught up with themselves and feel that no compliment is too great. This should not be interpreted as pure vanity. The Leo person has a clear understanding of his own superiority and worth.

In spite of the fact that he is generous in most things, the person born under Leo may not appreciate others making demands of him. He may not mind offering favors, but he does not like them to be asked of him.

Leo men and women feel that it is important to be your own boss. He does not like others to tell him what to do. He is quite capable, he feels, of handling his own affairs—and quite well. If he has to work with others, he may become impatient, especially if they are somewhat slow or unsure. He does not like to be kept waiting. Teamwork for the Lion is sometimes a very frustrating experience. He likes to be on his own.

Health

The Leo person is generally well built. He is a sturdy person, capable of taking a lot of stress and strain if necessary. Still, he may take on more than he can manage from time to time, and this is likely to exhaust him physically. He enjoys challenge, however, and finds it difficult to turn down a proposition which gives him a chance to demonstrate his worth—even if it is beyond his real capabilities.

Although he is basically an active person, he does have his limits. If he refuses to recognize them, he may become the victim of a nervous disorder. Some people born under this sign are fond of keeping late hours, especially in pursuit of pleasure or of fame. They can keep this up for some time, but in the end it does have a telling effect on their health. People born under this sign often wear themselves out by going from one extreme to the other.

The weak parts of the Leo are his spine and heart. He should see to it that he does nothing that might affect these areas of his body. In many instances, the Leo has to restrain himself in order to protect his health. Heart disease or rheumatic fever sometimes strikes people born under this sign. In spite of this, the Leo generally has a strong resistance to disease. His constitution is good. Whenever he does fall ill, he generally recovers rather quickly. The Leo man or woman cannot stand being sick. He has to be up and around; lying in bed is quite bothersome for him.

On the whole, Leo is a brave person. However, he may have to learn the art of being physically courageous. This is generally not one of his natural attributes. When physical dangers threaten, he may be somewhat paralyzed by fear. But intellectually Leo is fearless. If ideas or principles are at stake he is not afraid to stand up and let others know his opinion.

The Leo man or woman has a deep love of life. He can be quite pleasure-oriented. He likes the good things that life has to offer. Sometimes he is overenthusiastic in his approach to things, and as a result accidents occur. Under certain conditions he may take chances that others wouldn't. It is important that the person born as a Lion or Lioness learn how to curb impulsiveness, as often it works against him.

Even when they become older, Leo people remain energetic. Their zest for life never dies. They can prolong their lives by avoiding excesses in drinking or by adopting a balanced and moderate lifestyle.

Occupation

Leo seems to gravitate to jobs where he will have a chance to exercise his ability to manage. He is best suited to positions of authority; people respect the decisions he makes. He seems to be a natural-born leader. He knows how to take command of any situation in which he finds himself. The decisions he makes are usually just. He is direct in the way he handles his business affairs. When dealing with others he is open. He says what he means—even if he runs the danger of being blunt or offensive. He is the kind of person who believes that honesty is the best policy. Lies don't go down well with him. The truth—even if it is painful—is better than a kind lie.

In spite of the fact that the Leo man or woman is sometimes critical to a fault, the people who work under him generally respect him and try to understand him. They seldom have reason to question his authority.

In work situations, Leo always tries to do his best. His interest in being the top person has considerable motivational force. He is not interested in second place; only the top position is good enough for him. He will strive until he gets the position he feels is his due. The Leo individual generally has a good understanding of the way things work and how to improve work situations so that better results can be obtained. He knows how to handle people—how they think and how they behave. His understanding of human nature is considerable. He is not the kind of person to rest on his laurels. He is always in search of ways to better an existing situation. He knows how to move along with the times and always tries to keep abreast of new developments in his field.

Leo is proud. In every struggle—be it physical or intellectual—he fights to win. Failure is something he finds difficult to accept. He seldom considers the possibility; success is the only thing he keeps in mind as he works. He coordinates all of his energies and efforts so that success is almost guaranteed. Dull, routine work he is glad to leave to others. His interest lies in the decision-making area of business. He wants to discuss important issues and have a hand in making policies.

Leo leads things well; there can be no question of that. He or she is deeply interested in people's welfare. Leo would never abuse his position as supervisor or manager, but would use it to help those working under him.

On the whole, Leo is a responsible person. He handles his duties capably. He does not, however, enjoy being told what to do. When others try to lord it over him, he is likely to resent it—sometimes quite violently. He feels that no one is in a position to lead him. He often finds fault with the way others try to run things; sometimes he is quite just in his criticism.

The person born under this fifth sign of the Zodiac usually does well in a position where he has to deal with the public. He knows how to be persuasive in his argument. Others seldom have reason to doubt his word, for he is usually sure of what he has to say. A Leo person is likely to do well in any kind of business where he is given an opportunity to make use of his managerial skills. Politics is another area where the man or woman born under the sign of the Lion is apt to do quite well.

As was mentioned before, many Leos seem to be natural-born actors. They have convincing ease when on the stage. They know how to immerse themselves completely in a dramatic role. They do well in almost any kind of creative work. They have the soul of an artist or poet. In whatever field he enters—theater, art, politics, advertising, or industrial management—the Lion or Lioness will do what they can to occupy the top position. If they do not have it in the beginning, you can be sure they are working toward it.

The Leo person is far from being stingy. He loves entertaining his friends and relatives in a royal manner. Generous, sometimes to a fault, he is far from being careless with his money. He has a deep-hidden fear of being poor. He'll do what he can to protect his interests. The Leo man or woman is generally fortunate enough to occupy a position that pays well. If he earns a lot, he is apt to spend a lot. He does not like to have to count pennies. Luxurious surroundings give him the feeling of success. Money is seldom a problem to the wise Leo man or woman. Some of them wind up considerably well-off early in life. They usually don't mind taking chances with their finances. Quite often they are lucky in speculation or gambling.

If Leo feels that someone is in serious financial trouble, he does not mind helping out. He is generous and good-hearted when it comes to lending money. But he doesn't like to be taken advantage of. If someone makes unnecessary demands of him financially, he is apt to become disagreeable.

Leo likes to treat the people he cares for and to give them presents. The gifts he gives are usually expensive and in good taste. He likes to please others—to make them grateful for the gifts he has given them. He likes others to think well of him and that is perhaps why he is eager to give presents. He likes to be the one others turn to when in trouble or lean on for support.

A show of wealth makes Leo men or women feel important. The cultivated Leo sees to it that their extravagance never becomes unreasonable or unbearable.

Home and Family

The Leo man or woman needs a place where he can relax in peace and quiet. His home is his castle. He likes to live in a place that radiates comfort and harmony. Home life is important to the Leo person. He likes to feel that his family needs him—financially as well as emotionally. He likes to be the one who runs things at home. He expects his standards to be upheld by the other members of his family. He is generally a good provider.

The Leo individual makes an excellent host. He knows how to make his guests feel at home. He likes to entertain his close friends quite often. The Leo woman does everything she can to make her guests feel they are liked and cared for. She is usually a very attentive hostess.

When the Leo person spends money, it is often to show that he is capable of spending it. For him it is a display of power or success. It lets others know what he is worth. He sees to it that his home has all of the latest appliances and luxuries. He enjoys impressing others by his clothes and furnishings, even though this may encourage them to envy him.

The woman born under this sign usually enjoys dressing well. Her wardrobe is apt to be large. If she is able, she may not wear the same thing more than once or twice. She is very conscious of being in style. If her husband is not a big earner, she may be quite a burden, for her extravagance is sometimes boundless. If she is married to a man who is not in a top earning position, she will do what she can to help him achieve it.

The Leo person is fond of children. Leos enjoy taking care of them and seeing them grow up. Sometimes, however, they are too forceful as parents and don't give their children a chance to develop their own potential. They like to be proud of their children and appreciate it when others pay them compliments about their children's behavior.

Some Leo parents love their children so much that they are blind to their faults. They become angry if others should accuse them of spoiling their children. They are anxious to see their children succeed and sometimes expect too much of them too soon. When the children reach adulthood and assert their own will, the Leo parent is apt to feel that his children are not appreciative of all that he has done for them. He may resent the youngsters' show of independence.

Social Relationships

Leo people have no trouble making friends. People seem to gravitate to them. It is unusual for someone born under this sign not to be popular. They are warm, friendly, and considerate. People like them because of their sure, authoritative ways. Leo people know how to keep the friends they make. They are outgoing, open, and helpful. They never refuse someone in real need.

They usually have what is popularly known as "personality". They are never dull or retiring people. They are always out front where they can easily be seen. They like having a rich and active social life. Sometimes they make considerable gains in their business affairs through social activities. For them, business and pleasure can mix. They are never short of important contacts.

Those who love Leos accept their leadership without having any qualms. They trust Leos' good judgment and their ability to regulate things.

Leo is tremendously loyal to true friends, so firm friendships may last a lifetime. But a problem can arise in finding true friends. Because Leos believe everyone is as noble as they are, a naive belief at best, they often immediately claim an associate or casual acquaintance as a friend. The trouble begins when the person does not live up to Leo's expectations of what a friend should be.

Such disappointing experiences prove to be useful lessons for the young Lion. As they mature, and as a defense against hurt or betrayal, Leos will maintain a measure of aloofness in many of their personal relationships. For that reason, many Leo men and women have few really intimate friends or close confidantes. Leo likes to mix with people, but he or she may feel it necessary to keep some distance.

The Lion's desire to win in any situation makes for a very competitive personality. This basic competitive nature sometimes interferes with an ability to get along with teammates. Also, many people who are peers and might become good friends may be regarded as rivals on any playing field. Of course, Leos are just as likely to compliment a worthy rival as to criticize a weak and undeserving one.

But Leo is all heart. Leo is deeply sympathetic with anyone who is perceived to lack the advantages. Leos go out of their way to nurture, aid, and lead this person to a richer, fuller life. Some of Leo's friends are those unfortunates who need a helping hand. Family members or associates may pick on Leo for such unconventional choices. But a generosity of spirit rises above what Leos consider to be petty considerations of wealth, class, and rank.

Love and Marriage

Leo is the sign of life and love of life. Leo is also the sign of pleasure and of children. Love together with love of life linked in the union of two loving individuals is the basis for pleasure and children. The supreme force of love motivates the Lion or Lioness in every aspect of living. But Leo's love is not strictly sexual nor earthly sensual nor purely mental. Leo's love embraces each kind yet extends to the romantic, idealistic, unrestrained, universal love that sustains all of humankind.

Because of love's impelling force, it can hardly be said that Leo men and women are cool, easygoing lovers. Quite the contrary! Most Lions are incredibly impulsive, even unpredictable, in affairs of the heart—and as a result Leos are very vulnerable.

With their intense emotionality, Leos are apt to get carried away in love. They throw caution to the winds. They take all kinds of risks in order to win someone they are chasing. When amorous and ardent, Leos may lose all sense of what is wrong and what is right.

Leos are sentimental and easily moved. Every love affair is serious to them. They may flirt from time to time, but when earnest in love they do what they can to make it permanent.

A Leo is very affectionate by nature and he displays this in private. He or she is not fond of being demonstrative in public places. Somehow Leo feels this is undignified. Love and affection should be kept between two people in private.

When in love, Leos are faithful. They do not believe in cheating. Constancy is important to the Lion and Lioness. But if a lover cheats, Leo cannot endure such unhappiness even long enough to resolve what might be only a testing situation. Leo quickly switches interest to another potential mate and wholeheartedly resumes the chase. The same is true of unrequited love. If the adored one is not responding, Leo doesn't hang around acting like a pest. He or she eagerly looks for another beloved on whom to lavish attention and affection.

Generally, Leo individuals are attractive and are never at a loss for company. The opposite sex falls under the charm of a Leo person quite easily.

When looking for a permanent mate, the wise and cultivated Leo chooses someone who is not jealous or possessive—someone who won't suspect him of infidelity if he finds someone else attractive and is quite frank about it.

Romance and the Leo Woman

The Leo woman is often charming and beautiful. She seldom has any trouble in finding a mate. Men are drawn to her almost automatically because of her grace and poise. Lady Lions are known for their attractive eyes and regal bearing. Their features are often fine and delicate. There is seldom anything gross about a woman born under the sign of Leo, even when they tend to be heavy-set or large. There is always something fine that is easy to recognize in their build and carriage.

The Leo woman is passionate by nature. She is very warm and giving when in love. Men find her a very desirable creature and are apt to lose their heads over her when in love. She has an undeniable charm for the opposite sex. Other women are not apt to care for her when men are in the vicinity, for she has no trouble in outshining them all. She is serious when it comes to love. She may have many love affairs before she settles down, but all of them will be serious. She almost never flirts. She doesn't like a jealous or possessive man. She wants the person she loves to trust her implicitly. She doesn't like her love to be doubted.

She likes to be active socially. She enjoys being catered to by the man who loves her. She is fond of parties and entertainment. The man who courts her may have to spend quite a bit of money in order to please her. Sometimes, she is dreamy and idealistic when in love, and so chooses the wrong man for a partner.

She is the kind of woman who stands behind her man in all that she does. She does what she can to help him ascend the ladder of success. She is an intelligent conversationalist and can often entertain her husband's business associates in such a way that her husband can make important gains. She is a charming hostess.

The Leo mother is affectionate and understanding. She will do all she can to see to it that her children are brought up properly.

Romance and the Leo Man

The Leo man is considered a real Casanova by many. He is passionate when in love and will stop at nothing to please the object of his affection. Women love his fiery, sure nature. They feel safe and secure when they are with him. He is a difficult person for many a woman to resist. When romancing someone, Leo does what he can to keep the affair exciting and happy. He lavishes gifts on the person he loves. Dining and dancing at the best places in town are something that Leo is fond of when dating.

If Leo loves someone, he is likely to be blind to her faults. He may be more in love with his idea of a person than with the person herself. So caught up is he in his passion that he is likely to forget all practical matters. Sometimes Leo marries unluckily because of this. He idolizes his love to such an extent that he feels she is incapable of human faults and weaknesses.

The Leo man is a passionate lover. He woos the woman of his choice until he wins her. It is important for him to love, and to have that love returned. Women are easily attracted to him because of his charming ways. He knows how to make a woman feel important and wanted.

He is serious about love. He doesn't believe in meaningless

flings. He is very concerned with appearance and is easily attracted to a good-looking woman. He is apt to build a certain fantasy world around the woman he loves and set her on a high pedestal. He will do everything he can to make her happy. He is an attentive lover and is fond of presenting his loved one with presents. He does not like possessive or jealous women. He wants his sweetheart or wife to give him the freedom he feels he is entitled to. Although he may be attracted to other women after marriage, it is unlikely that he will ever be unfaithful.

As a parent and husband Leo is an excellent provider. He likes to be admired by his family. He may become quite irritable if he feels his family is not as loving and as affectionate as he is. He wants his family to be one he can be proud of.

Woman—Man
LEO WOMAN
ARIES MAN
The man born under the sign of Aries is often attracted to the Leo woman. After all, you are both fire signs. In you he can find that mixture of intellect and charm that is often difficult to find in a woman.

In some ways, the lamb and the lion are an idealized union. Your lively Ram lover may even lead the way. Aries has an insatiable thirst for knowledge. He is ambitious and is apt to have his finger in many pies. He can do with a woman like you—someone attractive, quick-witted, and smart.

He is not interested in a clinging vine for a wife. He wants someone who is there when he needs her; someone who listens and understands what he says; someone who can give advice if he should ever have to ask for it—which is not likely to be often. The Aries man wants a woman who is a good companion and a good sport.

He is looking for a woman who will look good on his arm without hanging on it too heavily. He is looking for a woman who has both feet on the ground and yet is mysterious and enticing—a kind of domestic Helen of Troy whose face or fine dinner can launch a thousand business deals if need be. That woman he is in search of sounds a little like you, doesn't it? If the shoe fits, wear it. It will make you feel like Cinderella.

The Aries man makes a good husband. He is faithful and attentive. He is an affectionate kind of man. He'll make you feel needed and loved. Love is a serious matter for the Aries man. He does not believe in flirting or playing the field—especially after he's found the woman of his dreams. He'll expect you to be as constant in your affection as he is in his. He'll expect you to be one hundred percent his; he won't put up with any nonsense while romancing you.

The Aries man may be pretty progressive and modern about many things. However, when it comes to wearing the pants he's downright conventional; it's strictly male attire. The best role you can take in the relationship is a supporting one. He's the boss and that's that. Once you have learned to accept that, you'll find the going easy.

The Aries man, with his endless energy and drive, likes to relax in the comfort of his home at the end of the day. The good homemaker can be sure of holding his love. He's keen on watching news programs and special reports from a comfortable armchair. If you see to it that everything in the house is where he expects to find it, you'll have no difficulty keeping the relationship on an even keel.

Life and love with an Aries man may be just the medicine you need. He'll be a good provider. He'll spoil you if he's financially able.

The Aries father is young at heart and can get along easily with children. His ability to jump from one activity to another will suit and delight a young child's attention span.

LEO WOMAN
TAURUS MAN
If you've got your heart set on a man born under the sign of Taurus, you'll have to learn the art of being patient. Taurus take their time about everything—even love.

The steady and deliberate Taurus man is a little slow on the draw. It may take him quite a while before he gets around to popping that question. For the Leo woman who doesn't mind twiddling her thumbs, the waiting and anticipating almost always pay off in the end. Taurus men want to make sure that every step they take is a good one, particularly if they feel that the path they're on could lead to the altar.

If you are in the mood for a whirlwind romance, you had better cast your net in shallower waters. Moreover, most Taurus prefer to do the angling themselves. They are not happy when a woman takes the lead. Once she does, he's likely to drop her like a dead fish. If you let yourself get caught on his terms, you'll find that he's fallen for you—hook, line, and sinker.

The Taurus man is fond of a comfortable home life. It is very important to him. If you keep those home fires burning, you will have no trouble keeping that flame in your Taurus lover's heart aglow. You have a talent for homemaking; use it. Your taste in furnishings is excellent. You know how to make a house come alive with inviting colors and decorations.

Taurus, the strong, steady, and protective Bull, could be the answer to your prayers. Perhaps he could be the anchor for your dreams and plans. He could help you acquire a more balanced outlook and approach to your life. If you're given to impulsiveness, he could help you to curb it. He's the man who is always there when you need him.

When you tie the knot with a man born under Taurus, you can put away fears about creditors pounding on the front door. Taurus are practical about everything including bill paying. When he carries you over that threshold, you can be certain that the entire house is paid for, not only the doorsill.

As a homemaker, you won't have to worry about putting aside your many interests for the sake of back-breaking house chores. Your Taurus husband will see to it that you have all the latest time-saving appliances and comforts.

You can forget about acquiring premature gray hairs due to unruly, ruckus-raising children under your feet. Papa Taurus is a master at keeping the youngsters in line. He's crazy about kids, but he also knows what's good for them.

LEO WOMAN
GEMINI MAN

The Gemini man is quite a catch. Many a woman has set her cap for him and failed to bag him. Generally, Gemini men are intelligent, witty, and outgoing. Many of them tend to be versatile and multifaceted. The Gemini man could easily wind up being your better half.

One thing that causes a Twin's mind and affection to wander is a bore, and it is unlikely that an active Leo woman would ever allow herself to be accused of that. The Gemini man who has caught your heart will admire you for your ideas and intellect—perhaps even more than for your homemaking talents and good looks.

The Leo woman needn't feel that once she's made her marriage vows that she'll have to store her interests and ambition in the attic somewhere. The Gemini man will admire you for your zeal and liveliness. He's the kind of guy who won't scowl if you let him shift for himself in the kitchen once in a while. In fact, he'll enjoy the challenge of wrestling with pots and pans himself for a change. Chances are, too, that he might turn out to be a better cook than you—that is, if he isn't already.

The man born under the sign of the Twins is a very active person. There aren't many women who have enough pep to keep up with him. But pep is no problem for the spry Leo woman. You are both dreamers, planners, and idealists. The strong Leo woman can easily fill the role of rudder for her Gemini's ship-without-a-sail. If you are a cultivated, purposeful Leo, he won't mind it at all.

The intelligent Twin is often aware of his shortcomings and doesn't resent it if someone with better bearings gives him a shove in the right direction—when it's needed. The average Gemini does not have serious ego hang-ups and will even accept a well-deserved chewing out from his mate quite gracefully.

When you and your Gemini man team up, you'll probably always have a houseful of people to entertain—interesting people, too. Geminis find it hard to tolerate sluggish minds and impassive dispositions.

People born under Gemini generally have two sides to their natures, as different as night and day. It's very easy for them to be happy-go-lucky one minute, then down in the dumps the next. They hate to be bored and will generally do anything to make their lives interesting, vivid, and action-packed.

Gemini men are always attractive to the opposite sex. You'll perhaps have to allow him an occasional harmless flirt—it will seldom amount to more than that if you're his proper mate.

The Gemini father is a pushover for the kids. He loves them so much, he generally lets them do what they want. Gemini's sense of humor is infectious, so the children will naturally come to see the fun and funny sides of life.

LEO WOMAN
CANCER MAN

Chances are you won't hit it off too well with the man born under Cancer if love is your object, but then Cupid has been known to do some pretty unlikely things. The Cancer man is very sensitive. He is thin-skinned and occasionally moody. You've got to keep on your toes—and not step on his—if you're determined to make a go of the relationship.

The Cancer man may be lacking in many of the qualities you seek in a man, but when it comes to being faithful and being a good provider, he's hard to beat.

It is the perceptive Leo woman who will not mistake the Crab's quietness for sullenness or his thriftiness for penny-pinching. In some respects, he is like that wise old owl out on a limb; he may look like he's dozing but actually he hasn't missed a thing. Cancers often possess a well of knowledge about human behavior. They can come across with some pretty helpful advice to those in trouble. He can certainly guide you in making investments both in time and in money. He may not say much, but he's always got his wits about him.

The Crab may not be the match or the catch for many a Leo

woman. In fact, he is likely to seem downright dull to the on-the-move Leo girl. True to his sign, he can be fairly cranky and crabby when handled the wrong way. He is perhaps more sensitive than he should be.

Leo people are usually as smart as a whip. If you're clever, you will never in any way convey the idea that you consider your Cancer a little slow on the uptake. Browbeating is a surefire way of sending the Crab angrily scurrying back to his shell. And it's quite possible that all of that lost ground will never be recovered.

The Crab is most himself at home. Once settled down for the night or the weekend, wild horses couldn't drag him any farther than the gatepost—that is, unless those wild horses were dispatched by his mother. The Crab is sometimes a Momma's boy. If his mate doesn't put her foot down, he will see to it that his mother always comes first. No self-respecting Leo would ever allow herself to play second fiddle, even if it's to an elderly mother-in-law. If the Lioness is tactful, she'll discover that slipping into the number-one position is as easy as pie (that legendary pie his mother used to bake).

If you pamper your Cancer man, you'll find that "mother" turns up less and less both at the front door as well as in conversations.

Cancers make protective, proud, and patient fathers. But they can be a little too protective. Sheltering may interfere with a youngster's burgeoning independence. Still, the Cancer father doesn't want to see his youngster learning about life the hard way.

LEO WOMAN
LEO MAN

You probably won't have any trouble understanding the Leo man as you were born under the same sign. Still, some conflict is possible due to the fact that you both are very much alike. Be tactful and tolerant in a Leo-Leo relationship.

For many women, Leo is the sign of love. When the Lion puts his mind to romance, he doesn't stint. If he has it his way, he will be wining, dining, and dancing with his Lioness till the wee hours of the morning.

The Leo man is all heart and knows how to make his woman feel like a woman. More often than not, he is a man a woman can look up to. He's a man who manages to have full control of just about any situation he finds himself in. He's a winner.

The Leo man may not look like Tarzan, but he knows how to roar and beat his chest if he has to. He's the kind of man you can lean upon. He'll also give you support in your plans and projects. He's often capable of giving advice that pays off. Leo men are direct. They don't pussyfoot around.

Leo men often rise to the top of their profession, and through their examples prove to be great sources of inspiration to others.

Although he's a ladies' man, Leo is very particular about his ladies. His standards are high when it comes to love interests. He believes that romance should be played on a fair give-and-take basis. He won't put up with any monkey business in a love relationship. It's all or nothing.

You'll find him a frank, honest person. He generally says what is on his mind.

If you decide that a Leo man is the one for you, be prepared to stand behind him full force. He expects it—and usually deserves it. He's the head of the house and can handle that position without a hitch. He knows how to go about breadwinning and, if he has his way (and most Leos do have their own way), he'll see to it that you'll have all the luxuries you crave and the comforts you need.

It's unlikely that the romance in your marriage will ever die out. Lions need love like flowers need sunshine. They're ever amorous and generally expect equal attention and affection from their mate. Lions are fond of going out on the town. They love to give parties as well as go to them. You should encounter no difficulties in sharing his interests in this direction.

Leo fathers can be strict when they think that the rules of the royal kingdom are being broken. You'll have to do your best to smooth over the children's roughed-up feelings.

LEO WOMAN
VIRGO MAN

The Virgo man is all business—or he may seem so to you. He is usually very cool, calm, and collected. He's perhaps too much of a fussbudget to wake up deep romantic interests in a Leo woman. Torrid romancing to the Virgo man is just so much sentimental mush. He can do without it and can make that quite evident.

The Virgo man regards chastity as a virtue. If necessary, he can lead a sedentary, sexless life without caring too much about the fun others think he's missing. In short, you are apt to find him a first-class dud. He doesn't have much of an imagination; flights of fancy don't interest him. He is always correct and likes to be handled correctly. Almost everything about him is orderly. There's a place for everything and everything in its place is likely to be an adage he'll fall upon quite regularly.

He does have an honest-to-goodness heart, believe it or not. The Leo woman who finds herself strangely attracted to his cool, feet-flat-on-the-ground ways will discover that his is a constant heart, not one that goes in for flings or sordid affairs. Virgos take an awfully long time to warm up to someone. A practical man, even in matters of the heart, he wants to know just what kind of a person you are before he takes a chance on you.

The impulsive Leo girl had better not make the mistake of kissing her Virgo friend on the street—even if it's only a peck on the cheek. He's not at all demonstrative and hates public displays of affection. Love, according to him, should be kept within the confines of one's home—with the curtains drawn. Once he believes that you are on the level with him as far as your love is concerned, you'll see how fast he can lose his cool. Virgos are considerate, gentle lovers. He'll spend a long time, though, getting to know you. He'll like you before he loves you.

A Leo-Virgo romance can be a sometime—or, rather, a one-time thing. If the bottom ever falls out, don't bother reaching for the adhesive tape. Nine times out of ten he won't care about patching up. He's a once-burnt-twice-shy guy. When he crosses your telephone number out of his address book, he's crossing you out of his life for good.

Neat as a pin, he's thumbs-down on what he considers sloppy housekeeping. An ashtray with just one stubbed-out cigarette in it can annoy him even if it's just two seconds old. Glassware should always sparkle and shine.

If you marry a Virgo man, instill a sense of order in the kids, or at least have them behaving by the time he gets home. The Virgo father wants his children to be kind and courteous and always helpful to the neighbors.

LEO WOMAN
LIBRA MAN

If there's a Libra in your life, you are most likely a very happy woman. Men born under this sign have a way with women. You'll always feel at ease in a Libra's company. You can be yourself when you're with him.

Like you, he can be moody at times. His moodiness, though, is more puzzling. One moment he comes on hard and strong with declarations of his love, the next moment you find that he's left you like yesterday's mashed potatoes. He'll come back, though; don't worry. Libras are like that. Deep down inside he really knows what he wants even though he may not appear to.

You'll appreciate his admiration of beauty and harmony. If you're dressed to the teeth and never looked lovelier, you'll get a ready compliment—and one that's really deserved. Libras don't indulge in idle flattery. If they don't like something, they are tactful enough to remain silent.

Libras will go to great lengths to preserve peace and harmony—even tell a fat lie if necessary. They don't like showdowns or disagreeable confrontations. The frank Leo woman is all for getting whatever is bothering her off her chest and out into the open, even if it comes out all wrong. To the Libra, making a clean breast of everything seems like sheer folly sometimes.

You may lose your patience while waiting for your Libra friend to make up his mind. It takes him ages sometimes to make a decision. He weighs both sides carefully before committing himself to anything. You seldom dillydally—at least about small things—and so it's likely that you will find it difficult to see eye-to-eye with a hesitating Libra when it comes to decision-making methods.

All in all, though, he is kind, gentle, and fair. He is interested in the "real" truth. He'll try to balance everything out until he has all the correct answers. It is not difficult for him to see both sides of a story.

He's a peace-loving man. The mere prospect of an explosive scene will turn him off.

Libras are not show-offs. Generally, they are well-balanced people. Honest, wholesome, and affectionate, they are serious about every love encounter they have. If he should find that the woman he's dating is not really suited to him, he will end the relationship in such a tactful manner that no hard feelings will come about.

The Libra father is gentle and patient. He can be firm without exercising undue strictness. Although he can be a harsh judge at times, with youngsters growing up he will radiate sweetness and light.

LEO WOMAN
SCORPIO MAN

Many people have a hard time understanding a man born under the sign of Scorpio. Few, however, are able to resist his magnetic charm.

When angered, he can act like an overturned wasps' nest; his sting is capable of leaving an almost permanent mark. If you find yourself interested in a man born under this sign, you'd better learn how to keep on the good side of him. If he's in love with you, you'll know about it. Scorpio men let no one get in their way when they are out to win a certain heart. When it comes to romance, they never take no for an answer.

The Scorpio man can be quite blunt when he chooses. At times, he'll strike you as being a brute. His touchiness may get on your nerves after a while. If it does, you'd better tiptoe away from the scene rather than chance an explosive confrontation. He's capable of a firestorm of emotion that drives even fiery Leo away.

You're the kind of woman who can put up with almost anything once you put your mind and heart to it. A stormy Scorpio relationship may be worth its ups and downs. Scorpio men are all quite perceptive and intelligent. In some respects, they know how to use their brains more effectively than others. They believe in winning in whatever they do. And in business, they usually achieve the position they want through drive and intellect.

He doesn't give a hoot for home life, generally. He doesn't like being tied down. He would rather be out on the battlefield of life, belting away at what he feels is a just and worthy cause.

Many women are easily attracted to him. You are perhaps no exception. Know what you're getting into before you go making any promises to him. Women who allow themselves to be swept off their feet by a Scorpio man soon find that they're dealing with a pepper pot of seething excitement. He's passion with a capital P, make no mistake about that.

Scorpios are straight to the point. They can be as sharp as a razor blade and just as cutting. Don't give him cause to find fault with you, and you'll do just fine.

If you decide to marry him and take the bitter with the sweet, prepare yourself for a challenging relationship. Chances are you won't have as much time for your own interests as you'd like. Your Scorpio man may keep you at his beck and call.

In spite of the extremes in his personality, the Scorpio man is able to transform conflicting characteristics when he becomes a father. He is adept with difficult youngsters because he knows how to tap the best in a child.

LEO WOMAN
SAGITTARIUS MAN

If you've set your cap for a man born under the sign of Sagittarius, you may have to apply an awful lot of strategy before you can persuade him to get down on bended knee. Although some Sagittarius may be marriage-shy, they're not ones to skitter away from romance. You'll find a love relationship with a Sagittarius—whether it is a fling or the real thing—a very enjoyable experience.

As a rule, Sagittarius are bright, happy, and healthy people. They have a strong sense of fair play. Often they are a source of inspiration to others. They are full of drive and ideas.

You'll be taken by the Archer's infectious grin and his lighthearted friendly nature. If you do wind up being the woman in his life, you'll find that he's apt to treat you more like a buddy than the love of his life. It's just his way. Sagittarius are often more chummy than romantic.

You'll admire his broad-mindedness in most matters—including those of the heart. If, while dating you, he claims that he still wants to play the field, he'll expect you to enjoy the same liberty. Once he's promised to love, honor, and obey, however, he does just that. Marriage for him, once he's taken that big step, is very serious business.

The Sagittarius man is quick-witted. He has a genuine interest in equality. He hates prejudice and injustice. Generally, Sagittarius are good at sports. They love the great out-of-doors and respect wildlife in all its forms.

He's not much of a homebody. Quite often he's occupied with faraway places either in his daydreams or in reality. He enjoys being on the move. He's got ants in his pants and refuses to sit still for long stretches at a time. Humdrum routine—especially at home—bores him. At the drop of a hat, he may ask you to put on your party clothes and dine out for a change. He likes surprising people. He'll take great pride in showing you off to his friends. He'll always be a considerate mate. He will never embarrass or disappoint you intentionally.

His friendly, sunny nature is capable of attracting many people. Like you, he's very tolerant when it comes to friends. You will probably spend a great deal of time entertaining.

The Sagittarius father will dote on any son or daughter, but he may be bewildered by the newborn baby. As soon as the children are old enough to walk and talk, the Sagittarius dad encourages each and every visible sign of talent or skill.

LEO WOMAN
CAPRICORN MAN

A with-it Leo woman is likely to find the average Capricorn man a bit of a drag. The man born under the sign of the Goat is often a closed person and difficult to get to know. Even if you do get to know him, you may not find him very interesting.

In romance, Capricorn men are a little on the rusty side. You'll probably have to make all the passes.

You may find his plodding manner irritating, and his conservative, traditional ways downright maddening. He's not one to take chances on anything. He believes in the motto: If it was good enough for my father, it's good enough for me. He follows a way that is tried and true.

Whenever adventure rears its tantalizing head, the Goat may turn the other way. He's more interested in succeeding at what he's already doing.

He may be just as ambitious as you are—perhaps even more so—but his ways of accomplishing his aims are more subterranean or, at least, seem so. He operates from the background a good deal of the time. At a gathering you may never even notice him. But he's there, taking in everything and sizing up everyone—planning his next careful move.

Although Capricorns may be intellectual to a degree, it is generally not the kind of intelligence you appreciate. He may not be as quick or as bright as you; it may take ages for him to understand a simple joke.

If you decide to take up with a man born under this sign, you ought to be pretty good in the cheering-up department. The Capricorn man often acts as though he's constantly being followed by a cloud of gloom.

The Capricorn man is most himself when in the comfort and privacy of his own home. The security possible within four walls can make him a happy man. He'll spend as much time as he can at home. If he is loaded down with extra work, he'll bring it home instead of working overtime at the office.

You'll most likely find yourself frequently confronted by his relatives. Family is very important to the Capricorn—his family, that is. They had better take a pretty important place in your life, too, if you want to keep your home a happy one.

Although his caution in most matters may all but drive you up the wall, you'll find his concerned way with money justified most of the time. He'll plan everything right down to the last penny.

The Capricorn father's empire is rather like the Leo mother's royal realm. There are goals to be achieved, and there is the right way to achieve them. He can be quite a scold when it comes to disciplining the youngsters. You'll have to step in and bend the rules sometimes.

LEO WOMAN
AQUARIUS MAN
Aquarius individuals love everybody—even their worst enemies, sometimes. Through your relationship with an Aquarius man, you'll find yourself running into all sorts of people, ranging from near-genius to downright insane—and they're all friends of his.

As a rule, Aquarius are extremely friendly and open. Of all the signs of the Zodiac, they are perhaps the most tolerant. In the thinking department, they are often miles ahead of others.

You'll most likely find your relationship with this man a challenging one. Your high respect for intelligence and imagination may be reason enough for you to settle your heart on a Water Bearer. You'll find that you can learn a lot from him.

In the holding-hands phase of your romance, you may find that your Water Bearer friend has cold feet. Aquarius take quite a bit of warming up before they are ready to come across with that first goodnight kiss. More than likely, he'll just want to be your pal in the beginning. For him, that's an important first step in any relationship—love, included.

The poetry and flowers stage—if it ever comes—will be later. The Aquarius is all heart. Still, when it comes to tying himself down to one person and for keeps, he is apt to hesitate. He may even try to get out of it if you breathe down his neck too heavily.

The Aquarius man is no Valentino and wouldn't want to be. The kind of love life he's looking for is one that's made up mainly for companionship. Although he may not be very romantic, the memory of his first romance will always hold an important position in his heart. Sometimes Aquarius wind up marrying their childhood sweethearts.

You won't find it difficult to look up to a man born under the sign of the Water Bearer. But you may find the challenge of trying to keep up with him dizzying. He can pierce through the most complicated problem as if it were a simple math puzzle. You may find him a little too lofty and high-minded—but don't judge him too harshly if that's the case; he's way ahead of his time—your time, too, most likely.

If you marry this man, he'll stay true to you. Don't think that once the honeymoon is over, you'll be chained to the kitchen sink forever. Your Aquarius husband will encourage you to keep active in your own interests and affairs. You'll most likely have a minor tiff now and again but never anything serious.

The Aquarius father can be a shining example for the children because he sees them as individuals in their own right, not as extensions of himself. Kids love him and vice versa. He'll be as tolerant with them as he is with adults.

**LEO WOMAN
PISCES MAN**
The man born under Pisces is quite a dreamer. Sometimes he's so wrapped up in his dreams that he's difficult to reach. To the average ambitious woman, he may seem a little passive.

He's easygoing most of the time. He seems to take things in his stride. He'll entertain all kinds of views and opinions from just about anyone, nodding or smiling vaguely, giving the impression that he's with them one hundred percent while that may not be the case at all. His attitude may be why bother when he is confronted with someone wrong who thinks he's right. The Pisces man will seldom speak his mind if he thinks he'll be rigidly opposed.

The Pisces man is oversensitive at times. He's afraid of getting his feelings hurt. He'll sometimes imagine a personal injury when none's been made at all. Chances are you'll find this complex of his maddening; at times you may feel like giving him a swift kick where it hurts the most. It wouldn't do any good, though. It would just add fuel to the fire of his persecution complex.

One thing you will admire about Pisces is his concern for people who are sickly or troubled. He'll make his shoulder available to anyone in the mood for a good cry. He can listen to one hard-luck story after another without seeming to tire. When his advice is asked, he is capable of coming across with some pretty important words of wisdom. He often knows what is bothering someone before that person is aware of it himself. It's almost intuitive with Pisces, it seems.

Still, at the end of the day, the Pisces man looks forward to some peace and quiet. If you've got a problem on your mind when he comes home, don't unload it in his lap. If you do, you're likely to find him short-tempered. He's a good listener, but he can only take so much.

Pisces men are not aimless although they may seem so at times. The positive sort of Pisces man is quite often successful in his profession and is likely to wind up rich and influential. Material gain, however, is not a direct goal for a Pisces who devotes his life's work to helping people in need.

The weaker Pisces is usually content to stay put on the level where he finds himself. He won't complain too much if the roof leaks and the fence is in need of repair. He'll just shrug it off as a minor inconvenience.

Because of their seemingly laissez-faire manner, Pisces individuals are immensely popular with children. For tots the Pisces father plays the double role of confidant and playmate. It will never enter his mind to discipline a child, no matter how spoiled or incorrigible that child becomes.

Man—Woman

LEO MAN
ARIES WOMAN

The Aries woman is quite a charmer. When she tugs at the strings of your heart, you'll know it. She's a woman who's in search of a knight in shining armor. She is a very particular person with very high ideals. She won't accept anyone but the man of her dreams.

The Aries woman never plays around with passion; she means business when it comes to love.

Don't get the idea that she's a dewy-eyed damsel. She isn't. In fact, she can be pretty practical and to the point when she wants. She's a woman with plenty of drive and ambition. With an Aries woman behind you, you can go far in life. She knows how to help her man get ahead. She's full of wise advice; you only have to ask. In some cases, the Aries woman has a keen business sense; many of them become successful career women. There is nothing hesitant or retiring about her. She is equipped with a good brain and she knows how to use it.

Your union with her could be something strong, secure, and romantic. If both of you have your sights fixed in the same direction, there is almost nothing that you could not accomplish.

The Aries woman is proud and capable of being quite jealous. While you're with her, never cast your eye in another woman's direction. It could spell disaster for your relationship. The Aries woman won't put up with romantic nonsense when her heart is at stake.

If the Aries woman backs you up in your business affairs, you can be sure of succeeding. However, if she only is interested in advancing her own career and puts her interests before yours, she will surely be rocking the boat. It will put a strain on the relationship. The overambitious Aries woman can be a pain in the neck and make you forget that you were in love with her once.

The cultivated Aries woman makes a wonderful wife and mother. She has a natural talent for homemaking. With a pot of paint and some wallpaper, she can transform the dreariest domicile into an abode of beauty and snug comfort. The perfect hostess—even when friends just happen by—she knows how to make guests feel at home.

You'll also admire your Aries because she knows how to stand on her own two feet. Hers is an independent nature. She won't break down and cry when things go wrong, but pick herself up and try to patch things up.

The Aries woman is skilled at juggling both career and motherhood, so her kids will never feel that she is an absentee parent. In fact, as the youngsters grow older, they might want a little more of the liberation that is so important to her.

LEO MAN
TAURUS WOMAN

The woman born under the sign of Taurus may lack a little of the sparkle and bubble you often like to find in a woman. The Taurus woman is generally down to earth and never flighty. It's important to her that she keep both feet flat on the ground. She is not fond of bounding all over the place, especially if she's under the impression that there's no profit in it.

On the other hand, if you hit it off with a Taurus woman, you won't be disappointed at all in the romance area. The Taurus woman is all woman and proud of it, too. She can be very devoted and loving once she decides that her relationship with you is no fly-by-night romance. Basically, she's a passionate person. In sex, she's direct and to the point. If she really loves you, she'll let you know she's yours—and without reservations. Better not flirt with other women once you've committed yourself to her. She is capable of being jealous and possessive.

She'll stick by you through thick and thin. It's almost certain that if the going ever gets rough, she'll not go running home to her mother. She can adjust to hard times just as graciously as she can to the good times.

Taurus are, on the whole, pretty even-tempered. They like to be treated with kindness. Pretty things and soft things make them purr like kittens.

You may find her a little slow and deliberate. She likes to be safe and sure about everything. Let her plod along if she likes; don't coax her but just let her take her own sweet time. Everything she does is done thoroughly and, generally, without mistakes. Don't deride her for being a kind of slowpoke. It could lead to flying pots and pans and a fireworks display that would light up the sky. The Taurus woman doesn't anger readily but when prodded often enough, she's capable of letting loose with a cyclone of ill will. If you treat her with kindness and consideration, you'll have no cause for complaint.

The Taurus woman loves doing things for her man. She's a whiz in the kitchen and can whip up feasts fit for a king if she thinks they'll be royally appreciated. She may not fully understand you, but she'll adore you and be faithful to you if she feels you're worthy of it.

The woman born under Taurus will make a wonderful mother. She knows how to keep her children well-loved, cuddled, and warm. She may find them difficult to manage, however, when they reach the teenage stage.

LEO MAN
GEMINI WOMAN

You may find a romance with a woman born under the sign of the Twins a many-splendored thing. In her you can find the intellectual companionship you often look for in a friend or mate. A Gemini partner can appreciate your aims and desires because she travels pretty much the same road as you do intellectually—that is, at least part of the way. She may share your interest but she will lack your tenacity.

She suffers from itchy feet. She can be here, there, all over the place and at the same time, or so it would seem. Her eagerness to be on the move may make you dizzy. Still, you'll enjoy and appreciate her liveliness and mental agility.

Geminis often have sparkling personalities. You'll be attracted by her warmth and grace. While she's on your arm you'll probably notice that many male eyes are drawn to her. She may even return a gaze or two, but don't let that worry you. All women born under this sign have nothing against a harmless flirt once in a while. They enjoy this sort of attention. If she feels she is already spoken for, however, she will never let it get out of hand.

Although she may not be as handy as you'd like in the kitchen, you'll never go hungry for a filling and tasty meal. She's as much in a hurry as you are, and won't feel like she's cheating by breaking out the instant mashed potatoes or the frozen peas. She may not be much of a cook but she is clever. With a dash of this and a suggestion of that, she can make an uninteresting TV dinner taste like a gourmet meal. Then, again, maybe you've struck it rich and have a Gemini lover who finds complicated recipes a challenge to her intellect. If so, you'll find every meal a tantalizing and mouth-watering surprise.

When you're beating your brains out over the Sunday crossword puzzle and find yourself stuck, just ask your Gemini mate. She'll give you all the right answers without batting an eyelash.

Like you, she loves all kinds of people. You may even find that you're a bit more particular than she. Often all that a Gemini requires is that her friends be interesting—and stay interesting. One thing she's not able to abide is a dullard.

Leave the party organizing to your Gemini sweetheart or mate, and you'll never have a chance to know what a dull moment is. She'll bring the swinger out in you if you give her half a chance.

A Gemini mother enjoys her children, which can be the truest form of love. Like them, she's often restless, adventurous, and easily bored. She will never complain about their fleeting interests because she understands the changes they will go through as they mature.

LEO MAN
CANCER WOMAN

If you fall in love with a Cancer woman, be prepared for anything. Cancers are sometimes difficult to understand when it comes to love. In one hour, she can unravel a whole gamut of emotions that will leave you in a tizzy. She'll keep you guessing, that's for sure.

You may find her a little too uncertain and sensitive for your liking. You'll most likely spend a good deal of time encouraging her, helping her to erase her foolish fears. Tell her she's a living doll a dozen times a day, and you'll be well loved in return.

Be careful of the jokes you make when in her company. Don't let any of them revolve around her, her personal interests, or her family. If you do, you'll most likely reduce her to tears. She can't stand being made fun of. It will take bushels of roses and tons of chocolates—not to mention the apologies—to get her to come back out of her shell.

In matters of money managing, she may not easily come around to your way of thinking. Money will never burn a hole in her pocket. You may get the notion that your Cancer sweetheart or mate is a direct descendent of Scrooge. If she has her way, she'll hang onto that first dollar you earned. She's not only that way with money, but with everything right on up from bakery string to jelly jars. She's a saver; she never throws anything away, no matter how trivial.

Once she returns your love, you'll have an affectionate, self-sacrificing, and devoted woman for life. Her love for you will never alter unless you want it to. She'll put you high upon a pedestal and will do everything—even if it's against your will—to keep you up there.

Cancer women love home life. For them, marriage is an easy step. They're domestic with a capital D. She'll do her best to make your home comfortable and cozy. She is more at ease at home than anywhere else. She makes an excellent hostess. The best in her comes out when she is in her own environment.

Cancer women make the best mothers of all the signs of the Zodiac. She'll consider every complaint of her child a major catastrophe. With her, children always come first. If you're lucky, you'll run a close second. You'll perhaps see her as too devoted to the children. You may have a hard time convincing her that her apron strings are a little too long.

LEO MAN
LEO WOMAN

If you can manage a woman who likes to kick up her heels every now and again, then Leo was made for you. You'll have to learn to put away jealous fears—or at least forget about them—when you take up with a woman born under this sign. She's often the kind that makes heads turn and tongues wag. You don't necessarily have to believe any of what you hear—it's most likely just jealous gossip. Take up with a Leo woman and you'll be taking off on a romance full of fire and ice. Be prepared to take the good things with the bad—the bitter with the sweet.

The Leo woman has more than a fair share of grace and glamour.

She is aware of her charms and knows how to put them to good use. Needless to say, other women in her vicinity turn green with envy and will try anything short of shoving her into the nearest lake, in order to put her out of commission.

If she's captured your heart and fancy, woo her full force if your intention is to eventually win her. Shower her with expensive gifts and promise her the moon—if you're in a position to go that far—then you'll find her resistance beginning to weaken. It's not that she's such a difficult cookie—she'll probably adore you once she's decided you're the man for her—but she does enjoy a lot of attention. What's more, she feels she's entitled to it. Her mild arrogance, though, is becoming. The Leo woman knows how to transform the crime of excessive pride into a very charming misdemeanor. It sweeps most men right off their feet. Those who do not succumb to her leonine charm are few and far between.

If you've got an important business deal to clinch and you have doubts as to whether or not it will go over, bring your Leo lover along to that business luncheon and it's a cinch that that contract will be yours. She won't have to do or say anything—just be there at your side. The grouchiest oil magnate can be transformed into a gushing, obedient schoolboy if there's a Leo woman in the room.

If you're rich and want to stay that way, don't give your Leo mate a free hand with the charge accounts and credit cards. If you're poor, the luxury-loving Leo will most likely never enter your life.

The Leo mother is strict yet easygoing with the children. She wants her youngsters to follow the rules, and she is a patient teacher. She loves to pal around with the kids, proudly showing them off on every occasion.

LEO MAN
VIRGO WOMAN

The Virgo woman may be a little too difficult for you to understand at first. Her waters run deep. Even when you think you know her, don't take any bets on it. She's capable of keeping things hidden in the deep recesses of her womanly soul—things she'll only release when she's sure that you're the man she's been looking for. It may take her some time to come around to this decision. Virgos are finicky about almost everything; everything has to be letter-perfect before they're satisfied. Many of them have the idea that the only people who can do things correctly are Virgos.

Nothing offends a Virgo woman more than slovenly dress, sloppy character, or a careless display of affection. Make sure your tie is not crooked and your shoes sport a bright shine before you go calling on this lady. Keep your off-color jokes for the locker room; she'll have none of that. Take her arm when crossing the street.

Don't rush the romance. Trying to corner her in the back of a cab may be one way of striking out. Never criticize the way she looks. In fact, the best policy would be to agree with her as much as possible.

Still, there's just so much a man can take. All those dos and don'ts you'll have to observe if you want to get to first base with a Virgo may be just a little too much to ask of you. After a few dates, you may come to the conclusion that she just isn't worth all that trouble. However, the Virgo woman is mysterious enough, generally speaking, to keep her men running back for more. Chances are you'll be intrigued by her airs and graces.

If lovemaking means a lot to you, you'll be disappointed at first in the cool ways of your Virgo lover. However, under her glacial facade there lies a hot cauldron of seething excitement. If you're patient and artful in your romantic approach, you'll find that all that caution was well worth the trouble. When Virgos love, they don't stint. It's all or nothing as far as they're concerned. Once they're convinced that they love you, they go all the way, right off the bat—tossing all cares to the wind.

One thing a Virgo woman can't stand in love is hypocrisy. They don't give a hoot about what the neighbors say, if their hearts tell them to go ahead. They're very concerned with human truths—so much so that if their hearts stumble upon another fancy, they're likely to be true to that new heartthrob and leave you standing in the rain.

She's honest to her heart and will be as true to you as you are with her, generally. Do her wrong once, however, and it's farewell.

The Virgo mother has high expectations for her children, and she will strive to bring out the very best in them. She is more tender than strict, though, and will nag rather than discipline. But youngsters sense her unconditional love for them, and usually turn out just as she hoped they would.

LEO MAN
LIBRA WOMAN

You'll probably find that the woman born under the sign of Libra is worth more than her weight in gold. She's a woman after your own heart.

With her, you'll always come first—make no mistake about that. She'll always be behind you 100 percent, no matter what you do. When you ask her advice about almost anything, you'll most likely get a very balanced and realistic opinion. She is good at thinking things out and never lets her emotions run away with her when clear logic is called for.

As a homemaker she is hard to beat. She is very concerned with harmony and balance. You can be sure she'll make your house a joy to live in; she'll see to it that the house is tastefully furnished and decorated. A Libra cannot stand filth or disarray. Anything that does not radiate harmony, in fact, runs against her orderly grain.

She is chock-full of charm and womanly ways. She can sweep just about any man off his feet with one winning smile. When it comes to using her brains, she can outthink almost anyone and, sometimes, with half the effort. She is diplomatic enough, though, never to let this become glaringly apparent. She may even turn the conversation around so that you think you were the one who did all the brainwork. She couldn't care less, really, just as long as you wind up doing what is right.

The Libra woman will put you up on a pretty high pedestal. You are her man and her idol. She'll leave all the decision making, large or small, up to you. She's not interested in running things and will only offer her assistance if she feels you really need it.

Some find her approach to reason masculine. However, in the areas of love and affection the Libra woman is all woman. She'll literally shower you with love and kisses during your romance with her. She doesn't believe in holding out. You shouldn't, either, if you want to hang onto her.

Libra is the kind of lover who likes to snuggle up to you in front of the fire on chilly autumn nights, the kind who will bring you breakfast in bed Sunday. She'll be very thoughtful about anything that concerns you. If anyone dares suggest you're not the grandest guy in the world, she'll give that person what-for. She'll defend you till her dying breath. The Libra woman will be everything you want her to be.

The Libra mother is sensitive and sensible, with an intuitive understanding of what a child needs. Her youngsters will never lack for anything that could make their lives easier and richer. Still, you will always come before the children.

LEO MAN
SCORPIO WOMAN

The Scorpio woman can be a whirlwind of passion—perhaps too much passion to really suit you. When her temper flies, you'd better lock up the family heirlooms and take cover. When she chooses to be sweet, you're apt to think that butter wouldn't melt in her mouth—but, of course, it would.

The Scorpio woman can be as hot as a tamale or as cool as a cucumber, but whatever mood she's in, she's in it for real. She does not believe in posing or putting on airs.

The Scorpio woman is often sultry and seductive. Her femme fatale charm can pierce through the hardest of hearts like a laser beam. She may not look like Mata Hari (quite often Scorpios resemble the tomboy next door) but once she's fixed you with her tantalizing eyes, you're a goner.

Life with the Scorpio woman will not be all smiles and smooth sailing. When prompted, she can unleash a gale of venom. Generally, she'll have the good grace to keep family battles within the walls of your home. When company visits, she's apt to give the impression that married life with you is one great big joyride. It's just one of her ways of expressing her loyalty to you—at least in front of others. She may fight you tooth and nail in the confines of your living room, but at a ball or during an evening out, she'll hang onto your arm and have stars in her eyes.

Scorpio women are good at keeping secrets. She may even keep a few buried from you if she feels like it.

Never cross her up on even the smallest thing. When it comes to revenge, she's an eye-for-an-eye woman. She's not too keen on forgiveness—especially if she feels she's been wronged unfairly. You'd be well-advised not to give her any cause to be jealous, either. When the Scorpio woman sees green, your life will be made far from rosy. Once she's put you in the doghouse, you can be sure that you're going to stay there awhile.

You may find life with a Scorpio woman too draining. Although she may be full of the old paprika, it's quite likely that she's not the kind of woman you'd like to spend the rest of your natural life with. You'd prefer someone gentler and not so hot-tempered; someone who can take the highs with the lows and not bellyache; someone who is flexible and understanding. A woman born under Scorpio can be heavenly, but she can also be the very devil when she chooses.

The Scorpio mother is protective yet encouraging. The opposites within her nature mirror the very contradictions of life itself. Under her skillful guidance, the children learn how to cope with extremes and grow up to become many-faceted individuals.

LEO MAN
SAGITTARIUS WOMAN

You'll most likely never come across a more good-natured woman than the one born under the sign of Sagittarius. Generally, they're full of bounce and good cheer. Their sunny disposition seems almost permanent and can be relied upon even on the rainiest of days.

Women born under this sign are almost never malicious. If ever they seem to be it is only unintentional. Sagittarius are often a little short on tact and say literally anything that comes into their minds no matter what the occasion. Sometimes the words that tumble out of their mouths seem downright cutting and cruel. Still, no matter what she says, she means well. The Sagittarius woman is quite capable of losing some of her friends—and perhaps even some of yours—through a careless slip of the lip.

On the other hand, you will appreciate her honesty and good intentions. To you, qualities of this sort play an important part in life. With a little patience and practice, you can probably help cure your Sagittarius lover of her loose tongue. In most cases, she'll give in to your better judgment and try to follow your advice to the letter.

Chances are she'll be the outdoors type. Long hikes, fishing trips, and white-water canoeing will most likely appeal to her. She's a busy person; no one could ever call her a slouch. She sets great store in mobility. Her feet are itchy and she won't sit still for a minute if she doesn't have to.

She is great company most of the time and, generally, lots of fun. Even if your buddies drop by for poker and beer, she won't have any trouble fitting in.

On the whole, she is a very kind and sympathetic woman. If she feels she's made a mistake, she'll be the first to call your attention to it. She's not afraid to own up to her faults and shortcomings.

You might lose your patience with her once or twice. After she's seen how upset her shortsightedness or tendency to blab has made you, she'll do her best to straighten up.

The Sagittarius woman is not the kind who will pry into your business affairs. But she'll always be there, ready to offer advice if you need it. If you come home with red stains on your collar and you say it's paint and not lipstick, she'll believe you.

She'll seldom be suspicious. Your word will almost always be good enough for her.

The Sagittarius mother is a wonderful and loving friend to her children. She is not afraid if a youngster learns some street smarts along the way. She will broaden her children's knowledge and see that they get a well-rounded education.

LEO MAN
CAPRICORN WOMAN

If you are not a successful businessman, or at least on your way to success, it's quite possible that a Capricorn woman will have no interest in entering your life. Generally speaking, she is a very security-minded female; she'll see to it that she invests her time only in sure things. Men who whittle away their time with one unsuccessful scheme or another seldom attract a Capricorn. Men who are interested in getting somewhere in life and keep their noses close to the grindstone quite often have a Capricorn woman behind them, helping them to get ahead.

Although she is a kind of social climber she is not what you could call cruel or hard-hearted. Beneath that cool, seemingly calculating exterior there's a warm and desirable woman. She just happens to think that it is just as easy to fall in love with a rich or ambitious man as it is with a poor or lazy one. She's practical.

The Capricorn woman may be keenly interested in rising to the top, but she'll never be aggressive about it. She'll seldom step on someone's feet or nudge competitors away with her elbows. She's quiet about her desires. She sits, waits, and watches. When an opening or opportunity does appear, she'll latch onto it. For an on-the-move man, an ambitious Capricorn wife or lover can be quite an asset. She can probably give you some very good advice about business matters. When you invite the boss and his wife for dinner, she'll charm them both.

The Capricorn woman is thorough in whatever she does: cooking, cleaning, making a success out of life. Capricorns are excellent hostesses as well as guests. Generally, they are very well mannered and gracious, no matter what their backgrounds are. They seem to have a built-in sense of what is right. Crude behavior or a careless faux pas can offend them no end.

If you should marry a woman born under Capricorn, you need never worry about her going on a wild shopping spree. Capricorns are careful with every cent that comes into their hands. They understand the value of money better than most women and have no room in their lives for careless spending.

Capricorn women are usually very fond of family—their own, that is. With them, family ties run very deep. Don't make jokes about her relatives; she won't stand for it. You'd better check her family out before you get down on bended knee; after your marriage you'll undoubtedly be seeing lots of them.

The Capricorn mother is very ambitious for her children. She wants them to have every advantage and to benefit from things she perhaps lacked as a child. She will train her youngsters to be polite and kind and to honor traditional codes of conduct.

LEO MAN
AQUARIUS WOMAN
If you find that you've fallen head over heels for a woman born under the sign of the Water Bearer, you'd better fasten your safety belt. It may take you quite a while to actually discover what this woman is like. Even then, you may have nothing to go on but a string of vague hunches. Aquarius is like a rainbow, full of bright and shining hues; she's like no other women you've ever known. There is something elusive about her—something delightfully mysterious. You'll most likely never be able to put your finger on it. It's

nothing calculated, either. Aquarius doesn't believe in phony charm.

There will never be a dull moment in your life with this Water Bearer woman; she seems to radiate adventure and magic. She'll most likely be the most open-minded and tolerant woman you've ever met. She has a strong dislike for injustice and prejudice. Narrow-mindedness runs against her grain.

She is very independent by nature and quite capable of shifting for herself if necessary. She may receive many proposals for marriage from all sorts of people without ever really taking them seriously. Marriage is a very big step for her; she wants to be sure she knows what she's getting into. If she thinks that it will seriously curb her independence and love of freedom, she's apt to shake her head and give the man his engagement ring back—if indeed she's let the romance get that far.

The line between friendship and romance is a pretty fuzzy one for an Aquarius. It's not difficult for her to remain buddy-buddy with an ex-lover. She's tolerant, remember? So if you should see her on the arm of an old love, don't jump to any hasty conclusions.

She's not a jealous person herself and doesn't expect you to be, either. You'll find her pretty much of a free spirit most of the time. Just when you think you know her inside out, you'll discover that you don't really know her at all.

She's a very sympathetic and warm person; she can be helpful to people in need of assistance and advice.

She'll seldom be suspicious even if she has every right to be. If the man she loves slips and allows himself a little fling, chances are she'll just ignore it—at least the first time. Her tolerance does have its limits, though, and her man should press never his luck fooling around.

The Aquarius mother is bighearted and seldom refuses her children anything. Her open-minded attitude is easily transmitted to her youngsters. They have every chance of growing up as respectful and tolerant individuals who feel at ease anywhere.

LEO MAN
PISCES WOMAN

Many a man dreams of an alluring Pisces woman. You're perhaps no exception. She's soft and cuddly and very domestic. She'll let you be the brains of the family; she's contented to play a behind-the-scenes role in order to help you achieve your goals. The illusion that you are the master of the household is the kind of magic that the Pisces woman is adept at creating.

She can be very ladylike and proper. Your business associates and friends will be dazzled by her warmth and femininity. Although she's a charmer, there is a lot more to her than just a pretty exterior. There is a brain ticking away behind that soft, womanly facade. You may never become aware of it—that is, until you're married to her. It's no cause for alarm, however; she'll most likely never use it against you, only to help you and possibly set you on a more successful path.

If she feels you're botching up your married life through careless behavior or if she feels you could be earning more money than you do, she'll tell you about it. But any wife would, really. She will never try to usurp your position as head and breadwinner of the family.

No one had better dare say one uncomplimentary word about you in her presence. It's likely to cause her to break into tears. Pisces women are usually very sensitive beings. Their reaction to adversity, frustration, or anger is just a plain, good, old-fashioned cry. They can weep buckets when inclined.

She can do wonders with a house. She is very fond of dramatic and beautiful things. There will always be plenty of fresh-cut flowers around the house. She will choose charming artwork and antiques, if they are affordable. She'll see to it that the house is decorated in a dazzling yet welcoming style.

She'll have an extra special dinner prepared for you when you come home from an important business meeting. Don't dwell on the boring details of the meeting, though. But if you need that grand vision, the big idea, to seal a contract or make a conquest, your Pisces woman is sure to confide a secret that will guarantee your success. She is canny and shrewd with money, and once you are on her wavelength you can manage the intricacies on your own.

Treat her with tenderness and generosity and your relationship will be an enjoyable one. She's most likely fond of chocolates. A bunch of beautiful flowers will never fail to make her eyes light up. See to it that you never forget her birthday or your anniversary. These things are very important to her. If you let them slip your mind, you'll send her into a crying fit that could last a considerable length of time. If you are patient and kind, you can keep a Pisces woman happy for a lifetime. She, however, is not without her faults. Her sensitivity may get on your nerves after a while. You may find her lacking in practicality and good old-fashioned stoicism. You may even feel that she uses her tears as a method of getting her own way.

The Pisces woman makes a strong, self-sacrificing mother. She will teach her children the value of service to the community while not letting them lose their individuality.

LEO
LUCKY NUMBERS 2007

Lucky numbers and astrology can be linked through the movements of the Moon. Each phase of the thirteen Moon cycles vibrates with a sequence of numbers for your Sign of the Zodiac over the course of the year. Using your lucky numbers is a fun system that connects you with tradition.

New Moon	First Quarter	Full Moon	Last Quarter
Dec. 20 ('06)	Dec. 27 ('06)	Jan. 3	Jan. 11
2 8 1 2	5 3 1 9	1 0 6 8	8 3 7 4
Jan. 18	Jan. 25	Feb. 2	Feb. 10
4 0 7 1	0 8 6 5	0 2 4 8	8 3 9 6
Feb. 17	Feb. 24	March 3	March 11
6 7 4 2	9 8 7 5	7 7 2 6	6 3 9 1
March 18	March 25	April 2	April 10
4 2 4 2	1 0 7 9	9 4 8 5	5 2 3 6
April 17	April 24	May 2	May 9
6 4 2 7	6 4 6 0	4 5 2 8	8 9 3 0
May 16	May 23	May 31	June 8
8 7 6 5	5 5 9 4	8 0 7 8	8 2 9 7
June 14	June 22	June 30	July 7
7 6 5 3	5 2 6 0	5 4 5 8	8 6 4 3
July 14	July 22	July 29	August 5
3 2 9 2	2 6 9 6	2 4 7 5	5 3 2 0
August 12	August 20	August 28	Sept. 3
1 8 0 5	5 9 1 7	3 2 9 7	7 6 5 3
Sept. 11	Sept. 19	Sept. 26	Oct. 3
3 5 9 4	4 1 7 9	6 0 8 7	7 6 4 6
Oct. 11	Oct. 19	Oct. 26	Nov. 1
6 1 5 2	2 8 9 6	4 2 1 0	9 7 9 4
Nov. 9	Nov. 17	Nov. 24	Dec. 1
4 8 5 2	2 3 6 7	2 4 0 3	1 0 3 7
Dec. 9	Dec. 17	Dec. 23	Dec. 31
2 8 5 6	6 9 7 0	1 0 8 6	8 8 3 7

LEO
YEARLY FORECAST 2007

Forecast for 2007 Concerning Business and
Financial Affairs, Job Prospects,
Travel, Health, Romance and Marriage
for Persons Born with the Sun
in the Zodiacal Sign of Leo.
July 21–August 21

For those born under the zodiacal sign of Leo, ruled by the Sun which is the life force of the universe and the source of vitality and zest, 2007 will be a time of extreme highs and lows. The coming year promises to assist the talented to achieve goals in artistic and creative expression. Many Lions are likely to receive public recognition or media coverage for specific expertise. As the year gets under way Mars, Jupiter, and Pluto congregate in your house of fun, children, romance, creation, and recreation. This indicates that plenty of activity will be taking place in this sector of life. Energy will focus on children, a lover, social activities, and your favorite hobbies and pursuits. New births surround you and the family, bringing joy as well as special celebrations. You can make significant headway by correctly utilizing your unique creative and innovative flair. Your ability to host a gala event or social gathering is likely to be called upon regularly. Leos who do this for a living should have a very successful year providing trustworthy and reliable tradespeople are hired to assist.

Responsibilities for children that have impacted on your social life could lift, providing more time for leisure fun and to socialize with other people. With Saturn, the planet of structure and disciplinary action, residing in your sign of Leo until September, your house of personality and self is heavily accentuated. Lions should be taking a more conservative and practical approach to many areas of life. Continue to apply organization and hard work to career and business affairs. Your determination and passion to succeed will produce the personal and professional rewards you are aiming for. Successfully dealing with limitations, delays, obstacles, and disputes depends on how you manage your temperament, utilize patience, and allot energy.

Difficulties come from overestimating capabilities or taking on too much. Superiors, competitive associates, or bureaucrats might cause some problems and setbacks. Low self-esteem will be counteracted by increased social popularity. Promotion, changes at work, or opportunities to move out and up into the world of self-employment could arise. Employers and heads of organizations are more likely to approach or pursue you with career opportunities and openings. Earnings are strongly connected to your ability to put creative expertise into practical form.

Flexibility, something that Leos are not always comfortable with, will be required when it comes to monetary affairs throughout 2007. Uranus, the planet of cosmic disruptions and innovations, remains in your Pisces house of joint finances and long-term financial stability. Being thorough and checking all monetary details, both large and small, and examining all angles with care and patience are musts in the year ahead. Changes are indicated in the amount of joint income received in the household. A partner's circumstances could alter, affecting you. Finances will fluctuate due to a break in income, pregnancy, leaving a job, or working casual hours. Money could also come in unexpectedly. Be flexible where finances are concerned, but also be organized. During May delays or adjustments to a property settlement, inheritance, divorce settlement, or child support are likely. Unexpected expenses regarding children and education could cause extra strain and stress on the budget. Financial challenges require that you correctly support your aims and avoid wasting resources. The money sector of your Leo horoscope will be highly energized when Saturn enters the Virgo second house of money in September. This is a major shift and brings an opportunity to consolidate finances.

Health generally remains favorable providing common sense prevails to prevent problems before they begin. The key to good health throughout the year is to pace yourself, avoid overindulging, eat healthy, and stick to a balanced diet. Listen to your body. Too much work or too much play is likely to result in immediate feedback from your body. Mental tension and lack of sleep can bring on anxiety. Protect your health through regular stress-relieving exercises and practices such as yoga and meditation. From September until the end of December when Mars transits your twelfth sector is an excellent time to plan a vacation or to go away to a quiet location and revitalize your energy. Leos without children may make a decision to change this status either through natural means or by adoption. Weight-loss efforts should be extremely successful throughout this year. Any accident will most likely be related to bone fractures or bruising. Regular dental checkups are advised. You are also apt to worry more, suffer from lower self-esteem, and occasionally fall behind in your work due to attempting more than you can comfortably handle. More will be demanded of you in the way of duties, obligations, and responsibilities, causing temporary bouts of physical and emotional exhaustion.

At the beginning of the year a bevy of planets greets you in the romance sector of your chart. This is a time when any outstanding issues can be resolved and mutual goals worked out to ensure progress in the right direction. Neptune represents inspiration, imagination, spiritual pursuits, and escapism. Throughout 2007 and beyond, this planet will be in your house of other people. Pleasure comes from increased focus on romantic and professional relationships. Although the romantic atmosphere contains change and some confusion, there is good chance of a beautiful new relationship. A partnership that is not open to change and renewal could end, allowing a new love affair to start. However, this will only occur if it has served its cosmic purpose. Sacrificing your own needs for a partner is possible, although this can add increased sensitivity to the relationship. For much of the year Saturn challenges Neptune, bringing uncertainty and unsettled feelings in many of your relationships. Take the time to examine how you are relating with other people.

A problem is likely to develop within a significant relationship that upsets the status quo. Willingness to accommodate changes is necessary or partnerships will end. Increased stress in this area is foreseen in mid-June. Husband-and-wife teams need to develop clear boundaries to circumvent potential problems. Otherwise resentment might emerge over equality of labor or power. Some opposition regarding your personal plans is unavoidable. The merging of reality and fantasy in your love life could leave you confused. The Venus retrograde period provides a chance to reevaluate and clarify your priorities according to changing values. This could end or strengthen ties of affection. If you can make it to September when Venus goes direct, fragile relationships have a greater chance of succeeding. You might need to support a sibling or friend through a romantic breakup or divorce. Although some single Leos will be happy to remain footloose and fancy-free, marriage is highly likely for many others.

The Mercury retrograde phases this year are February 14 to March 8, June 15 to July 10, and October 12 to November 2. During these periods expect transportation stoppages, delays, and crossed wires in communications. Defer signing important contracts, buying a home or property, or negotiating a commercial lease. However, this time can be used to complete outstanding work or continue on with a long-term project. Leo authors and writers finalizing a manuscript will be assisted under the Mercury retrograde. Take notice of the Moon phases in beginning and culminating projects. Each month the New Moon signifies a time of renewal, making this the perfect opportunity to begin something new. The Full Moon is the time to focus on completion.

The best time to expand your knowledge is during the early part of the year, although the urge to travel and broaden your horizons will be present for the whole of 2007. This year is also excellent for exploring the world, which should be both an adventure and a learning experience. Dealings with the public need to be handled with care. Opportunities exist to be highly creative and productive. Your ability to put your personal talents and expertise to practical use can produce emotional and financial rewards as well as enjoyment and benefits to yourself and to others.

LEO
DAILY FORECAST

January–December 2007

JANUARY

1. MONDAY. Stimulating. This first day of the New Year is a good time to throw out the old and bring in the new. Once your head is cleared of last night's celebration, get busy on your resolutions. If life has been running off track, now is the time to make changes and create your own positive destiny. For Leos who love to entertain, be prepared for the party to continue. The Moon is in the chatty sign of Gemini, so everyone around you will feel sociable. If expecting guests, keep catering arrangements simple so you can experience the joy of mixing with family members and special friends. Use extra tact this afternoon, especially if you are tired.

2. TUESDAY. Satisfying. Diminished energy is your body's way of telling you it is time to take it easy. Rest and recuperate to restore vitality if excessive socializing over the past few weeks has taken a toll. From midmorning onward is a very good time to finish up regular responsibilities and meet deadlines. If you have some time off or are currently on vacation, take over a comfortable chair and enjoy a good book, an interesting television documentary, or a favorite companion. A pleasant surprise involving your mate or partner's income or company profit could put a smile on your face, providing a great start to the year.

3. WEDNESDAY. Stressful. Foolish mistakes and errors are likely to occur, especially during the morning hours. Make sure you have your keys before shutting the front door and have mailed off bills due soon. This morning's Full Moon in the Cancer twelfth house brings an urge to be away from other people as much as possible. Try to arrange to work in quiet surroundings, or better still in complete solitude. That way petty annoyances, interruptions, and needless arguments can be kept to a minimum or totally avoided. For Leos who are on vacation, entertainment that is quiet, relaxing, and not very active would be the best way to spend leisure hours.

4. THURSDAY. Expansive. An unexpected opportunity could be very lucrative. Do the research, and then if everything looks good go for it. Venus, goddess of love and values, is now settled in your seventh house of Aquarius until January 27, putting the focus on personal and professional partnerships. Relationships that have been under a cloud should vastly improve if both you and the other party make an effort to restore harmonious vibes. Leos in a business partnership should also experience better relations and a possible boost of profits while dealing directly with the public. Be prepared to socialize more with work colleagues and other people you see on a regular basis.

5. FRIDAY. Pleasant. The Moon in your own sign of Leo encourages all types of creativity and enjoyable pursuits. For Leos who are back on the job, the prospect of a weekend full of fun and social activity will be inviting. Try to do important tasks early in the day. The hours are likely to drag from midmorning on, with the possibility of making more errors. These minor mistakes could quickly expand out of proportion if extra focus is not applied. This evening do some of the things that you must or that make you feel good. Leos in a romantic relationship should spend time planning a future weekend away just for the two of you.

6. SATURDAY. Accomplished. Your energy level should remain high throughout the day, providing the chance to apply sustained effort and exertion toward your important duties. Time and work put into a personal creative project should be emotionally and financially rewarding. With life beginning to move in the right direction, don't be put off by any minor setbacks. A more serious mood is likely to develop after lunch, bringing an urge to engage in practical pursuits rather than frivolous activities. Visiting grandparents or an elderly relative would satisfy your desire to do your duty as well as please those you go to see.

7. SUNDAY. Sensitive. Financial issues are likely to demand some of your free time. If you overdid on festive spending you are apt to be dreading the arrival of credit card and bank statements. Cutting back on leisure activities could help reduce the expected deficit. If organizing plans to entertain, make preparations in advance and avoid inviting guests who you know are inclined to be picky or to want an elaborate spread. A casual gathering with close friends will be most rewarding. Returning unwanted gifts or items that are faulty can be done without a hitch even if you don't have the receipts.

8. MONDAY. Rewarding. You are likely to feel more in control of your life. An opportunity to boost your investment portfolio is worth looking into. If this involves commercial property or other real estate, financial gains in coming years are likely. Leos who are in a committed union should not let their partner spend too much money. Stick to your budget despite advertised sales. Attention to detail is heightened, making this an excellent day to undertake work of an intricate or delicate nature. Entertaining guests in your own home or hosting a special event should prove successful and rewarding, especially if you add your own creative touches.

9. TUESDAY. Good. Take a slow and steady approach to the day. Routine activities can be accomplished without too many difficulties. Beginning a new project or trying to get one moving will probably be unsuccessful until later in the afternoon. This is also a good time for Leos who are scheduled to make a speech or present a sales report. A team or other business meeting could make progress if the discussion is focused on completing tasks already on the go or on making changes to current processes. Advancement may be limited if new initiatives are implemented. Inaccurate information could cause an argument that disturbs tranquility. Make sure data is correct before confronting your mate, partner, or boss.

10. WEDNESDAY. Soothing. Be prepared for long-winded phone conversations. Even if you are busy or not interested, you might have to listen carefully in order to successfully resolve the complaint or situation. Networking with coworkers on the job can bring you into contact with someone who can provide guidance. Read a book or watch a television show that takes you away from stress or overwork this evening. Let family members know that you are not interested in discussing today's events, so your mind can close off at least until tomorrow morning. The benefits will be evident when you return to work raring to go.

11. THURSDAY. Cautious. Patience is needed throughout the day. Appointments or meetings are likely to take longer than expected, so be prepared in advance. Everyone in attendance could demand to be heard, dragging out the process. Over the next few days it would be advisable to avoid attending any social activity after dark on your own. By taking extra precautions with your personal safety, the chance greatly diminishes of problems arising through this period of possible nasty incidents. If engaged in a body-contact sport, be sure to wear proper safety gear. In general, avoid high-risk recreational activities.

12. FRIDAY. Satisfactory. You or other people around you could be on edge today. Endeavor to remain calm. Explosive eruptions with loved ones will take some time and a lot of effort for wounds to heal. Younger Leos can utilize this potentially destructive energy in a positive manner by participating in physical activities or an organized sporting event. Don't believe everything you are told. People may be tempted to tell a few minor lies or to expand the truth. You might not be receiving the recognition you crave or feel you deserve on the job. Be prepared to challenge and stretch yourself more, and the resulting rewards should eventually come your way.

13. SATURDAY. Trying. This is the type of day when it is best to keep a low profile. People are likely to be more secretive and not as outgoing as usual. Take care not to push anyone unnecessarily, especially a lover or a child. Even if family members normally give in to you, this is unlikely to be the case today. Leo shoppers should take care if making a large purchase. Don't trust the word of salespeople. Check paperwork thoroughly if purchasing on credit, and verify warranties. Take extra care if driving in heavy traffic. Be sensible and obey all rules of the road. Don't become involved in any verbal confrontation with another motorist. Love and passion will be intense.

14. SUNDAY. Enjoyable. Focus on difficult tasks early in the day. Leave the more enjoyable activities for later on. Fast, accurate thinking will help you make snap decisions or choices on the run. If you are out driving, take extra care to watch out for crazy driving or the rash behavior of other motorists. Experimenting in the kitchen cooking something you have never tried before can liven up the day. Family members or friends may lavish you with compliments on your expert culinary skills and flair. The solo Leo could find interesting romantic possibilities at a function attended by family members and friends.

15. MONDAY. Constructive. Today's cosmic influences favor tasks that have a creative theme. The morning hours are the best time to seek information and helpful guidance. Extra work or a lucrative contract could help boost the bank account for self-employed Leos. Watch for opportunities to come your way. You are likely to rebel if tasks are boring, especially after lunch. Schedule challenging and interesting activities to help you maintain focus. Mercury, planet of all forms of communication, moves into your house of relationships, joining Chiron, Venus, and Neptune. Partners come to the fore now and can provide excellent advice and guidance.

16. TUESDAY. Sparkling. Leo businesspeople or company directors could experience a boost in profits through entertaining and mixing with those who can provide information or influential contacts. Tact and diplomacy are the only way to handle a situation that involves an authority figure. Otherwise you could be on the receiving end of an unpleasant experience. It would be wise to defer seeking a loan from the bank, credit institution, or a friend because the terms will probably not be in your favor. Leos currently in a romantic relationship should arrange a dinner for two tonight, with sparkling silverware and mood-making candles. Prepare for a love fest.

17. WEDNESDAY. Calm. This should be an uneventful day providing you don't look for drama. Avoid skipping meals. Keep up a regular intake of fluid, preferably of the nonalcoholic variety. Even if you are busy on the job, neglecting your health can have serious consequences later on. A headstrong attitude won't be helpful at home. Compromise and cooperation will get you further than aggression or bullying tactics. For those not on the job, performing domestic duties will provide a sense of comfort and security. Keep busy reorganizing your closets, removing clutter, and giving away old clothing to a local charity or selling it at a consignment shop.

18. THURSDAY. Harmonious. If the weather is not inclement, set aside time to get out in nature even if you just take a stroll around the neighborhood. With this evening's New Moon in the health and well-being sector of your solar chart, this is an excellent period to begin a new physical exercise program and a diet to increase vitamin intake. Leos wishing to lose or gain weight have an increased chance of staying with a dietary regime begun now. Poetry, beauty, and creative activities are likely to appeal as the preferred method of entertainment. Lovers could find excitement through romantic fantasy.

19. FRIDAY. Manageable. Warn family and friends in advance that you might arrive home later than usual from work or your daily routine. A public meeting or group activity is bound to run past the expected time. Work or team building exercises could take longer than normal. Cooperating with your mate or partner will lead to accomplishment as you view your shared visions and goals more clearly. For many Leos excitement will be building as that very special day draws closer. Some might be experiencing the joy of an engagement or the birth of a much wanted bundle of joy, while others join in the celebration.

20. SATURDAY. Cautious. If you are in the habit of having a few extra alcoholic drinks over the weekend, you might need to slow down now. There is a danger of overindulging, possibly embarrassing yourself or other people. The Sun charges out of stable Capricorn into radical Aquarius today, highlighting the area of partnerships and your personal relations. Situations that have been stalemated could begin to move forward, although not necessarily in the way you had envisioned or hoped. This is a period when you need to go with the flow. Be prepared to embrace change, which is not always easy for the fixed Leo.

21. SUNDAY. Helpful. Your compassion and sensitivity to the plight of the needy is enhanced. Be prepared to perform a few good deeds for and with other people. You may decide to visit an elderly relative and do some odd jobs around the house, or volunteer to take a neighbor shopping. Whatever you do, be sure to follow through on what you start. There is a tendency to leave activities half-finished. Be wary about making important decisions, especially if these are connected with joint finances or tax matters. Wait a few more days since all relevant information needed to make informed choices is not available just yet. Expect an unusual surprise or small windfall.

22. MONDAY. Unpredictable. A bevy of planetary activity ensures that your day will be anything but ordinary. Remain cool, calm, and collected even in situations where you feel you have no control or are about to be overwhelmed. Try to adapt to whatever occurs and you should experience fewer problems and less stress. Your mind could slip into overdrive, but beware of jumping to unfounded conclusions. Accusing other people of unsavory activities should also be avoided unless you have concrete proof. Otherwise you may be wrong. Be prepared for a possibly unpleasant letter from your bank.

23. TUESDAY. Active. Everyone around you might seem to be on the move and in a hurry. With the Moon in fellow fire sign Aries, your energy level will rise over the next two days. This influence also encourages action and activity, so you will need to keep busy focusing on stimulating tasks. Be very careful what you say and how you approach other people. Arguments and disagreements are most likely to erupt later this afternoon. That is also the time to expect delays or minor frustrations if you are setting off on a long-distance trip. Have your tickets and relevant paperwork where you can get to them quickly to avoid problems and hassles.

24. WEDNESDAY. Guarded. Expect a little vagueness from those you deal with today. You might also experience some deception as someone tries to pull the wool over your eyes. If you are prepared at least it won't come as a shock. Leos in a partnership either of an intimate or professional nature need to realize that their partner is only human. Take off the rose-colored glasses and bring down the other person from the pedestal before you become disillusioned or disappointed. If seriously considering enrolling in a formal course of study, you should be successful if you begin the process now. However, be realistic about how much extra work you can cope with.

25. THURSDAY. Tricky. With deceptive influences still swirling all around you, don't sign any legally binding agreement. Take the time to research, think things through, and obtain expert advice. This is also not the best period to consider going into business or commercial partnership. Career-minded Lions need patience right now. Forging ahead and moving up the ladder takes time, preparation, and planning. Use restraint without letting this dampen your enthusiasm and progress can be made. Sedentary social activities will be most appealing tonight. Socializing after hours with work colleagues should be enjoyable if you want to unwind a little before heading home.

26. FRIDAY. Passionate. Bundles of love and passion are heading your way. This is a perfect day to organize a weekend getaway with that special person or arrange an intimate dinner for two at a favorite restaurant followed by a trip to the local movie house or theater. If you have children, pack them off for a sleepover and set the scene for a night of romance. All that could spoil your evening would be talk that turns to career or business problems. Switch off from thoughts of employment as soon as you walk in your front door. Meditation could be especially helpful for Leos who are staying home alone. Your ability to receive insightful messages is enhanced.

27. SATURDAY. Variable. Stress from studies or work might cause you to feel under the weather. This is a good time to catch up on your sleep. Staying in bed for a little longer than usual will give you extra energy to put into various personal pursuits. Emphasis now falls on partnership finances and money handling as Venus, the planet linked to romance and values, moves into your house of sex and shared resources. Give special attention to joint accounts, confidential business, and tax issues. This is also a good period to reorganize or restructure your monetary affairs and also to spice up your love life. You won't need a lot of money to have a lot of fun.

28. SUNDAY. Mixed. Concentration is not your strong suit today. Focus on routine tasks as well as fun activities. Errors are likely to creep in if you try to act on mental tasks or jobs that demand attention to detail. If you are staying home to finish up household chores, do one thing at a time. In this way you can best make a dent in tasks waiting for completion. Differences of opinion with your mate or partner are likely to surface. Minimize disputes by keeping talk on a superficial level. Avoid topics that are likely to cause heated debated or outright confrontation. Spend time with friends who offer the opportunity for a pleasant interlude and congenial company.

29. MONDAY. Accomplished. As this new workweek begins you will be on the go more than usual. Two heads are better than one, so ask a friend or a trusted colleague to listen to a speech or lecture you have prepared. Advice you receive will tell you whether your words are informative as well as entertaining. Expect faster than usual answers to problems and queries, but take care if you are giving information to other people. Confirm data first since inconsistencies or errors are possible. If these are not detected now they could cause larger problems later on. Contact an old friend for an evening out if you feel the need to socialize.

30. TUESDAY. Subdued. Best results will be obtained by putting your effort into completing outstanding chores and other activities. Effort devoted to new ventures will just cause confusion and stress because of all the unfinished business already waiting for your action. If the day seems a bit slow or you have a bad dose of winter blues, think positively. It won't be long until spring arrives and the world appears much happier and brighter. Lend your support to the goals of your mate or partner. Their instincts are likely to be right on target. Don't become distressed over a lost or misplaced item, which will be found if you just keep looking.

31. WEDNESDAY. Changeable. Mixed trends prevail today. Your mind is in full analytical mode, ready to research or debate topics of specific interest. The actions of other people could take you by surprise. Accept that this behavior is their choice, not something you can do anything about. Distance yourself and move on with your own tasks. Self-employed Leos and those on the rise up the ladder of success can make significant headway by mixing business with pleasure. Just be careful what you say if discussion turns to your own many accomplishments. Be proud and truthful without displaying a boastful manner.

FEBRUARY

1. THURSDAY. Rejuvenating. With the Moon gliding through your own sign of Leo, this is the right time to discard old, outdated clothes by giving to charity. A more modern hairstyle, clothes, and makeup can have you feeling like the regal person you really are. Talking to your mate or partner to resolve any outstanding issues or grievances can produce positive results. Leos involved in advertising or promotional work should go with clever and innovative ideas, which are most likely to lead to financial gains or increased benefits. Recapturing the passion of an exciting romance would be a special and thrilling way to spend the evening.

2. FRIDAY. Sensitive. Sensitivity and emotional feelings are the theme of the day. The Full Moon culminates in your own sign of Leo, bringing touchy issues to the fore. A person close to you could be more demanding, or extra commitments that take up your free time might threaten to overwhelm you. When you realize that everyone around you might also be emotionally demonstrative and irritable, coping should be easier. This may be the time to let go of plans, ideas, or projects that have stalled and are obviously not going anywhere. Even if the decision is difficult to adjust to, you will be better off in the long term to forget and to move on to more worthwhile and viable activities.

3. SATURDAY. Manageable. A confident and optimistic atmosphere prevails. If you put your mind to it, most things on your weekend to-do list can be achieved today. This will leave enough time to indulge in your favorite activities. Later in the day an urge to splurge brings a relaxing interlude. Just make sure to limit how much you spend. Trickster Mercury is now settled into your Pisces eighth house of debts, collections, and shared finances. Be extra attentive to tax and estate matters and also to paperwork involving insurance or a legal settlement. Seek advice if you don't understand the fine print or the process involved. Confusion is a possibility with all monetary affairs over the next few weeks.

4. SUNDAY. Variable. Restlessness encourages you to be up and active early this morning. This also emphasizes your desire to possess, which could lead to overspending. Decide if you really need any more nonessential items and, if purchased, will these be used to full capacity. Small, petty differences of opinion could easily be magnified, leading to dissension with your loved ones. If financial matters must be discussed, a calm and sensible attitude should produce the desired results. The best time for an in-depth conversation involving monetary matters is midafternoon. Any other time today may result in arguments and a stalemate.

5. MONDAY. Important. Beware of a tendency to overreact or go to extremes, especially in regard to spending on leisure activities. There is also a need to be more moderate with food and drink since your inclination to indulge remains strong. Do not saddle yourself with an overload of employment duties and responsibilities as you begin the new working week. Set priorities and don't get caught up with unnecessary activities. Keep communications light and ongoing as a way to improve relations with other people, especially if cooperation has been in short supply lately. Let others know you are prepared to put any tension or disputes in the past and move on.

6. TUESDAY. Hectic. If possible, put off any major decisions. Today's celestial influences are not conducive for making clear choices. An abundance of e-mails, phone calls, and other communication needs to be handled with patience and care. When time permits, write your thoughts and ideas down on paper, to be reviewed by you during a more relaxing period. You might be amazed by what you wrote when reading it back at your leisure. Spending on other people might crimp your budget. Curb your generosity unless you have plenty of cash to spare. Try to rise above any upsets or problems that erupt throughout the day.

7. WEDNESDAY. Fortunate. Keep a cool head especially early this morning. The remainder of the day is likely to progress without too much drama or challenging incidents. Contact important people who might offer assistance in promoting or advertising your products or services. To increase your chances of receiving an unexpected windfall, purchase a lottery ticket, enter a raffle, or fill out the form for a magazine competition. You have nothing to lose and could receive a pleasant boost to your savings. A new relationship may blossom into a lingering and passionate union. Leo couples should also experience happy rapport.

8. THURSDAY. Insightful. Younger Lions heading out to socialize should be sure to tell someone where they are going. This will keep worry to a minimum. Any concern from parents should be viewed as stemming from love, not overprotective feelings. Make sure that you clear your desk of important paperwork before next Tuesday, when Mercury turns retrograde. Pay particular attention to financial matters, including insurance, tax, or joint loans. Heightened imagination and creativity provides the power to put inspirational ideas and plans into action. Set aside time this evening to do something that is important to you and displays your creative flair.

9. FRIDAY. Mixed. Beware an overconfident and overly optimistic attitude. Fighting for justice involving a person or a situation could occupy your thoughts and time. Efforts devoted to this cause are worthwhile, so continue despite personal hardship. Benefits should come eventually if not immediately. Now is not the right time to ask anyone for assistance. You might wind up having to give more than you receive. For this reason defer applying for a bank loan or overdraft protection at least until Monday. Otherwise repayments might be more than you can comfortably afford. There is a strong possibility that self-indulgent tendencies could prove challenging if you are trying to reduce your intake of carbs and alcohol.

10. SATURDAY. Sluggish. Your energy is at a lower level, with moving around seeming to take twice as long as usual. The Sun, planet of vim and vitality, clashes with debilitating Saturn, placing additional obstacles and limitations in your path. Leos who are organizing a public event or social function need to be up and about early to make sure everything is ready and will run smoothly. Check the time helpers are expected, and be prepared to hurry along those who are in charge of setting up the venue. Unless you have a prearranged social engagement, it might be better to opt for a quiet night at home with the family.

11. SUNDAY. Focused. Although it will be difficult for outgoing Leos, avoiding the limelight and not socializing is the only way to get all your chores completed. If you become caught up on the phone or answering e-mails, any hope of finalizing weekend tasks will quickly vanish. Later, a family get-together or other important gathering will be joyful as well as possibly tense. Steer clear of those who are inclined to overindulge, and make sure you don't fall into that trap. Emotional outbursts and impulsive actions could prove embarrassing. Shopping for bargains at secondhand stores or thrift shops could be just the place to find exactly what you are looking for.

12. MONDAY. Helpful. Speculative investments and interests could help swell your bank balance providing you have some expertise in this area. For best results keep the amount you invest small. Then, if you are inclined to worry at all, stress will be kept to a minimum. Making contact with older family members can bring pleasure. Leo parents may want to take young children to visit grandparents. Or go on your own to share your latest news and gossip. This evening a passionate mood prevails. Enjoy time at a romantic venue with your mate or partner. If this is not possible, a night at home for just the two of you should be happy and relaxing.

13. TUESDAY. Variable. Today's practical Capricorn Moon provides assistance to Leos experiencing problems on the job or with domestic issues. Shoppers who look hard and compare costs should find quality products at bargain prices. Mercury will soon go into backward motion, creating possible confusion and irritation. Information will take longer to arrive and might be incorrect when it gets to you. Expect delays with important decisions, especially in relation to corporate financial dealings or matters involving a personal loan or insurance. Entertaining in the comfort of your own home should provide enjoyment this evening. For those at home alone, listening to favorite music will be calming.

14. WEDNESDAY. Renewing. If you know that you should be exercising more and taking better care of your health, try an invigorating walk to reenergize and restore motivation. Breaking an old unhealthy habit should be easier if you are serious about making changes to your lifestyle. Be careful if socializing. Talking too much could result in an argument or heighten the tension already in the air. Even Leos who opt to stay home rather than going out should curb a know-it-all attitude in order to avoid domestic friction. A special romantic dinner will help celebrate Valentine's Day in style.

15. THURSDAY. Happy. Amicable relations with those in your environment make this a mostly pleasant day. From around midday onward creative and innovative ideas are likely to burst to mind. Agreements regarding basic issues make this a productive time for Leos who are on the job or teaming up with others. Financially there could be a business matter to sort out or a situation involving home insurance to resolve. Better results are likely if action in this regard is taken during the morning hours. It would be wise to check your mate or partner's needs and desires before making a decision or choice without prior consultation.

16. FRIDAY. Interesting. Prioritize and do first things first so that you finish most of your tasks early enough to thoroughly plan weekend activities. Socially you are in demand. Invitations could be pouring in, with unusual and interesting choices of entertainment for you to sample. Investigative efforts should prove very successful if you are interested in uncovering specific information or data. Your imagination will be activated more than usual, inspiring you to aim higher. Put aside some free time throughout the day or evening to enjoy a favorite hobby or artistic pursuit. Socializing with a group of friends would also be a pleasant option.

17. SATURDAY. Lively. Today's New Moon in your opposite sign of Aquarius marks the beginning of a sociable period for Lions. Just be sure to include your significant other in all the expected fun and frivolity. Leos who like to participate in sports or are planning a day at the racetrack should experience minor success. Prevailing cosmic influences assist your ability to research the field and to make final selections. Those who need to catch up on endless household chores should get started early. Put on your favorite music and dance your way through the various tasks. In this way you can finish in half the time and increase your physical fitness as well.

18. SUNDAY. Liberating. Over the next four weeks pay special attention to joint bank accounts, tax matters, and any confidential issues. The Sun travels into your Pisces eighth house, providing the opportunity to restructure financial affairs, insurance coverage, and mortgage payments so that you are receiving maximum benefits. Investigative efforts are likely to reveal information that has been intentionally hidden or at least difficult to locate. This is an excellent period for clearing your life of anything that seems outmoded or outdated. Energy and enthusiasm will assist those wanting to also remove accumulated clutter and items no longer required.

19. MONDAY. Passionate. Money and emotions are usually not a good mix. Leos who are feeling the heavy weight of outstanding loans need to review these thoroughly and realistically in order to move to a more comfortable level of living within current means. Leos who have reached a stage where paying bills is not a major concern should be alert for opportunities to expand investments or add to savings. A passionate encounter is foreseen for those involved in a romantic relationship, so be prepared. Leave work early to make the most of this pleasant interlude. Leo singles will also find that love is in the air.

20. TUESDAY. Sizzling. Wrestling with vacation plans, organizing travel arrangements, and trying to catch up with a friend or relative from overseas are all possible activities that keep you occupied today. There is something you need to learn to upgrade your employment or business expertise or broaden your overall knowledge. Do something positive about this. Even if you are inexperienced or unprepared, it will not take long for you to grasp the concept, theory, or skill. The mood for love remains, with a sizzling romantic encounter high on the wish list of Leo singles as well as those already in a committed union. Guard against overpossessiveness or jealousy, which will turn a lover off.

21. WEDNESDAY. Favorable. Patience may be in short supply, especially through the morning hours. If you can steer clear of volatile family members, arguments should be averted. Venus, which is linked to love and money, is now visiting impulsive Aries and your philosophical belief and travel house. A thirst for adventure and romance could be quenched for the traveling Lion who finds new love while on vacation. This is very likely for the unattached. If you decide to form an intimate romantic connection, make sure that honest and open communication is one of your prerequisites for a harmonious relationship. Saving for a long-distance vacation should be easier for the committed Leo anxious to expand horizons.

22. THURSDAY. Auspicious. Leos who are learning to drive, have just obtained a driver's license, or have been driving for years should seriously consider adding a defensive driving course to their list of achievements. Watch your behavior as well as what you say if socializing with an associate or someone you wish to impress. Out-of-line remarks will not endear you to anyone. Financially your bank balance could receive a welcome boost. A wage increase, large bonus, promotion, or new job could provide the means for you to generate extra income. Then you can begin to live in a style that you would like to become accustomed to.

23. FRIDAY. Rewarding. Motivation to reach for your professional goals is strong now. Taking the reins with a business or career matter is likely to prove hugely successful if you can sustain the effort. Leos seeking to expand their horizons should look no further than a vacation abroad to increase worldly knowledge. Plan an itinerary or pay a deposit as the first step toward realizing a dream. An outing with friends or entertaining them in your home will give you a glow of pleasure this evening. Wining and dining an associate or valued clients could give the self-employed Lion a jump on competitors.

24. SATURDAY. Cautious. A group activity or event that has a philosophical or spiritual theme might interest pleasure-seeking Lions. However, beware any request for you to take on a leadership position or other role that involves a heavy commitment. Unless you have plenty of leisure time available, it would be wiser to say no even if being the center of attention is part of the package. On the home scene a domestic appliance could break down, upsetting the household budget if a replacement needs to be bought quickly. Give yourself the necessary time to obtain comparison prices before purchasing any new equipment.

25. SUNDAY. Manageable. You are likely to be in the hot seat regarding a decision to postpone or cancel plans that also involve a partner. Quick thinking could help you come up with another good idea, or at least an acceptable reason why you need to take the action you have decided upon. Energetic Mars travels into your seventh house of Aquarius until April 6, indicating that business or personal partnerships could be the source of conflict or tension. If this energy is utilized positively, you could reach a higher level of understanding with your mate or partner thanks to conciliation and collaboration.

26. MONDAY. Sensitive. Squabbles concerning old issues could surface, bringing a sense of unease. Try not to let problems trouble you. Realize that some people just never want to let go. Spending time in a place or with a person you find uplifting will help dispel confusion and refresh your body and spirit. Trying to absorb an unexpected bill into the family household budget could be worrisome.

To resolve this matter, talk it over with other members of the family to find ways to trim current expenses. The health of a relative could be of concern. A visit to the hospital or nursing home might be required for your peace of mind.

27. TUESDAY. Unsettling. Although it is not your favorite spot, Leo people need to take a backseat today. The planetary combinations are likely to cause annoyance, irritation, and frustration. You will be able to handle this easier if you are out of the spotlight. There could also be some uncertain factors that take time to clarify, so defer making choices until all options have been presented and considered. Take extra care with your health. You could feel both physically and emotionally drained. With energy at a lower ebb than usual, it might be time to visit a health spa or go for a revitalizing massage or reflexology treatment to get your body back in good shape.

28. WEDNESDAY. Positive. Expect a change of pace and energy this morning as the Moon sweeps into your regal sign of Leo. If you know what needs to be done, get to it. Finish up tasks so that you can then begin new ones under today's positive vibes. Your ability to understand complex situations is enhanced, with a complicated or confusing personal matter now beginning to at last make some sense. Achieving a mutual goal requires working closely with a partner or associate. Compromise will be necessary to achieve desired results. Stimulating communication with your significant other will promote warmth and appreciation, giving you a good reason to stay home tonight.

MARCH

1. THURSDAY. Mixed. Trying to remain upbeat and cheerful is likely to test your resolve. Instead you are apt to feel tired and cranky as the new month gets under way. Best results can be obtained by concentrating on personal projects and endeavors. Cooperation will be lacking. Spend time revamping your appearance or improving your grooming. Make that overdue hair appointment, visit a massage therapist, or venture to the local boutique to purchase some interesting clothing accessories suitable for spring. This evening you might suffer a bout of guilt or mild depression. Retire to bed early and this uncomfortable energy can be avoided. Family friction will also be lessened if you are out of sight.

2. FRIDAY. Interesting. As much as possible cater to your own needs rather than running around fulfilling the demands of other people. Even if this appears selfish, you need to concentrate on yourself occasionally. If you have to prepare a lecture or sales presentation, ask a learned associate to give you some advice. With financial matters beckoning, this afternoon is the best time to organize bills and all paperwork relating to your monetary concerns. Stand back from an emotional issue involving your mate or partner so you can gain a more rational perspective. Separating your heart from your head will prompt clearer vision.

3. SATURDAY. Renewing. Guard against displaying a picky or pedantic attitude. Allowing your irritability to be evident could have a boomerang effect, causing other people to also become cranky and upset. Today's eclipsed Virgo Full Moon raises everybody's standard, which could also lead to a hypercritical approach. Leos who are spending the day at home might get the urge to clean away clutter and discard articles of clothing and furnishings that are no longer serving a useful purpose. Set aside time to check the progress of special projects or assignments to ensure that correct procedures are being followed.

4. SUNDAY. Guarded. Unless you have a full day of social activities planned, focus on a detail-oriented project or other important endeavor. Otherwise you could scatter your efforts on a wide spectrum of activities and make very little progress. Avoid any tendency to criticize, which is likely to be a waste of time. If you must offer advice, make sure it is constructive rather than petty censure. Financial issues could come to a head, especially if you share expenses within your household. This is a favorable time to construct a more workable budget that will lead to repaying all money that you owe.

5. MONDAY. Revealing. Remain open to all possibilities. A spur-of-the-moment day trip to visit friends or take advantage of some advertised sales is likely to appeal if you are not fully occupied on the job. Communication issues or technical problems could result in confusion if you are waiting for financial statements or records. Leos working on a computer can lessen stress by saving data regularly. Back up your work to safeguard against loss of important information. A secret could unexpectedly be revealed, coming as a shock to many people and upsetting your equilibrium. Go with the flow and most problems will be successfully resolved.

6. TUESDAY. Energetic. For much of the day you will be inclined to rush in or somehow act in a foolish manner. Although your mind should be sharp, concentrating on practical details or concerns is unlikely to be a priority. Finally building up the courage to say what is on your mind to a sibling or neighbor will be a relief. Once the air is cleared your relationship should move on to a new level of understanding and respect. Your confidence and belief in yourself has been severely tested over the past few weeks due to the challenging cosmic aspects. This influence will pass, so try not to let little things get the better of you.

7. WEDNESDAY. Unpredictable. Nothing is likely to go exactly as planned. You might have to run a number of errands even though you would prefer staying close to home. Perform these active duties early in the day so your evening can be spent enjoying home comforts with your loved ones. Mercury moves forward in the zodiac tonight and ongoing misunderstandings should miraculously be resolved. Stalled projects are likely to begin to make progress. You may be tempted to go to extremes, becoming overly excessive in romance or leisure pursuits. Avoid putting yourself in any situation where you must make quick decisions or hasty choices.

8. THURSDAY. Productive. An expensive or expansive day awaits you. It is your choice. Leos seeking knowledge and wisdom should experience insight and understanding. If planning to take a vacation in the near future, you can find plenty of travel bargains online. Decide on your destination of choice and then begin the exciting task of organizing an interesting itinerary. Travelers setting off on an overseas journey should make it a point to check out the duty free shops, where you can make some extra good purchases at very affordable prices. A loved one could easily become upset and cranky. Exert personal effort to calm them down rather than becoming involved in any squabbles.

9. FRIDAY. Fortunate. This could be a lucky day if you are realistic and refrain from going overboard, which is your normal Leo fashion. If applying for a new position or seeking a promotion you are apt to receive a positive reply. An active and organized approach encourages home dwellers to initiate projects or act on new ideas around the house. Those on a fact-finding mission could encounter a brick wall when investigating some resources. You could also come up against secretive types who are not willing to divulge relevant information. You would be better off moving on and then coming back to this source in a few weeks. Harmonious vibes highlight the romantic scene.

10. SATURDAY. Eventful. Everyday boring or routine tasks are likely to irritate outgoing Leos. Act on what is vital and leave the rest of your chores for another time. It is better to use the social energy conveyed by the Sagittarius Moon for meeting friends, relaxing with a favored leisure activity, or playing a sport. Leo parents should be thrilled with the results of a sporting competition that a child participates in. Even if they do not win, let them know how proud you are of their gallant effort. Social activities this evening, although enjoyable, could come very close to breaking the budget.

11. SUNDAY. Encouraging. Your opportunities to connect with other people are enhanced today. For single Leos hoping to change that status, there is a strong possibility of surprising developments. To ensure success you need to make the effort to get out and mingle. Take part in a new sports activity or leisure pursuit. If you are financially limited, use restraint or your funds will soon run low. Those who are trying a new recreational or hobby pursuit but not experiencing the expected excitement should give it a little longer before throwing in the towel. Keep in mind that practice may not make perfect but will enhance fun.

12. MONDAY. Joyous. Today's upbeat trends put optimism, confidence, fun, love, and romance on your agenda. If you are seeking favors from other people, this is a propitious time to make a move. Your eager, confident mood will prevail for most of the day. Competition should be a source of joy, especially for the Leo who loves to win. Business efforts are sure to provide success, with a social event presenting an opportunity to increase commercial contacts and clientele prospects. Conveying ideas to partners or associates will be easier if language and plans are kept simple, clear, and concise.

13. TUESDAY. Powerful. This is the time in the lunar month when your health and well-being increases in importance. Study your lifestyle, diet, and exercise regime to discover areas where you could be doing better. Discard an unhealthy habit such as smoking or drinking too much or not getting sufficient sleep. Make the most of your increased energy, especially if you need to get through a large list of chores and work tasks. Your ability to think clearly late this afternoon aids business activity and should help avoid any last-minute calamity before you leave work. With regular rest breaks to recharge your battery, you can return to your duties refreshed and freshly motivated.

14. WEDNESDAY. Favorable. If interest on your home mortgage, business loan, or credit card is currently keeping you poor, now is a good time to do something about it. Look for a way to put the cash back in your wallet instead of someone else's. This will be a positive investment for your future. Call the bank or credit association and compare current rates. During the middle part of the day much progress can be made. This is also a good period to present a training seminar, apply for a promotion, send a resume, or go on a job interview. A medical procedure conducted in this period should also proceed smoothly.

15. THURSDAY. Sensitive. A joint venture or team effort that involves money and time is bound to arouse frustrations. Try to let matters evolve naturally at their own pace rather than rushing or pushing for results. A partner or loved one might not be easy to deal with, which is bound to be upsetting. Be cool, calm, and sensible, especially during the evening hours. Even Leos who are not usually fiery by nature could be unusually cranky and fierce tonight. The best course of action is to remove yourself from the scene so you are not tempted to have a temper tantrum in front of others. A leisurely dinner and a warm bath will refuel your depleted enthusiasm and energy.

16. FRIDAY. Opportune. A large number of cosmic influences are affecting your sign of Leo, so anything and everything could happen. Although most of the energy is positive, this is not the day to push anyone else's buttons. Self-promotion should be extremely successful providing you don't try too hard to get what you want. Softly, softly is the right approach for a positive outcome. Business meetings should move along at a quick pace, with attendees prepared to embrace new or radical ideas designed to improve the bottom line. This evening is promising for Leo lovers, with passion and desire enhanced.

17. SATURDAY. Empowering. If a special project to be completed around the house requires the input or labor of a number of people, this is an excellent day to arrange a working bee. Invite your friends to come over, stock the fridge, throw some hamburgers or sausages on the barbeque, and get everyone motivated to work. Venus, the planet of pleasure and romantic love, moves into sensuous Taurus and your professional sector, increasing the chance of finding love on the job for Leos who are single and looking. Even those not actively seeking a new relationship could find that opportunities abound in the working environment.

18. SUNDAY. Dynamic. If you haven't already begun the process of reorganizing and restructuring your financial accounts and investments, Mercury's reentry into your joint monetary sector of Pisces now gives you another chance to take action. Pensions, loans, annuities, and tax matters all add to your financial security and status. A proactive approach ensures that you will know if you are receiving the best deals for increasing funds and making long-term savings. With a Pisces New Moon eclipse also culminating in this sector, new monetary projects begun now have an excellent chance of succeeding. An unexpected gift will put a smile on your face.

19. MONDAY. Invigorating. If unpaid bills or joint monetary problems are sending shivers up your spine, it might be time to seek professional advice. A counselor can help you determine the best way to get your finances back to a more manageable level. Enroll in a course that can expand your knowledge of economics if you want a more in-depth understanding of monetary matters. Insight can come through informal or formal teaching. A spiritual retreat or a New Age seminar or conference could be a memorable indulgence for Leos who have some cash to spare. A good time is promised for those heading overseas. However, you could be confronted with some unexpected adventures that you were not counting on.

20. TUESDAY. Extraordinary. Today marks the beginning of the spring equinox with the entry of the Sun into your ninth house of Aries. On this happy day you can expect to accomplish a lot thanks to good planning and concerted effort. Habits and attitudes that in the past you were resistant to change may now be obviously outdated and therefore easily discarded. Long-distance travel is highlighted. You could be preparing a journey that leads to expansion of your knowledge and experience. This is an excellent time to plan a vacation itinerary, apply for a passport, purchase luggage for your trip, or sign up to learn the basics of a foreign language.

21. WEDNESDAY. Excellent. With the Moon gliding through the sign of sensuous Taurus, this is a time for self-indulgence. Just remember to do this on a small scale without going overboard. Travel as well as spiritual and New Age practices are likely to claim attention as you seek ways to broaden your knowledge in one of these areas. A mention in the local paper of a course could spark your interest and develop into a lifetime hobby or passion. Employed Leos may receive an offer of employment or a promotion that has considerable future earning potential. Your challenge is not to begin spending the increased income before you have earned it. Your love life will soon get a boost.

22. THURSDAY. Bumpy. This could be a difficult day as cosmic forces bring impatience and irritability to the surface. Tread warily with loved ones, a partner, or business associate. Otherwise you will need to make amends or an apology tomorrow. Don't allow other people to pressure you into making quick decisions. These are not likely to be correct or the right choices for you at this time. This is also not the right time to push yourself or to take part in any activity that requires a great deal of physical exertion. Otherwise your energy will soon disappear. Work that demands meticulous attention to detail can be performed since your concentration is enhanced.

23. FRIDAY. Favorable. Creative expression is yours to use as you like. If this talent is needed in your employment, expect to make good progress today. Public speaking and taking the lead in a community group or campaign are also areas where you can excel. Taking a seat on the sidelines won't sit well with the outgoing Lion. However, those involved in a romantic relationship need to make a special effort to display love and affection. Otherwise you could have something to worry about, especially if your mate or partner accuses you of neglect or of emphasizing the needs of other family members or work colleagues.

24. SATURDAY. Uplifting. For single Lions, joining a new social group or volunteer organization will bring a welcome change from the same old conversations and faces. Look for a group that offers change and variety so your mind is continually stimulated. A new romance or reigniting the spark in an existing relationship is a possibility. Stopping by a large department store could be fun if you like to sniff out bargains. However, unless you are extremely careful when choosing your shopping companion, there is a likelihood that a big dent could be made in your bank balance. Put yourself on a financial limit and stick with it.

25. SUNDAY. Subdued. Your energy and tolerance level are at a low par. Confine today's efforts to routine tasks for best results and less fatigue. Don't skip meals. Maintain a healthy diet and get plenty of rest and relaxation. Then you will be ready to face the new working week come tomorrow morning. A relative could try to influence you, but only if you allow this. Reclaim your power through articulate words or passive actions. Laugh off taunts or ignore the antics of other people altogether. Having faith in your own abilities inspires others to be equally positive. Lose yourself in a romantic comedy or fantasy film this evening.

26. MONDAY. Uneasy. This is not a good time to begin any new undertaking. Your energy level remains at a low ebb. Concentrate on finalizing uncompleted tasks and work projects. Straighten up your desk, act on personal obligations, and finish domestic duties waiting for attention. Leos employed in areas where physical labor is required should seek work that is less taxing or take the day off. All tense or stressful situations ought to be avoided. A part-time or volunteer position assisting other people to overcome traumatic or worrisome situations could lift your spirits if you are not currently employed full-time.

27. TUESDAY. Expansive. Better time management is the key to increasing the amount of prime time available just for you. Opportunities to make good on a personal objective or endeavor are present. Avoid interfering in the problems or disputes of other people. Even if asked for advice, tread warily. A noncommittal response would be the best response. Don't be afraid to be yourself. Dress to impress in order to attract the attention of someone special. This will enhance your personal esteem, which in turn conveys increased self-confidence in your own abilities and skills. Upsets or complications are likely if you insist on socializing this evening. Have alternative plans in place to avoid disappointment.

28. WEDNESDAY. Manageable. If your significant romantic relationship is currently floundering, now is the time to take action. Clearing the air with honest, open communication would be a major step in the right direction. Someone important is likely to keep you waiting or might be too busy to get back to you. Be patient and everything should be satisfactorily resolved. With the Moon in your own sign of Leo, establishing a positive new habit or breaking a negative old one should be easier. A child might be demanding, inconsiderate, or just prone to bad behavior. Sit down together and revisit the ground rules, explaining exactly what will not be tolerated.

29. THURSDAY. Tricky. Be prepared for the unexpected to occur. Rapport with your business partner, significant other, or an important client could be strained. A clash of wills is likely to cause tension. Take your time before making decisions regarding a legal matter, confidential issues, or expensive purchases. Something is not quite right, but this may not be evident or clear just yet. Delays are likely for Leos who have been waiting for a refund on merchandise or a special delivery. Be wary of what seems to be a get-rich-quick scheme. What sounds too good to be true will be just that. Tension eases by nightfall, so plan a romantic evening when you can let go of built-up stress.

30. FRIDAY. Encouraging. Life should be back on track today, or at least not as tricky as yesterday. A work assignment needs your undivided attention if good progress is to be made. Be discerning if you go on a shopping trip. Second thoughts about one of your purchases could emerge when you discover that the item was overpriced, faulty, or doesn't fit in with your current decor. Leos going out to socialize should first come up with a rough idea of how much the night's amusement is likely to cost. Otherwise you might suffer some embarrassment when you can't pay your fair share.

31. SATURDAY. Lucky. Look forward to a lucky day. Start off on a good note by sleeping a little later this morning. You are apt to feel more like playing than taking care of routine obligations. If you don't have to be anywhere special, take a break and give yourself a treat. Recognition or an honor bestowed for your efforts, possibly in some type of community role, could come as a pleasant surprise for deserving Leos. For those on the job, a pay increase could come in the form of a better than expected bonus or sales commission. Entertaining a special person, relaxing with a lover, or socializing with friends would all be excellent choices for tonight's amusement.

APRIL

1. SUNDAY. Challenging. Staying still is apt to prove challenging. Keeping on the move should help you to avoid restlessness. If staying home, focus on tasks that need physical input such as cleaning out the garage, straightening cupboards, or catching up on housework. Those requiring less strenuous and more mental activities should ensure that all financial correspondence and bookkeeping are in order and up to date. Avoid making rash or impulsive decisions during the next few days. A long walk, a bike ride, or a trolley trip could also create calmness instead of agitation. Intellectual pursuits that stimulate your mind are also likely to appeal.

2. MONDAY. Tricky. Problems involving a loan or mortgage repayment could surface. If you attend to this as soon as it comes to your notice, it will keep problems from escalating any further. Otherwise you might incur extra charges or a fine. Leos who are planning to seek a pay increase or promotion should put this on hold right now. With the Full Moon energy culminating, even though in the placid sign of Libra, the only response you receive might be a tirade from your boss as to why higher wages are out of the question right at this moment. Be alert for road rage from some other motorist if driving any time during the day.

3. TUESDAY. Useful. The current lunar influences focus on all aspects of communications. If you need a new phone, fax, or computer, make your move during the morning hours. With emotions still high because of yesterday's Full Moon energy, steer clear of contrary people and those who are quick to anger. Leisure periods can be used to catch up on reading and answering correspondence. Resist the temptation for sarcasm, especially with loved ones and particularly if they are emotionally fragile right now. Avoid idle gossip, even if rumors seem to have some foundation. You are better off staying away from innuendo since feelings could end up being hurt and relationships strained.

4. WEDNESDAY. Romantic. A quest to acquire more possessions could find Leos heading for the department store. Your desire for beautiful acquisitions is stimulated. If you cannot do without your retail fix, be discerning or you might be sold a dud or be taken in by a smooth-talking salesperson. Your thoughts turn to love as your romantic imagination escalates. If single, enjoy time with someone you just met. A long-term union might not be the result, but memories of the encounter will linger. Leo couples should take a break from the rat race and spend time at home alone, enjoying being together surrounded by home comforts.

5. THURSDAY. Insightful. Today's influences encourage investigation and research work. You might need to push and dig a little harder to obtain all the information you want. Examine long-range plans to make sure you are still heading in the right direction. There is a tendency for daydreaming or overlooking the obvious. Contemplating ways to improve your domestic environment would be a constructive use of current influences. Once daily errands and tasks are completed, go home and look at your living quarters and home comforts with a critical eye. Domesticated Leos might find spring cleaning, baking a cake, or restoring an old piece of furniture increases home pleasure.

6. FRIDAY. Practical. Home, family, and property matters remain a focus again today. If your decor is still languishing with last century's fixtures and appliances, it may be time to revamp and refurbish. Even if money is tight, making inexpensive small changes can add value to your property while pleasing you. Expect more fireworks and explosions in your love life now that Mars has entered your Pisces house of sex and passion. Conflict with someone you share your possessions or finances with could escalate. A patient, calm attitude will be of more value and get you further than a stubborn or fiery approach.

7. SATURDAY. Renewing. Ongoing stress can take a toll on your health. Release built-up pressure by taking off for the weekend or at least for the day. Escape dilemmas and dramas by going off by yourself or as a family unit to explore places and sights you have not seen before. Romance looks very promising for Leos in love and for those seeking emotional contact. Communication is vital to continue harmonious vibes, so make a point of talking heart-to-heart to your mate or partner. A creative period prevails, and several opportunities to realize potential in this area could arise. Insight into financial issues is likely if you take the time to do some Internet research.

8. SUNDAY. Rewarding. Remove whatever is no longer adding to your life, even a person or possessions. Good vibes exist for Leos who have planned a family day, especially if in involves youngsters.

Lion parents love their cubs, so treat children to a special outing. Bring along your camera to record happiness of all members of the clan. If you yearn to mingle with children but don't have any of your own, offer to baby-sit a niece, nephew, or a friend's child. You can have fun and will give the parents a much needed break. Chances of a romantic connection are high for Leos singles who go out mingling with a crowd.

9. MONDAY. Fortunate. Life often delivers what you ask for, so today ask for what you need. Luck is on your side, bringing possible good fortune. A long-held desire or wish could finally be granted. A prize in a competition or a financial windfall might arrive in the mail, so keep an eye out for the mail carrier. Or you may receive a wage increase, a larger than expected bonus, or promotion to a higher-paying position. Jetting off into the sunset or finalizing vacation plans is favorable for Leo travelers. A radical health or diet change can now be considered if you believe it would improve the quality of your life.

10. TUESDAY. Uncertain. Murphy's Law reigns today, indicating that what can go wrong probably will. The best way to handle this is with a smile and a shrug. Don't let work colleagues or associates know of your plans until you have outlined thoughts to the boss or some other authority figure. Otherwise someone could steal your ideas or get in before you do. Communicative Mercury enters your house of travel and education, conveying an urge to roam and learn. Plan a few trips out of town over the next three weeks to experience new vistas and to expand your knowledge. The state of a relative's health might be of concern but try not to worry because your fears may be unfounded.

11. WEDNESDAY. Pleasurable. Venus, the goddess of love, money, art, and beauty, moves into your Gemini eleventh house of your hopes, wishes, and future goals. Leos involved in community efforts are likely to receive pleasure as well as prestige from now until May 8. Doors could open, bringing increased opportunities for financial and business deals. Your ability to attract resources and people to assist you in obtaining special goals is enhanced. This is a favorable period to promote your services, especially if you are now self-employed. Put your creative flair to work preparing unique promotional and advertising material that clearly describes what you have to offer potential clients.

12. THURSDAY. Mixed. An agreement made today is likely to lead to increased responsibilities, one of which could involve a professional role. Before going ahead make sure you are prepared for increased work and will be able to handle extra duties. Be aware of an inclination toward extravagance, especially if you are going shopping. You might set out just to purchase life's necessities but return home with expensive luxury items. This could lead to a dispute with your significant other, particularly if you are spending joint funds. A big hug for your mate or partner might just do the trick to restore harmony.

13. FRIDAY. Tense. Work and professional matters could clash with social activities. Attend to urgent duties early in the day to reduce the likelihood of having to spend longer hours on the job. Money problems involving a friend might cause an upset early this afternoon. You need to decide which is more important, your friendship or the quick return of money that was borrowed. Either way there may be a loss, so it is up to you to choose what action to take. Leos involved in collecting money owed for goods or services should have more luck pursuing overdue debts during the earlier part of the day.

14. SATURDAY. Enjoyable. People are likely to talk a lot without saying much. Expect confusion and misunderstandings in some if not all of your communications. Someone is also likely to do something unusual, perhaps altering social plans at the last minute. Remain calm and go with the flow. Whatever you end up doing will be better than staying home alone. If you are half of a couple, your mate or partner could be full of surprises. There is the chance of a special gift arriving at your door. Or you might be treated to a special night out on the town. Don't spoil the occasion by overindulging and having too much of a good time.

15. SUNDAY. Favorable. This is a good day to take part in a cultural event or education program. Make sure to limit your spending if there are lots of places and areas where you could purchase goodies. If you take cash only and leave the credit cards at home, temptation will be reduced. Steer clear of potentially difficult or controversial topics, including politics and religion, when socializing. Even if your words are articulate and nonjudgemental, someone is likely to take offense. Try your best to avoid causing dissent and possible tension. Students with a heavy or difficult academic workload can make steady progress by pacing the work throughout the day. Take regular rest breaks to increase your powers of concentration.

16. MONDAY. Daring. Today's adventurous mood urges Leos to do something different and challenging. Any activity that takes you out of a rut is likely to appeal. The possibility of overseas travel could be tempting. Planning a vacation with a local travel agent or researching interesting destinations on the Internet could provide the excitement you crave. Imagination should flow late this evening, assisting Leo writers and those involved in creative activities of all varieties. Keep a record of themes and ideas that come to mind so these can be studied or put to productive use at a later time.

17. TUESDAY. Pleasant. The silver ruler of your emotions, the Moon, begins a new cycle now, culminating in the sign of assertive Aries. This is an excellent period to plan or depart on the trip of a lifetime. Approaching the boss for time off, applying to an educational institution, and beginning a new course of study are all areas where favorable results are likely. Problems with in-laws or a legal situation can be more easily resolved, especially during the morning. That is also the best time to hold a meeting or financial discussion, particularly of a confidential nature. Business and pleasure will mix happily and successfully.

18. WEDNESDAY. Expansive. Luck is on your side, especially in the areas of love and romance. Many Leos will be walking on air where matters of the heart are concerned. Avoid colleagues or workmates who have a habit of telling you what to do. They might think they are steering you in the right direction, but you are likely to think otherwise. Excitement may arrive in the form of a wedding invitation for a relative currently living abroad. Try to take advantage of the opportunity to expand your horizons. Even if you have to overuse your credit cards, the trip will be worthwhile for personal growth as well as pleasure.

19. THURSDAY. Promising. This is an excellent period to concentrate time and energy on one or several of your important friendships. If time constraints or other obligations have been the reason for neglecting a certain person, do something to change this now. Call to chat, send a long e-mail, or drop by for a surprise visit. Saturn, planet of structure, discipline, and obstacles, begins marching forward now in your solar house of self. Your energy level and enthusiasm should begin to rise, especially if these have been flat lately. Personal projects that have been at a standstill will now begin to make some significant progress.

20. FRIDAY. Opportune. With the entry of your ruler into the money sign of Taurus and your vocational sector, be ready to grasp life-changing opportunities that come your way. This is the time for Leo individuals to shine. Do not sit back and rest on your laurels. Reputation and prestige can be enhanced as your business and professional life advances. Valuable contacts can be made and cultivated to enhance your opportunities. Get together with friends after dark. Meet up for dinner, drinks, or the movies and celebrate whatever good luck has come your way recently. Romance looks promising for Leo singles providing long-term commitment is not a must-have for you now.

21. SATURDAY. Reflective. Withdrawing into your own space is likely even for the most outgoing Leo. Spend time alone over the next two days, delving into your own thoughts and goals. If you feel the need to socialize, opt for less stressful recreational pursuits rather than heavy physical activities. This is the time of the month when your body is urging you to slow down and take a breather. If this seems foreign to you, at least plan relaxing social periods, possibly including a dinner for two at a fancy restaurant, a romantic movie, or a trip to the theater or opera house.

22. SUNDAY. Emotional. The last thing on your mind will be work, and that is the way it should be providing you are not on the job. Enjoy yourself by taking off for the day. Finish household tasks early, pack a picnic lunch, and head for the hills, lake, or park. If lucky enough to own a boat, you could go for a joy ride and then enjoy a delicious fresh seafood lunch. This might be an emotional or sentimental day, so keep tissues within easy reach. Don't make decisions now because these are more likely to be based on emotion rather than logic. If you are staying home, finish up outstanding chores rather than starting something new.

23. MONDAY. Vexing. Stay calm and focused even as unexpected twists come at you from all angles. Turn a deaf ear if a friend hints about wanting a loan. The mood for love and passion may sweep over you. Show your romantic side, but avoid possessive and clingy tendencies. Don't allow jealousy to spoil your chance of emotional fulfillment. Even a long-term commitment may become tense due to the potential for disputes and stress. Someone could cause a scene and become melodramatic. Early this evening the pace of life picks up and your need to socialize and interact with other people will return.

24. TUESDAY. Perplexing. A workplace error regarding a schedule could throw your social plans into disarray. Make this a priority first thing this morning so arrangements can be altered. Self-employed Leos might find that getting the job done seems to be much harder than usual. It may be easier on your stress level to accept this fact. Just do as much as you can, as quickly and efficiently as you can, in the time available. If you are romantically attracted to a workmate or client, some development in this area could occur. However, a potential relationship might not be clear-cut, so you may need to wait before taking the next step.

25. WEDNESDAY. Renewing. The Moon is gliding through your own sign of Leo, assisting you with your personal plans. If you are bored or tired with your appearance, now is the time to revamp your image and style. Make an appointment at the beauty salon, visit your favorite boutique, and step up the fitness program. Leos who are already in a committed relationship should tread gently. Make love, not war. Avoid risking your relationship with potentially damaging fallout. Mutual harmony is most important during this time, so avoid subjects that might lead to tension or discord. Learn to say no, and delay making promises that you cannot easily keep.

26. THURSDAY. Tempting. A number of events or situations will occur today. Apart from a possible upset involving a daughter or women friend over money, most of the day favors organizing or handling financial matters. Mixed signals with a romantic relationship are a possibility. Avoid impulsive actions, in particular with issues regarding your love life. The temptation to flirt should be resisted if you or the other party are not free to engage in this type of behavior. Someone's feelings are bound to be hurt, or a relationship almost certainly will be jeopardized. A discussion or lecture with a philosophical theme is likely to appeal this evening.

27. FRIDAY. Diverse. This is one of those days when money is likely to slip through your fingers if you do not take extra care. However you can make a long-term investment. Just avoid buying frivolous items. Mercury, the talkative planet, is now lighting up your solar tenth home of business and professional activities. A senior staff member or other higher authority could put in a good word regarding your achievements or work ethic. Leo people already in a position of power are apt to be very hard to please right now. Try to ease up on yourself and on those who work for you. Have faith that everything should eventually fall into place.

28. SATURDAY. Vigilant. Leos who are in the market for a new car or want to upgrade to a later model should begin checking out what is being offered. However, postpone making financial decisions under current trends. Research prices and inspect what is available, but wait until next week before coming to a final decision. Don't be distracted when talking to other people. There is a chance that you might blurt out something controversial or make a statement that a listener finds offensive. Give family or loved ones more space and you will avoid disputes or friction. Take extra care if you are driving since other motorists might not be as diligent on the road as you are.

29. SUNDAY. Revealing. Providing you keep discussions light and without any hint of criticism, this is a good time to reveal your thoughts, ideas, or plans. Trying to do too much, to fit everything that needs to be done into your day off, is likely to bring on a bout of crankiness or bad temper. Set priorities, then leave everything else for another day. Leos involved in a sports competition can expect success. Even if your team doesn't win, your own performance should be noticed and praised. A social event could turn out to be a lot more expensive as well as less enjoyable than you expected.

30. MONDAY. Successful. Today is a better day than yesterday for airing your views in public. Have the courage of your convictions, saying what you feel needs to be said. This attitude will be especially helpful with a career or business proposition. Leos going on interviews for a job or on an audition for a television or movie role should be happy with the results. Even if the position you are offered is not the same as what you applied for, it is likely to be something similar. Local travel, or just visiting relatives who live nearby, will brighten up your evening. Keep in mind that tomorrow is a workday so don't stay out too late.

MAY

1. TUESDAY. Cautious. To avoid an accident, walk don't run. Over the next few days Leos young or old need to ensure that all safety equipment, headgear, and mouth guards are firmly in place if involved in rough-and-tumble sports events or similar activities. Trying to evade obligations relating to home and family will be futile. Face up to your responsibilities and get these accomplished early in the day. Finances and friendships don't mix. Pass up socializing with anyone who is inclined to take advantage of your generous nature by asking for a donation or loan. Your tolerance level for this type of behavior is low and you could say something hurtful though unintended.

2. WEDNESDAY. Sensitive. Try not to take yourself too seriously throughout the day. Also be extra sensitive when dealing with other people. You might dismiss their opinions as of little consequence or not relevant, which could get their backs up. Insisting on having the last word is also unwise if you want to stay in their good graces. With today's Full Moon culminating in Scorpio, choose your company carefully. Sensitivity is increased, and someone's emotional outburst could prove unsettling because your own feelings are also a little fragile. Take advantage of a new offer involving a career or business venture.

3. THURSDAY. Unsettled. It is important to continue to smile throughout the day. Otherwise your mood could quickly deteriorate. For every household or work job completed, two more are likely to pop up just when you think everything is accomplished. Your enthusiasm and optimism will return eventually, but not until early this evening. Don't count on getting your ideas across to other people. Even the simplest message possibly will be misconstrued. Writing your thoughts down on paper can help you sort through any skeptical feelings that you may be harboring. A group activity will be much more enjoyable than expected, particularly if this is held in the comfort of your own home.

4. FRIDAY. Mixed. This is another day that could be unsettled unless you add some zest and zing to get things moving. As a Leo you will have the happy knack of bringing the best out in other people. Use this ability constructively and you will be rewarded with significant progress. Relationships among team members or at a staff meeting will benefit from your upbeat input. Freelance workers should put extra energy into chasing down new contracts and jobs. Success in this is foreseen providing effort is applied without letup. A change of management might bring about a job reshuffling. Make sure your star is shining when the top jobs open up.

5. SATURDAY. Unpredictable. Self-imposed rules and regulations need to be reviewed and possibly removed in order to make progress. Go with the flow. By accepting challenges you will be able to move ahead further and faster than you now think. Canceled social plans are likely to throw arrangements for today's entertainment into disarray, but this could turn out to be a blessing in disguise. Being free to do your own thing should be more fun, allowing you to choose your companions as well as you want to do. If you become the designated driver for family or friends, keep your mind on what you are doing. There is a possibility of an accident if your concentration lapses because you are talking too much.

6. SUNDAY. Frustrating. Money matters are problematic. If you are considering asking someone in the family for a loan, today is not a good day to do so. All you might receive is a lecture on how you should be more responsible in handling your finances. Jealousy, that green-eyed monster, could be let loose. If you or your mate or partner are the jealous type, this could be a very tricky time. It may be better to stay away from persons, places, or situations that have given rise to this type of behavior in the past. Opt for a day out together, sightseeing, viewing a movie, or visiting relatives who need cheering up. Or focus on completing some odd jobs around the house.

7. MONDAY. Distracting. Confusion reigns today. It is likely to be difficult keeping your mind on what you are supposed to be doing. The challenge is to stop your thoughts from wondering off in many different directions. If this proves to be a lost cause, it would be wise to postpone complex tasks until you are less easily distracted. Dealing with the public or just with your significant other should be done with care. Be at your best diplomatic self to make sure that communications flow smoothly, with no misunderstandings or tensions developing. Caution is recommended with finances, particularly with any advice given regarding money matters.

8. TUESDAY. Variable. Feelings of insecurity could overcome you. Even Leos who present an outwardly optimistic demeanor might be suffering from lack of confidence. Lots of cuddles, hugs, and affection will be spread around among loved ones now that Venus, goddess of love, has moved into the family sign of Cancer. Parenting your spouse could become an issue if your mate or partner prefers to remain independent and to have their own space. Your feelings are likely to be more easily hurt as sensitivity increases, so try to overlook minor criticism or sarcastic comments probably only made to make the other person feel superior. On the plus side, an unexpected windfall, promotion, or bonus can make this a lucky time.

9. WEDNESDAY. Frustrating. Your energy and vitality might be limited throughout the day. Motivation to remove obstacles in your path could be lacking, which may increase your frustration. This cosmic influence will pass quickly, so adapt as best as you can and wait it out. Relationships with those in authority might not be very amicable. A clash is likely. Maintain a low profile if you don't want to be singled out for any special duty or task. Also be wary of the resentment of an associate or colleague. Equipment breakdowns are possible if regular maintenance is not kept up to date. Hire a service company to keep essential parts in good working order.

10. THURSDAY. Vigilant. The best way is the slow way. Caution is needed. Today's cosmic atmosphere encourages going over the top, overindulging or promising more than you can possibly deliver. In order to advance, you need to base your decisions on logic and reason. Avoid wishful thinking. In-depth discussion rather than superficial conversation will be more appealing if you go out to socialize this evening. Such entertainment could be found at a public lecture, New Age seminar, or mixing with friends who share your interests. Venturing out unaccompanied after dark entails an element of risk. Avoid public transportation, and stay away from dimly lighted areas.

11. FRIDAY. Productive. Don't take no for an answer if you are trying to collect an overdue debt. If nonpayment threatens to jeopardize your financial status, insist that anyone who owes you money pay up in full. Mercury now moves into the air sign of talkative Gemini, accentuating social contacts, friends, and unique opportunities from today until May 28. Your intellectual energy and debating power increase along with your ability to succinctly articulate your views and opinions. Leos involved in selling, speaking, or writing for financial gain are entering a very productive period. Auditions and job interviews are also starred, although the result may not be known for a while.

12. SATURDAY. Stimulating. Friendships mean a lot to Leo people, so put mixing and mingling high on your list of priorities. Social obligations related to career or business interests are an excellent way to receive information and iron out a contract that otherwise could prove difficult to obtain. A target deadline set for a work project is likely be unrealistic. It would be wiser to review time constraints and possibly lower current expectations. Even though letting other people down is something you do not take lightly, an adjustment would be preferable to not doing the job properly. Opportunities exist for romance, but be discerning if currently solo.

13. SUNDAY. Unstable. There is increased need to keep your temper under control. Slow down as well. More can be accomplished if you maintain a steady rate, and there will also be less chance of an accident. If you have an interest in economics and the stock market, look into ways to increase your knowledge in these areas. You might arrange a trip to Wall Street, or enroll in a local class that teaches basic ways to grow your wealth. Sitting for an exam, digging for information, and becoming involved or in some type of detective work are particularly favored activities.

14. MONDAY. Manageable. Your mate or partner might accuse you of neglect or a lack of affection, adding to the list of things that you could be stressing about. Talk openly since you do not need other people's issues weighing you down right now. Overseas travel or contact with someone from abroad may occupy the mind and thoughts of many Lions. Although there may be a few slight glitches, Leos who are setting off on a long journey should expect a fairly routine trip. Add a few treats to the pantry shelf because unexpected guests could drop by right at dinnertime. Being able to fix a nourishing meal in a hurry will make a positive impression on them and may even amaze yourself.

15. TUESDAY. Energetic. A massive injection of energy is very probable now after a period when your vim and vitality have been at a low ebb. Mars, planet of risks and male energy, zooms into the impulsive and fiery sign of your Aries ninth sector, adding zest to your drive and motivation. Activities center on travel, academic plans, and legal proceedings, all of which can make favorable progress. Your patience and self-control might be lacking at times, so try to be more tolerant of other people. Unless you focus on tasks and projects that provide a challenge, motivation can soon fly straight out the door. Find the balance and use this energy in a constructive manner.

16. WEDNESDAY. Beneficial. If you want to add another language to your list of achievements, the current period is favorable for this. Enroll at a local educational center, visit your local library, or purchase a set of foreign language CDs, then begin to expand your horizons. Benefits could come at a later time from increased professional opportunities thanks to your newly acquired skills. Today's Taurus New Moon urges employed Lions and those actively seeking to join the workforce to focus on career advancement and business options. This is the time to push for a favor or other consideration from someone who is higher up than you.

17. THURSDAY. Expansive. Speak up today. Extra resources or financial benefits are likely to be granted if you seek these or seek other assistance in the working environment. Leo shoppers who want to upgrade household products and equipment should proceed with caution to make purchases. The potential to overcommit on loans or credit cards is high. Be moderate in your approach by looking for items that can perform just like the more expensive product, even if the visual appeal is not the same. Rapport with other people is strengthened, ensuring that any discussion should be friendly and harmonious. Leo couples are likely to share common views and opinions.

18. FRIDAY. Useful. If you are looking for something fulfilling to do, consider visiting and spending time with a sick or lonely friend or relative. Unexpected rewards should be forthcoming for both of you. The reappearance of a former lover could bring on doubts and confusion regarding whether you have taken the right romantic path. Don't make any decisions either way for the next few days. Contemplate where you are, where you have been, and where you intend to go. Make choices based on what is the best direction for you, not for others. Be wary when considering any advice given by a friend because those views might be tinged with bias.

19. SATURDAY. Peaceful. As a Leo, being the center of attention is something you usually relish and enjoy. However, this might not be the case over the next few days. You are even likely to jump at any and all opportunities to spend time out of the limelight, on your own or with a close family member or friend. Energy could fall below par, so conserve it throughout the day, especially if you intend on having a big night of socializing. Proceed with extra caution in matters of romance. Resist the temptation to take advantage of a situation if you or the other person is not single or free to become involved.

20. SUNDAY. Attentive. Your mind should be very mentally active and alert. This increases the possibility of short-circuiting your mental power as you struggle to decipher the overload of information and ideas. Rebelliousness and nervousness are likely if you try to action everything all at once. Slow down and maintain a moderate pace. More haste will definitely equal less speed. Don't become overly excited by promises made to you because these might not eventuate. Creative imagination should be working well. Paint, sculpt, or record your thoughts in a journal to capture ideas for review at a later time.

21. MONDAY. Cooperative. Relationships improve today, which is just as well since you must cooperate with colleagues and clients. There is still a need to keep arrogance and tactlessness in check. However, other people are more likely to take notice of your ideas and views. From now until June 21 your ruler, the Sun, is dazzling the Gemini sector of friends, group activities, and your hopes and wishes. During this period success comes by implementing projects designed to increase business income, promote your goals, and add new clients to your network of contacts. Restlessness increases along with intellectual clarity.

22. TUESDAY. Spirited. This is another day when you will have a strong desire to participate in an unusual activity or project. Your thinking should be quick, with bright ideas and plans flooding in. Be sure to write these down so you remember every little detail. Avoiding a showdown with a business client or partner might be difficult if you are involved in financial negotiations. Being diplomatic and attempting to cooperate will at least ensure that recriminations are kept to a minimum. When the dust settles with the Moon in your own sign of Leo, vitality and charisma will be magnified, increasing the demand for your presence at social occasions.

23. WEDNESDAY. Uplifting. Add a relaxing massage to your list of things to do today. As a Leo you succumb to stress more easily than some other zodiac signs. Giving yourself a treat every now and then is what life is all about, and this type of therapy could add years to your life. Focus on an employment project that needs a creative approach or your unique touch. This will receive a boost of productivity if work is begun right away. Your artistic flair is heightened, ensuring that inspiration arrives when needed. If you don't allow anyone to take over or interfere, on-the-job rewards should come winging your way.

24. THURSDAY. Confusing. Neptune, the planet of illusion and escapism, begins trekking backward in your solar seventh house of other people. From now until the end of October be more attentive to what other people are saying. Confusion and misunderstandings will multiply if you do not listen, especially to a business or personal partner. Mix-ups with clients and customers could also increase unless you pay close attention. Orders could be forgotten or not delivered on time. Issues with money owed to you for work performed might claim a lot of your attention. If you have supplied labor and materials, don't be badgered into reducing the amount you have billed.

25. FRIDAY. Valuable. Today's benefits come through studying your current financial situation. If you are trying to figure out how to maintain your current lifestyle or how to afford something expensive that you desire, consider financial counseling. Expert advice can result in better money management in the long term. An assertive attitude will help you make gains right now. Your talent for negotiating increases as the day progresses and helps you obtain the best possible terms in a business deal, wage discussion, or career move. Leo singles are blessed with unexpected romantic opportunities tonight. You will be in the right place at the right time to increase your luck.

26. SATURDAY. Exhilarating. An exciting opportunity, rewarding social experience, or financial windfall will brighten your day. Luck and love still surround you. A new joint business venture looks promising if you and your partner are willing to take a small but well-calculated risk. The afternoon hours usher in a period when family resentment or insecurities could lead to some nasty words or other unpleasantness. If possible, get out of the firing line before this occurs. Go out with friends or lock yourself away in the bedroom or computer room to avoid becoming entangled in the emotional drama going on in the household.

27. SUNDAY. Invigorating. Mixed trends prevail. A lovers' tiff could spoil what can be a good day, so think before you speak. Don't throw away a valued relationship due to a fit of temper or anger. Curbing your tongue will save the marriage or friendship. At the same time let other people know that you value a certain amount of privacy and independence. This is an excellent day to put your intellectual processes to the test. Research, detective work, a challenging crossword puzzle, or computer games are some areas where you can proudly display your abilities. You should also excel at debating or public speaking now.

28. MONDAY. Smooth. Mercury joins Venus in family-loving Cancer tonight, increasing your interest in the creature comforts of home. This is a period when plans can be initiated to renovate or refurbish your residence. Cleaning up around your home to make use of all available space is also likely to appeal if you prefer your home to be functional as well as visually appealing. Leos who are involved in organizing a special family function or celebration should find that plans proceed smoothly. Purchase new dinnerware and tidy up the garden since there is a good likelihood that entertaining at home will increase.

29. TUESDAY. Enjoyable. Keeping in touch with relatives and social contacts assumes more importance for you. This is an excellent period to increase goodwill and trust with others. If you haven't seen certain loved ones recently, drop a line, make a phone call, or plan a visit. Sentiment rises to the surface, making this a perfect time to organize a family outing or domestic chores. Leos with time to spare could arrange to have old family videos transferred to DVD or could update the photo collection. Favorite pastimes will be enjoyed more, so allow plenty of time to indulge in pleasant leisure pursuits later in the day.

30. WEDNESDAY. Variable. Expect an up-and-down day. The morning hours could include misunderstandings and confusion, especially with matters relating to a partnership or legal issue. Later in the day positive vibes are likely to reverse any negative situation, so try to remain calm and optimistic. An inability to make up your mind may hamper important negotiations. Plans to socialize with members of your extended family might be spoiled this evening by someone who knows how to push your buttons. Laugh off any verbal digs and this person will soon get tired of trying to get the better of you. Go to bed early to restore your vitality and motivation.

31. THURSDAY. Favorable. Creative projects prosper under prevailing cosmic influences. As a Leo you are a leader by nature, so put yourself in this role and let your talents shine through. Musicians, painters, and all artistic types should experience a flow of inspiration that increases productivity. If you often buy a raffle or lottery ticket, bet on a horse, or visit a casino, spend a little on one of these activities today. Even a small win could add a few dollars to your bank account or assist in paying an overdue bill. Romantically and socially you should be a star, with your appearance at an event increasing happiness and enjoyment for other guests.

JUNE

1. FRIDAY. Sensitive. Last night's Sagittarius Full Moon is bound to have a flow-on effect today. Tread carefully around family members and friends who have a short fuse or are easily wounded. Your love and affection for other people will be intensified. Couples anxious to expand the family circle or to begin one should put in extra effort this weekend. Pack your bags and head for some exotic location, or lock your front door and pretend no one is at home. Leo singles should relax and focus on personal enjoyment as a way to offset trying conditions encountered during the working day. Go dancing, enjoy the outdoors, or meet up with friends.

2. SATURDAY. Inspiring. Exhibiting patience pays off. Relationships with children should be excellent, although their expenses could make a large dent in your budget. Review upcoming commitments to ensure that money will be available to meet likely needs. With talkative Mercury and love goddess Venus in your house of solitude and secrets, express yourself more clearly, concisely, and honestly to your lover. Otherwise confusion will stem from mixed signals given and received. If you are in charge of entertainment, take advantage of the warmer weather. A casual brunch or outdoor barbecue should provide enjoyment for all.

3. SUNDAY. Mystifying. Some of what you hear could be a little puzzling. Don't be afraid to ask for clarification if you cannot make sense of what is being conveyed. Hidden costs relating to family issues or home and property matters might cause havoc for Leos desperately trying to stay within a set financial limit. Decisions based on emotions are not wise to make now. Wait until tomorrow, or at least later today, before making up your mind. An outburst of passion midafternoon would be upsetting for those with whom you share your life and love. Hop on the exercise bike instead and you will avert possible tension.

4. MONDAY. Creative. Today favors creative application rather than logical thinking or action. Written agreements and negotiations should be verified before you sign anything. If possible, avoid making concrete decisions or choices that cannot easily be reversed. An obviously enthusiastic approach when discussing philosophical beliefs, religion, or New Age topics can assist Leos who are presenting a lecture on those subjects to an audience that shares the same interests. However, take a more moderate approach if speaking to the nonconverted. Watch what you eat and drink. Stick to a healthy diet and drink plenty of water.

5. TUESDAY. Pleasurable. Leos are known to generally have a generous, loving, and giving nature. As a result you sometimes give too much of yourself and forget about you. Work at becoming more balanced. Socially you are in demand and can engage in activities held outside the home and family. Venus, goddess of the good things in life including love and money, moves into your own outgoing sign of Leo. You are now ready to really party, and other people will notice. Dress to impress. Make sure that personal appearance and grooming are at your usual high standard and people will flock to your side.

6. WEDNESDAY. Productive. If your current employment is not providing the stimulation you require to remain enthusiastic as well as motivated, chances of finding more suitable work now exist. There is a possibility that you will gain the support of someone who can benefit you financially or promote your special skills and expertise. An issue or situation that has been hidden might come out into the open. This will need your attention so it can be finally resolved and delegated firmly into the past, where it belongs. Romance, true love, and being swept off your feet by a desirable suitor are much more likely now.

7. THURSDAY. Demanding. Leos waiting for repayment of a debt from a family member, friend, or company should try hard to collect today. Make it clear that the money is owed and needed now. Once you understand the jargon, a new hobby or study should prove fascinating and well worth the time you devote to research and comprehension. It is that time of the month when clearing out accumulated clutter becomes easier as attachment lessens. In particular, concentrate on discarding clothes and footwear no longer in style. Don't forget all the other closets in the house also.

8. FRIDAY. Helpful. This is a day to flow with the tide. As a fixed sign Leo people are not always comfortable with change and accepting of the status quo. For the sake of your nerves and blood pressure, be as flexible as possible. Contact with an insurance broker could be less productive than you hope, especially if you are hoping to receive payment for a claim. If obtaining price quotations for insurance coverage, do not accept the first one given. Negotiate for a better deal and you should be pleasantly surprised with the result. An attraction to someone who was previously only a friend is apt to heat up now.

9. SATURDAY. Excellent. Make sure you have a stash of cash available to access over the weekend. You might also need to have luggage packed, ready to take off on an unexpected trip with a companion. Leos who are not jumping on a train, bus, or plane could use the current planetary influences to confer with future traveling companions and organize a sailing or backpacking itinerary. Friends or family members who share your tastes or are on the same wavelength will provide the best social company for going out tonight. News of receiving a lucrative contract could be the main reason for a celebration this evening.

10. SUNDAY. Manageable. Make decisions concerning travel, study, or educational plans. Lay out all of your available options so you can come to an informed choice. Take advantage of an offer from a relative or in-law. This would be a significant opportunity for you to expand and create a more fulfilling future. Entertainment plans should include activities that excite, stimulate, and challenge you. Competitive sports, either as a participant or spectator, should fit nicely into this category. If going to a large public venue, leave your car at home and opt for the train, bus, or taxi.

11. MONDAY. Bright. Professional opportunities are increasing. You could be offered the chance for new work-related training. Furthering your knowledge and adding to your skills base will enhance your value to a current or prospective employer. Money from parents, relatives, or a government authority is likely to come in or be offered just when you need it most. This should relieve a worrisome problem that has been the cause of ongoing upset. A legal issue can now be positively resolved. Your ability to see things from another person's perspective prompts a clearer picture and better understanding of the motives of your loved ones.

12. TUESDAY. Rewarding. Working with a group or organization in some type of humanitarian activity will be emotionally fulfilling and could even put you in front of a television camera, producing your fifteen minutes of fame. Make sure you are well groomed and well prepared so your point of view comes across in an articulate and professional manner. Grasp any opportunities to socialize with people who share your interests. Choose a venue that supports your favorite leisure pursuits, one where you can meet new people who expand your network of contacts. The potential for romance strengthens for the unattached Leo.

13. WEDNESDAY. Good. Ideas and plans ranging from beginning a new project to organizing a vacation or arranging a special celebration will keep you on the phone for a large chunk of the day. Consult with those who understand what you are endeavoring to do and will be inclined to go along with your wishes. Make sure that all arrangements are in place before Friday, when trickster Mercury begins tracking backward in the zodiac. Clear your desk of paperwork relating to property and family matters. Creative juices flow in whatever medium you choose to express your talents and expertise. Leo couples will share happy rapport.

14. THURSDAY. Constructive. Budding Leo authors are likely to make progress by putting pen to paper or fingers to the keyboard. Begin the novel, travel story, or scientific article that you are itching to write. If you have a manuscript ready to send, put it in the mail or send it by courier to the publisher, then sit back and wait for possible positive news. Tonight's New Moon in Gemini increases communication abilities. You know what to say and how to say it. Over the next two weeks push ahead with efforts to achieve your long-term goals. Your social life will keep you busy and on the move.

15. FRIDAY. Variable. If you discover that you have made a mistake on the job or on the home front, don't try to cover it up. Once you admit it without making a huge fuss, people will quickly and quietly forgive and forget. It is all part of the learning process and nothing to worry needlessly about. With a Mercury retrograde period beginning today and continuing until July 9, don't be surprised if snags, delays, and errors occur in paperwork, transportation, and equipment. Be extra careful with a faulty domestic product, discarding it if potentially dangerous. Defer signing a lease or other contract, in particular those relating to property or family matters.

16. SATURDAY. Reflective. Being alone doesn't mean being lonely. You will relish time spent away from the hustle and bustle of daily life. Relaxing beside a pool, at a spa, or at the beach can soothe your soul. Pulling a few strings behind the scenes should get things moving quicker if you have been frustrated by lack of action. Intuition, dreams, and first impressions are likely to be very revealing as well as accurate, so trust your instincts. Refrain from worrying about problems over which you have little control because doing so just creates anxiety and stress.

17. SUNDAY. Pleasant. Spend the morning at home or nearby. Stay in bed for an extra hour, enjoy a leisurely breakfast with the family, or finish personal chores. By midmorning you will be ready to face the world and socialize with loved ones or friends. Diplomatic skills might be needed, so jump right in if an argument requires your special touch. For Leos looking for a new romance, a sudden encounter could be the perfect answer. Harmony should reign on the domestic scene this evening, making this an ideal time to plan household activities and sort out an issue so that home life continues to flow smoothly.

18. MONDAY. Lively. With three planets in your sign of Leo and self, many Lions might feel like the king or queen of all they survey. Although you are a force to be reckoned with, it might be wise to refrain from letting everyone you meet be aware of this. Confirm all details of social plans before venturing out. Otherwise you might arrive at a function only to discover the plan or the venue has been changed. Check messages to guard against potential misunderstandings. A social lunch with business connections should produce rewarding gains. Put your best foot forward and other people will be charmed.

19. TUESDAY. Lucky. A little luck with love or money could come your way, a nice highlight for the day. Delay relating to a legal situation could begin to disappear as some outstanding issues are resolved. An aggressive approach or challenging the words of a superior or other authority figure would not be a wise career move.

Take a step in the right direction to turn a hobby into a profitable moneymaking operation. With thorough planning along with organizing promotional material and a display of products, you could be quickly on the road to a promotion or self-employment.

20. WEDNESDAY. Cautious. Early morning commuters need to be patient. Transportation delays could result from timetable and schedule adjustment. Think pleasant thoughts to calm your mind if you have to wait for any length of time. Concentrating on the current state of your love life may do the trick since it should be bubbling away very happily. As a safeguard, ensure that your medical insurance is paid up and coverage is sufficient for all possible emergencies. Illness, pregnancy, or an accident can strike at any time, draining your bank account if you are not sufficiently insured.

21. THURSDAY. Optimistic. Welcome to the summer solstice. With the Sun now visiting your Cancer twelfth house over the next four weeks, expect a period of heightened emotional sensitivity. Outgoing Leos as well as the more domesticated will probably prefer to spend extra time at home, puttering around the garden, cooking, or cleaning. This is the time of year to rest and relax before your next birthday. Socializing and entertaining family members and friends at home will be the choice for many. Be prepared ahead of your guests. Go shopping and fill up the pantry with an array of goodies. Feeding and catering will surely increase over the coming month.

22. FRIDAY. Favorable. Turn off your cell phone when you are on the job. Friends are likely to keep sending messages or calling to organize and reorganize weekend social plans. This could slow down your productivity, annoy coworkers, or worse still anger your boss. Talented Leos combining creative skills with ideas from other people could produce a moneymaking proposition. Once it gets off the ground, the potential for financial rewards could be unlimited. Hosting an intimate dinner party for a special companion would be preferable for the more mature Lion, while others will want the enjoyment of a group.

23. SATURDAY. Changeable. Making up your mind could be a challenge. Your ability to see and understand both sides of an argument can assist in a number of ways. Uranus, the planet of excitement and chaos, goes into reverse motion, bringing to the fore unexpected issues possibly relating to joint money and shared resources. Complications are likely for Leos engaged in a property settlement due to sale of a house or a divorce. This is a good period to renegotiate an ongoing lease agreement or loan if you hope to have monthly payments reduced. However, don't sign final paperwork until after July 9.

24. SUNDAY. Active. Energetic Mars now enters the stable sign of Taurus, bringing career and business ambitions to the fore. Motivation to move up the company ladder increases, with your ambition and success as the driving force. Time and effort applied to professional goals can lead to more perks or extra money in your monthly pay. Create an opportunity to get to know new neighbors. Invite them over for coffee or just to meet the rest of the family or household. A bus ride could provide a different adventure for Leos seeking to experience a new neighborhood. Try outdoor markets if you need to buy vegetables or crafts.

25. MONDAY. Manageable. Be steady and take a deep breath. Saturn, planet of constriction, is now challenging idealistic Neptune, producing inner conflict and uncertainty. Relationship issues might cause doubts and confusion. Leos may conjure up all kinds of worries, both real and imagined. The best defense for this type of thinking is to keep busy. Deal immediately with every situation on a practical and realistic level. Cutting through red tape is easy now, especially if you adopt a gentle approach. Landing an important contract could be the opening you have been waiting for.

26. TUESDAY. Unsettling. This is another day when you need to keep everything in perspective. Confusing issues are likely to surround partnership matters as you struggle for clarity regarding the motives of other people. The signals you are sending out could also be clouding the waters. Back off and wait until later in the week when the fog is likely to have disappeared enough for you to make sense of everything. Don't allow anyone to burden you with extra duties or responsibilities right now, when your coping mechanism is at a low ebb. Accept only an equal share of obligations. Calm down with a relaxing bath or shower before bedtime.

27. WEDNESDAY. Varied. Expect a topsy-turvy day. Absorbing moods and emotions works both ways. Your negative attitude could rub off on other people. Make a big effort to smile. Workmates and associates have probably been wondering what has happened to your sunny personality. Take a breather if you have been working extra hard. You can afford to relax and let your hair down. Be thankful for the opportunity to meet friends or colleagues for a drink or a meal after work. Even though the thought of socializing may not appeal as much as usual, you'll enjoy it if you make the initial effort.

28. THURSDAY. Uncertain. With many Leo people dealing with a heavier workload than usual, be wary of overdoing. Although this can be handled with relative ease, don't be a martyr. Set your own schedule, being sure to include plenty of family fun in your busy agenda. Seek guidance from a trusted friend or a member of your extended family if you do not want someone closer knowing about a personal issue. If your intimate relationship is shaky or suffering from indifference, improvements could occur if you exert the effort now. If you are honest with your mate or partner and keep expectations realistic, positive advances can be made.

29. FRIDAY. Beneficial. Unresolved conflicts within your significant partnership could come to light, so be ready to take positive action. If troubles and emotions are too deep to bring about an amicable resolution, separation for a few days or longer might be the answer. Leo teenagers could fall in love for the very first time but need to remember that being young and inexperienced can be a drawback to lasting love. Enjoy the romance without pushing for a commitment or assuming that the relationship will be forever. It might turn out that way, but it is more likely that this won't be the case. Social activities perk you up this evening.

30. SATURDAY. Mixed. Emotional issues are to be expected with a Full Moon culminating in the sign of Capricorn. Remain calm, if possible, when put in a position of having to explain your point of view. A female involved with a work project might use criticism as a way to get under your skin. Becoming angry or retaliating in a similar vein will put you in a bad light with other people. Upgrade your skills and inquire about participating in a first-aid course. The effort might challenge you but will be worthwhile, providing the rewarding knowledge of knowing what to do in an emergency situation.

JULY

1. SUNDAY. Promising. Discovering that your current earnings are not enough to cover debts and expenses could leave you a little upset. However, remain optimistic and frugal. You should receive a boost to your finances by the end of the month. Bouncing ideas off someone you love could produce some useful ways to implement cost-cutting measures. Benefits come from good eating habits, regular exercise, and spending time outdoors. Include an older family member in any social gathering, or invite a relative over for a meal. Leos who are in a long-term relationship could still be plagued by issues that need to be addressed.

2. MONDAY. Guarded. Romance and finances improve today, with the likelihood of more security and stability for most Leo people. A love affair that begins now has a strong chance of enduring providing everything is out in the open and there are no skeletons in the closet. Significant consequences can emerge from current action and behavior. Address any fears related to low self-esteem, and avoid putting yourself down in any fashion. Handle an irate customer with care if you are in charge of customer service. Displaying an overly assertive attitude could result in complaints directed at you.

3. TUESDAY. Chancy. Tread carefully with partners. Conflicts and clashes are more than likely. Issues concerning who is the boss could surface between couples who own a business. As a Leo you might naturally assume that being in charge is your role. Swallow your pride if your partner's leadership qualities are superior to yours. Focus on long-term mutual goals rather than short-term skirmishes. Extracurricular activities may be under a cloud. A planned event is apt to be canceled or rescheduled to another venue or another day. Self-employed Leos can make gains by reviewing and upgrading web site and advertising material. An original approach is bound to attract the attention of prospective clients.

4. WEDNESDAY. Enjoyable. A trip to the beach or lake could be a perfect way to celebrate this Independence Day. Pack a picnic lunch and fun items to keep everyone busy and head out early. A boat or canoe ride could also appeal. Don't forget to take along a camera to record family members experiencing and sharing this pleasant time. If you have some money to spare, consider donating to an organization that supports children's health and well-being.

Or you might prefer to help those with a drug or alcohol dependency achieve increased understanding and awareness. Show your compassion for the plight of those less fortunate than you.

5. THURSDAY. Astute. Hidden costs could quickly mount up. You may be appalled by the amount of joint money that is being spent on entertainment and leisure pursuits. Now that you are aware of this, quickly make changes to indiscriminate spending. Applying for one large loan to consolidate all of your debts might be worth considering. This could have the added bonus of reducing monthly payments and interest. There is a very good chance of receiving a favorable response from a bank or other financial institution. Spend time alone planning a romantic escapade for two for the upcoming weekend, when passion should sizzle.

6. FRIDAY. Cautious. A casual comment could develop into a philosophical debate, forcing you to defend your views. It would be best to keep opinions to yourself, as a way of saving time and perhaps face. There is also a possibility that you could clash with the law. To avoid this, be sure to follow the rules of the road and the laws of the land. Don't assume that you can get away with anything. Entertainment that includes action and variety would be most satisfactory. Dancing, indoor sports, or a session at the gym will appeal to the energetic Leo. If you prefer something more sedate, try a museum or watch an action-packed movie.

7. SATURDAY. Empowering. Spending money on yourself, whether to upgrade your knowledge and skills or to improve your health and well-being, is a worthwhile investment in your future. In addition, this will increase your value to prospective employers. Search the Internet or local newspaper for a class, workshop, or lecture that will enhance your expertise. Take out a gym membership, join a yoga group, or schedule a full beauty treatment. Leos in love should plan an overnight stay away from crowds. If that is not possible, at least arrange a special evening with all the trimmings including a candlelight dinner, soft music, and lots of love and affection.

8. SUNDAY. Passionate. Extra time in bed can bring the ultimate in pleasure, especially if you have created a seductive atmosphere just for two. This is also an excellent day to set off on a honeymoon or to exchange wedding vows. Your sense of fun is stimulated along with enough energy to engage in physical activity or sports. Leo parents can take children to wander around the zoo or cycle around a local bike track. Don't spoil youngsters with too many sweets or you will pay later when the child complains of a stomachache. Avoid spending too much time talking on the phone.

9. MONDAY. Constructive. If asked to assume a leadership role on the job, be quick to say yes. Even if the position is only temporary, the experience will be invaluable. Flirting with an attractive newcomer will be an enjoyable interlude providing you both act appropriately. Postpone fun and games until after work finishes for the day. Trickster Mercury now begins to move forward, setting in motion paperwork or communication that has been held up. A delayed contract, especially relating to sale of a property, should now be ready to settle. News of a career opportunity that you have been waiting to hear about might be received at last.

10. TUESDAY. Tricky. Avoid being selfish if loved ones are more demanding or request quality time alone with you. Plan a special treat for the weekend to make up for neglect if work commitments have been keeping you on the job later than ever before. Investments made now could be an asset for the future. Purchase a new painting, or search for a special item of furniture that will add to the beauty of your home as well as your financial future. Increased teamwork could translate into better earnings and a chance for a promotion. A financial shortfall could require reviewing and revising the budget for a special event.

11. WEDNESDAY. Favorable. Surprises are the order of the day. There is no knowing what could stem from them. Plans for a special function or celebration should proceed smoothly as original ideas and themes come flooding in. Keep these secret for now so other people don't have a chance to spoil a surprise. If you have money invested you could receive most welcome news. Check with your accountant or stockbroker. Property holdings in particular, might increase your current net worth. This is also a good time to make an appointment with a personal financial consultant to discuss where money can be successfully invested. Be sure your insurance coverage is adequate.

12. THURSDAY. Stimulating. A break from your normal routine can be rejuvenating. You are likely to struggle if expected to focus on complicated tasks because your mind won't be on the job at hand. However, if the work involves innovative thinking and planning, progress will be fast and furious. That is the type of challenge in which you will shine. Taking part in negotiations or discussions where thinking on your feet is a standard format is another activity that Leo people excel in now. An evening spent in the company of good friends, enjoying fine food and wine, is a perfect ending to the day.

13. FRIDAY. Renewing. Spending time alone could appeal to even the most social Lion today. With three planets in home-loving Cancer, you need to ensure that your nurturing instincts don't escalate into overly protective and possessive tendencies. Leo parents should allow children to display independence within a safe environment. You might hear from someone from your past. For your peace of mind, it will probably be better to leave the person as only a past memory. Move forward without regrets. A confidential deal could produce financial rewards that help build your business. Follow your good intuition.

14. SATURDAY. Prosperous. The New Moon in Cancer emphasizes home and family matters. Decisions in these areas can be made with a certain amount of assurance that you are making the right choices. Leos beginning the search for a new home should have success. This is also a favorable time to begin building a dream house or to present building plans and applications to local authorities. The goddess Venus is now visiting your Virgo second house of personal finances, increasing your ability to manage money and to attract the resources you need to generate extra income. Get set for a boost to your bank balance.

15. SUNDAY. Fulfilling. As a general rule Leo people are very creative, talented, and multiskilled. Turning your thoughts to finances, even on your day off, can display these characteristics to someone who counts. Innovative ideas and schemes can be developed to improve your current financial status. An anonymous e-mail or card could be an unexpected and pleasant surprise, especially if you have a very good inkling of who it is from. Remain coy, let the other person do the chasing. Social interactions, especially later in the day, should be very enjoyable. Solo Leos could meet a romantic interest who seems promising.

16. MONDAY. Ordinary. Leave home earlier than usual to avoid traffic problems this morning. A decision regarding an older member of the family might not be easy to make. If there is no alternative, go with your first choice. This is most likely to be best for all concerned. Maintain peace and cooperation through your willingness to compromise and to be considerate. If one of your colleagues seems particularly stressed, relieve them of some duties and let them go on an early lunch break. Their gratitude and appreciation will be evident, and the favor will be returned at a time when you need a break. Personal projects that are well organized will proceed smoothly.

17. TUESDAY. Trying. Today's influences bring money matters to the fore. Set aside some quiet time to consider your financial situation. If it is not as positive as you would like, take active steps to change this position. Once money matters have been resolved, moving forward toward your goals will be easier. If on the job you might not accomplish as much as you think you should, especially if money is a key to success. Be patient. Acceptance of your ideas or work is likely to come in time. A serious discussion with your mate or partner could be helpful in setting limits for leisure pursuits, especially if one of you seems to be spending more on nonessentials.

18. WEDNESDAY. Average. Guard against an overconfident attitude. If this is kept in check, good progress can be made in most areas of your daily life. Postpone decisions relating to buying or selling that will have a large impact on your finances. Finish tasks already begun. Be sure to keep relevant superiors fully informed of what is occurring on the job. Control the temptation to spend a lot, especially for social pursuits or hobby activities. Discord with a roommate or a significant other could arise later in the day due to mishandling of joint finances. Have good excuses ready if you are the guilty party.

19. THURSDAY. Uneasy. If you need to save money and are not heading off to work this morning, stay home until early afternoon. In that way you should be able to resist the lure of spending at large department stores. If you have to venture out to shop, limit purchasing or leave your credit cards at home. Lock up securely when leaving home, and consider upgrading security measures if these are not totally adequate. Your thoughts are inclined to wander or be interrupted by daydreams and fantasies, so avoid tasks that need concentration over a long period of time. Expect increased drama or intensity in a current love affair.

20. FRIDAY. Inspiring. As a Leo you are ruled by the Sun, which is the life force of the zodiac. This means that you usually stand out in a crowd and at times are given a leadership role or position of power allowing you to cater to the needs of other people. Acting as an emcee, guest speaker, host, or entertainer is your forte. If carrying out tasks such as these you should reap both financial rewards and personal enjoyment. Being flexible and open to change is often difficult for Leos, but this is necessary right at the moment. This is not the time for procrastination. You will tend to be in the right place at the right time to grasp a possible chance of a lifetime.

21. SATURDAY. Energetic. Going for a stroll around the park or to a local community center should be an enlightening experience. You are bound to meet friends, acquaintances, or local shop owners and have a lively gossip session. This is also a great day to window-shop, looking for some likely bargains to get your wardrobe ready for an increase in social activity. A strong belief in your own ability helps to remove some of the self-imposed limits that can hinder progress. Do one thing at a time. Establish stable future foundations, remembering to take notice of minor and major details.

22. SUNDAY. Encouraging. Remaining objective is today's challenge. You need to bring yourself fully into whatever you are doing in order to deal efficiently with the task at hand. The cosmic influences encourage Leos to work to highest standards. Aim to be the high-flying achiever that you know you can be. Resist the urge to make drastic changes at home without first consulting those who share the space with you. Their ideas and feedback should complement and add to your theme. Unless you avoid wasting financial resources, resentment is likely to intensify.

23. MONDAY. Rejuvenating. Life is about to shift into top gear as your ruler, the Sun, now beams in your own sign of Leo. Your social life will receive a massive boost, so make sure you are prepared to shine in your social circle. Revamp your style, image, and attire. Be ready to celebrate your upcoming birthday in style. Your confidence, vitality, and enthusiasm increases and gains momentum over the next four weeks. Exciting romantic and personal prospects are likely, so grasp opportunities, maximize chances, and make the most of this happy period. You will begin to feel much more confident and certain of your future.

24. TUESDAY. Upsetting. Irritability could strike even usually happy and easygoing Leos. Try to keep calm or you might blurt out caustic comments that you would normally not say. Today is not a favorable time to settle career or legal matters because confusion could muddy the waters. Don't trust anyone who tries to steer you in a certain direction if they have something to gain. Try not to overdo now. Be especially careful with your health. A minor infection could develop into a major problem if left unchecked. Don't take work problems home tonight. Leave them at the front door if you want harmony to prevail.

25. WEDNESDAY. Mixed. Every now and then even the king of the jungle gets pushed around. However, this is not the time to let loved ones continue to place their needs and wants above your own desires. Take back control, especially when someone tries to impose responsibilities on you that are not truly yours. Continue to be wary of the motives of business competitors or associates. There is a chance that you are being led down the garden path. Romance and recreation beckon those who are seeking fun times. Mysterious opportunities could appear, making this an exciting and exhilarating evening.

26. THURSDAY. Fair. A change of routine will add zest to your daily grind. Take a different route to work, act on chores out of their normal order, or perhaps take the day off. If this is not possible, be sure to allocate equal time to home, business, and social activities. Constantly working without a break dulls the senses. A different tactic taken toward discipline could prove productive for Leo parents whose youngsters are currently displaying bad behavior. Double-check an insurance claim before sending it in. You might have overlooked an important proof that could hold up payment to you.

27. FRIDAY. Manageable. Moneymaking plans and joint ideas probably need further investigation before making any firm decisions. Don't jump straight into the fray. Seek financial advice and stay realistic. Venus moves into retrograde motion now, bringing an opportunity to review issues related to finances, personal possessions, and relationships. This is a good time to negotiate a new wage package, increased perks, or a promotion. Chances are good that you will get most of what you ask for. Emotional upsets concerning money are likely to occur more frequently. A former lover could reappear on the scene and get in touch with you. Proceed slowly or you could be right back where you once were.

28. SATURDAY. Active. Restlessness is likely but can be used in a constructive way. However, there is also a need to control your enthusiasm to prevent spreading yourself too thin. Communicating with loved ones could be rough. Watch what you say and how you say it. Leos who are working in the area of publicity or advertising should find that ideas flow fast and furious. Buying products for business purposes, selling, and negotiating are also areas where productivity is on the rise. Don't rely on prearranged social plans to go as envisioned. Changes are likely to disrupt arrangements, but not to worry. You should have a number of invitations to choose from, so you won't be home alone.

29. SUNDAY. Tricky. Today's influences focus on sensitivities. Relationship issues could be intense and erratic as the Full Moon energies culminate in your opposite sign of Aquarius. Being pushed to the limit is an apt description, with the slightest annoyance likely to set you off. Calm down and take a long, deep breath. Avoid placing yourself in any situation where confrontation could occur. Think carefully before refusing to obey an order or an instruction just because you think the idea has little or no merit. This is not the time to become rebellious, since you are likely to regret your actions later on. Have a soothing bath at the end of the day to revitalize your energy.

30. MONDAY. Surprising. Your creative imagination should be working extremely well, although not all of your ideas will be well thought out or realistic. Write everything down, and then you can edit out what is unlikely to work. Overwork is a possibility, so make sure you are receiving needed support, especially if you must meet a set timetable or deadline. Someone in your circle of friends probably is very good at matchmaking or arranging a blind date. If you are single and looking, trust the judgment of this friend to find the right person for you.

31. TUESDAY. Satisfactory. Anger and irritability are likely to emerge. Don't let these emotions contribute to carelessness or an accident could occur. If you are overdue for a pay raise, an unexpected opportunity to talk to the boss could arise. State why you deserve special consideration and discuss future chances so you know what opportunities are likely to open up. Problems in a friendship could cause some confusion that will require a concerted effort to sort out. Keep an eye on your wallet or it could mysteriously disappear when you are not looking.

AUGUST

1. WEDNESDAY. Useful. Don't try so hard to get what you want. A soft approach can work just as well. There is a chance you might chase away exactly what you are seeking due to an overly aggressive attitude. Working with colleagues to achieve a unified goal is only possible if everyone is prepared to compromise. A task could take longer than anticipated, increasing pressure and stress. A family secret from the past that comes to the surface could at first be very disconcerting. Further investigation, however, might reveal that this can strengthen family bonding with the realization that past mistakes don't always have the power to retard positive growth.

2. THURSDAY. Fortunate. You will have extra bounce in your step as you get ready to face the day. Your ruler, the Sun, is happily connecting with Jupiter, the planet of abundance and grace. If celebrating your birthday, this should be a wonderful experience. Expect the arrival of a special gift, person, or a new bundle of joy. There is also a chance that you can make a name for yourself through your own initiative and enterprise. Financially, a stroke of good luck could be a windfall for your bank balance. An investment opportunity that carries only a small risk may fall into your lap, definitely worth a second look.

3. FRIDAY. Rewarding. This is another day when you can create your own opportunities. Push ahead to secure a special deal that you want. A special purchase will give you a dash of class and make you feel on top of the world. Plan a short getaway or an even longer vacation. Don't be afraid to be a little selfish and include a destination or activities that you as well as the family will enjoy. Aim for experiences that can set your imagination soaring. Teaching or training someone on the job will be a rewarding experience on both sides, with you also learning while you teach. Aim for precision, not guesstimates.

4. SATURDAY. Expressive. Keeping thoughts to yourself will be more difficult as Mercury adds power to your personality house of Leo. With creative flair one of your innate characteristics, put inspirational ideas and plans into action. Share confidences as well as harmless gossip with family members and friends. You might have to accept changes that are occurring in someone else's life. If this is a parent, be both supportive and patient. Exploring an unusual part of the city, a museum, or a theme park could interest Leos wanting to spend the day on the move. Or you might prefer to relax with a good book and a cold drink.

5. SUNDAY. Positive. Take a good look at your values and goals. If you truly are aware of what will make you happy, forward movement can be successful. It is vital to realize your potentials and to build on these. Social plans might have to be altered, possibly in midstream. Your willingness to cooperate and to change direction should impress other people. Leisure activities, whether planned or not, are likely to center around you. Suggest something out of the ordinary that is both stimulating and fun. If you are in the mood to celebrate, just take care not to overindulge. Recognize your limits and abide by them.

6. MONDAY. Promising. If you are unable to meet a particular criteria or challenge, don't panic. It is not worth stressing over if you have performed at your best. An experienced person in your line of work could be a guiding light. Suggestions and ideas put forward may include some you have not considered, easing your workload. A hobby or leisure pursuit might be the source of extra income. Talented Leos should investigate local outlets or consider selling online or through a party plan. Popping the question or saying yes to a proposal is very likely for the Leo in love.

7. TUESDAY. Exciting. Mars, the planet that makes things happen, visits your eleventh house of friends and associates from now until September 28. Put more of your energy into group activities and organizational meetings. Taking one step at a time can help you reach your goals better than acting on impulse. Be aware that someone might pretend to be your friend when in fact the opposite is more likely. A sale contract for a new home could be finalized, giving you the green light for the packing and moving to begin. Hiring a professional company to help you relocate might be a wise option for busy Lions.

8. WEDNESDAY. Active. Make the most of this successful period. Financial action should be sharper and problems can be solved with greater efficiency. The self-employed Leo business operator now has starred opportunity to build a good team of associates. Begin slowly and be selective. The core group will then become a solid foundation, giving you the ability to positively plan for the future. Friends could provide useful insights if you really listen. Do not just give lip service when offered well-intentioned advice. Sharing ideas and thoughts with those closest to you is important and can strengthen your bonds.

9. THURSDAY. Refreshing. Remember that many hours can be wasted chatting on the phone, surfing the Net, or writing and answering e-mails. Try to be more efficient to increase the chance of reducing your workload. Send short, friendly replies in preference to longer ones. Trust other people to perform some of your regular duties. Make good use of the answering machine. Reconciliation with a friend could make this a memorable and emotional day. Forgive and forget whatever problems existed in the past, and move your relationship to a new level. Mixing business with pleasure works well.

10. FRIDAY. Manageable. Personal commitments, domestic projects, and employment duties demand much of your time. Trying to make everyone happy will keep you hopping and increase stress. Move along at a steady pace, being sure to take rest breaks to keep your mind sharp and focused. A blast from the past could place you in a tricky position. If this involves a family issue, it might be better not to take sides until all the facts are available to you. Although you might be looking forward to entertaining at home, try to be flexible. If plans become muddled or food is not ready on time, laugh it off. The more you stress, the more things could go wrong.

11. SATURDAY. Pleasurable. Cosmic trends are especially promising for fun, romance, and creative ventures. Over this weekend five planets light up your Leo first house of personal plans and desires. Now you can have special fun. This is a time when you can roar, providing you direct your energy in the right areas. If you are not celebrating a birthday, wedding, or other special occasion, plan to participate in leisure pursuits or hobbies that get your adrenaline flowing. Leo singles can look forward to a romantic encounter with someone impressive, but you must mix, mingle, and get into the party spirit. A chance to increase the bonds of affection exists for Leo couples.

12. SUNDAY. Empowering. Leo people are in the driving seat, so be prepared to lead the way. Follow through with your ideas and plans. Your ability to make astute decisions is enhanced, especially involving creative projects. This evening's New Moon in your own sign of Leo triggers a new cycle with fresh beginnings. Personal plans and desires can gain added momentum if extra effort is applied. Lucky insights about career, business, and personal prospects assist you to move ahead quickly but with proper direction. There should be plenty of fun mixing socially with old friends and colleagues and also bringing new friends into your social circle.

13. MONDAY. Active. Leos will be dynamos in action, rushing around in circles and trying to do everything all at once as well as meet deadlines. You know it is impossible to be at two places simultaneously, so reschedule your calendar to release extra stress and strain. Finding practical solutions to your problems might not be appealing but is the most efficient way to handle things. Don't rely on a stroke of luck. There is a chance to get your creative and artistic talents more organized if you take stock of where you are heading. A relationship that begins now has a good chance of longevity.

14. TUESDAY. Average. Sort out your finances, being sure to ponder monetary decisions. Continue to view options from various angles until you have a good grasp of the situation. However, avoid becoming bogged down in minor details and methods. You also need to take time to view the bigger picture. A colleague is likely to rub you the wrong way. If this is an ongoing problem, now is the appropriate time to take action. If ignoring harassment has not worked in the past, consider taking your complaints to the boss or another higher authority. The judgment will be in your favor if you have right on your side.

15. WEDNESDAY. Passionate. Romance lights up your life as you star on the social circuit. As Venus, planet of pleasure, greets Pluto, planet of lust, be prepared for emotions to be intense and fiery. Passionate encounters are in the cards as many Leos flirt outrageously. Those who are not single should avoid this tendency, or at least be low-key about it. A public display of affection with someone other than your current mate or partner can lead to future drama. Avoid making frivolous purchases or unwise monetary decisions. If you are going out to shop, buy only essential items.

16. THURSDAY. Rewarding. Good study habits practiced regularly by Leo students ensure that cramming for exams will not be necessary. Focus on making this a daily routine. If you want to find out what is troubling a friend, the best approach is to come right out and ask. They will more than likely be pleasantly surprised that you care enough to be aware of their problems and mood swings. If you can help resolve issues for them, do so. If not, continue to at least offer moral support. Tempting delights will tantalize your taste buds and lure you to spend more money than you should. Romance is still high on your agenda.

17. FRIDAY. Bright. Important meetings and discussions should produce valuable results that are very promising for your future success. Leos going through counseling should find that progress is made. A new level of understanding can be reached at home. A romantic situation that develops might come as a big surprise to the solo Leo and could be the start of a wonderful love affair. Those in the mood for good times with friends and family members are in luck. Wining, dining, socializing, and shopping are all high on your list of favorite activities. Just take care and remember that moderation is the key to a healthy lifestyle and an equally healthy bank account.

18. SATURDAY. Busy. Lengthy discussions of goals and methods could take up a lot of time. Make sure that all ideas are given due consideration and that everyone has a chance to express their views. Stress could arrive this evening for the unprepared Leo, when guests turn up uninvited. Instead of being caught off guard, clean up around the house early, stock the pantry with suitable treats, dress in nice casual clothes, and put on a happy face. Everyone will be impressed by your ability to organize without becoming flustered. A celebration at home should prove to be a huge success, with much appreciation for the delicious food and good company.

19. SUNDAY. Excellent. You may wake up feeling a little under the weather this morning. Perform your daily exercises and you should soon be back to your old self. To a Leo success is not always complete unless sufficient financial rewards come with the achievement. Mercury, the planet of thought processes, moves into your Virgo second house of personal finances and assets, bringing monetary matters to the fore. The chance of increasing your income depends on applying more mental effort. Commitments that involve material resources can be explored with a view to identifying any areas that need immediate attention.

20. MONDAY. Astute. Your ability to give attention to both home and work is likely to be tested. Family matters might need your urgent input, clashing with time that should be devoted to employment tasks. Fortunately your ability to prioritize is enhanced, so you should be able to sort out what is important from what can be left for another time. Leo homeowners involved in unfinished renovations should apply extra effort to complete this task now. Call in a professional if needed to make one less responsibility that you have to shoulder. Enjoy a wholesome family dinner complete with dessert tonight.

21. TUESDAY. Unpredictable. An important personal project could be delayed, causing some upset. However this should only be a temporary setback, so don't despair. Delaying your own social or leisure plans to assist a client or higher-up is likely to bring rewards for the career-minded. Solo Lions could be spoiled as a number of romantic potentials become more readily available. Opt for someone who shares your likes and dislikes if looking for a relationship that has a chance of being long-term. Make dinner reservations and take family members out this evening if a home-cooked meal does not appeal.

22. WEDNESDAY. Favorable. An interest that begins to attract you might prove to be something you have the talent for but, until now, have never realized. This potential does exist, so explore, experiment, and discover what lurks within. This is a favorable day to get together with an investment planner and study options to achieve your long-term goals. Being shown a range of possibilities gives you the chance to have a big say in your financial security. This is also a good day to place a small wager at a casino or racetrack. Luck increases as the day goes on, but be discerning and only gamble what you can afford to lose.

23. THURSDAY. Encouraging. Your ruler, the Sun, is now glowing in the sign of the perfectionist Virgo, in your sector of monetary assets and possessions. This brings finances further into focus. You can seriously begin the process of tightening your financial spending and putting your affairs in order to make them run more smoothly. However, this process is not without a number of challenges. Your inclination to buy whatever you want without a second thought remains high. This is not the day to try to smooth over an argument with a friend or lover. Better results are likely if you put this off until next week.

24. FRIDAY. Satisfactory. The answer to a question you have been waiting to ask could come now. Although it might not be exactly what you want to hear, things will become clearer later on. Upsets are likely for Leos who share home life with a number of unrelated people. If talking to lazy roommates who are not pulling their weight doesn't have any impact, it might be time to consider moving back home or into your own place. Try not to stray from good eating habits. The best option for good health and vitality is a diet that does not include too many indulgences.

25. SATURDAY. Guarded. The people with whom you live could show a distinct lack of good humor. This might rub off on you unless you take care not to show annoyance. Artistic endeavors are enhanced and positive now, as imagination flows with vivid fantasy and flair. A romantic encounter might be magical but also contain issues of deception and confusion. Remember that no one can live up to a perfect ideal. If venturing out tonight be extremely careful because you are prone to impulsive actions. These can spell trouble with a capital T. Taking a break from usual Saturday night entertainment would do you a world of good.

26. SUNDAY. Chancy. Don't allow lack of confidence or nervousness to undermine a special talk in public that you are preparing to make. If you know your topic well, the reception you receive will be emotionally satisfying. Give yourself a rousing pep talk prior to the presentation to help control anxiety. A lovers' tiff could get out of hand in a public place this evening. The high cost of entertainment might be the impetus behind this dispute. To avoid possible embarrassment, stay home, choose inexpensive amusement, or limit spending. Listening to relaxing music, meditating, or walking in the park can help you get in the mood to face the new working week ahead.

27. MONDAY. Creative. The artist in you emerges with creative productivity that leads to pleasure and pride. The constant push-pull effect that has been occurring over the last few months has been mainly affecting business and personal relationships. This has probably been taking a toll on you, but this phase is nearly completed so hang in there. If you have realized that there is not enough communication going on within your relationship, take urgent steps to address this problem. Clean, clear, and sort through clutter. Start with the bedroom and systematically go through each room and out to the yard.

28. TUESDAY. Varied. Endeavor to keep your feet firmly placed on the ground despite the restless attitude that prevails. You are prone to going overboard, so take a moderate stance. This morning's eclipsed Pisces Full Moon conveys a financial theme. Benefits come by reviewing all aspects of your economic security. If bank charges are skyrocketing or service is nonexistent, now is the time to be proactive by complaining or changing banks or credit institutions. This is also the time to think about the best plans for retirement and old age. If a loved one is unpredictable and jittery, leave them alone until this mood passes.

29. WEDNESDAY. Insightful. Trust your own feelings and intuition when it comes to issues that can impact your financial security. Tax or insurance matters require extra attention. It is in your best interests to be thorough and detailed. Ethical practices are the only way to conduct business. Don't cut corners or attempt to take the easy way out when it comes to company financial matters. A difficult commitment could see you burning the midnight oil to complete the task on time. You won't relax until you reach your objective. Socially there is a nostalgic theme. Unattached Leos could meet someone special.

30. THURSDAY. Manageable. Keep an open mind. Establish priorities early in the day in order to act on as many tasks as possible. Your mind might be inclined to wander, making focusing a challenge. Avoid binding contracts. Also be careful with communications. Don't make any promise that you may not be able to keep. Leo people currently going through a divorce or lawsuit should hear some good news to lift spirits through this trying period. Travel plans are likely to be delayed or canceled. This might be linked to work commitments and should only be temporary. Get involved in extra study or training that will add to your skill base.

31. FRIDAY. Inspiring. Use your inspiration and ideas constructively. Obtaining knowledge is important. Write down spiritual experiences that have recently occurred. One day you could decide that these are of sufficient general interest to consider publishing. Your ability for in-depth study is enhanced due to your intuitive talents, making reading and researching beneficial. Attending a lecture, class, or workshop can provide interesting information that broadens your horizons. Leos with a political agenda should be successful addressing a group. A long-distance relationship could blossom. Socializing with people from overseas will be stimulating.

SEPTEMBER

1. SATURDAY. Lively. If celebrating a special occasion you can expect to be the star of your own show. Make sure you dress to impress other people. Be frugal with the amount of alcohol you consume, so that you stay in control and enjoy yourself. Volunteering with a youth team or becoming involved in any weekend fun activity for children will give you pleasure and possible recognition for your efforts. Leos who have been experiencing restless or sleepless nights should get help if this is becoming a problem. Mull over a proposition for a few days before coming to any definite conclusion.

2. SUNDAY. Dynamic. Today heralds a major change for Leos. Saturn, the planet of restriction and structure, has now entered Virgo, the money sector of your solar chart, and will stay there the next couple of years. Throughout this period Lions need to be alert for opportunities to increase finances or to change career direction. Timing is the key to making things work in your favor. Learning how to live with less out of necessity or choice is part of the experience of this transit. Financially a new moneymaking venture could come your way through a sideline business or an investment that slowly adds to your net worth.

3. MONDAY. Bountiful. With three planets in your personal money house, this is the time to build a substantial asset base that will create financial stability for your future. Be proactive. Record income and expenditures over the next month so you have clear documentation of where your money comes from and where it goes. Take stock of possessions, mortgages, and loans in both business and personal affairs to ensure that your assets are more than your liabilities. Your mind is likely to move faster than you can act.

A tendency to worry about anything and everything could reach a climax. To help release nervous anxiety, keep in mind that most of what you are currently stressing about is never likely to occur.

4. TUESDAY. Unsettling. Don't allow yourself to be dragged into other people's quarrels. Take a step back and let disputes take place without any input from you. If you suspect that your mate or partner is not being truthful, turn to a friend who is likely to have a very good idea of what is going on. However, there might not be much point asking questions right at this moment because people are likely to evade giving you a straight, honest answer. Bide your time and the truth will come out, just not yet. Catch up with friends and family members. Go out socially and mingle, or invite guests over to share your renowned Leo hospitality.

5. WEDNESDAY. Reassuring. The beginning of the day should find you in a good mood. Negotiations regarding property or a corporate deal should be making positive headway. An offer is likely to be accepted, although one party may decide to wait before announcing the decision. A thirst for knowledge and for keeping up with the latest gossip within your close circle of friends marks the next three weeks. Mercury, the planet of intellect and communication, enters your Libra third sector, bringing a deluge of invitations to a variety of social activities. Neighborhood get-togethers and spontaneous short trips can be lively and fun.

6. THURSDAY. Supportive. Tidy up loose ends and finish outstanding jobs. Remove old items that are no longer of any use, then update with better suited and higher quality gear. Take better care of personal possessions to guard against theft. This is a good time for Leo people in the market for a new or quality used vehicle to start checking the newspaper advertisements, auctions, or car lots. You may want to ask an older and wiser person to accompany you through the process to avoid being deceived by anyone. Staying home with the family is likely to be the most appealing entertainment this evening.

7. FRIDAY. Variable. You may feel a little crowded. Try to arrange some solo time where you can be alone. The planet of transformation, Pluto, now begins a forward march, stirring up your Sagittarius house of fun, romance, and creativity. Issues that concern these areas of your life should begin to clear up, with positive outcomes likely. Leo parents or those who have children in their care might start to see results from past actions taken to assist youngsters with behavior problems or if a tutor was engaged to help with an educational deficit. If you choose to spend time at home, enjoy puttering around doing a little of this and that.

8. SATURDAY. Positive. You should now be feeling more positive about your situation and more willing to accept challenges. Another planetary shift occurs as love goddess Venus moves in forward motion in your sign of Leo. A relationship that has been on the brink of breaking down but is still surviving should begin to experience a renewal. With tact, diplomacy, and the use of your intuitive abilities, you can zero in on the source of problems. Once you understand what is bothering your mate or partner, you can take steps to help resolve the situation. A wedding could become a social priority.

9. SUNDAY. Subdued. A somber atmosphere prevails. You could be better off spending time with just one person rather than becoming involved with a group or in a community environment. Gossiping over a cup of coffee with a trusted friend, sibling, or new neighbor, or sharing sightseeing experiences with a loved one, would be a great option. With physical appearance and grooming on your mind, wandering around trendy boutiques could put you in a perkier frame of mind. Treating yourself to a luxurious massage or facial is sure to do wonders for your body, mind, and spirit.

10. MONDAY. Variable. Keeping nervous energy to a minimum will help you make the best use of your time. Leo parents of young working adults living at home should make sure they are paying their way. You should not be expected to meet all household expenses. Discuss partnership issues with an open heart and mind. Avoid exaggerating or becoming overly judgmental in your assessment of a current situation. If you are planning to meet someone for drinks or dinner after work, ensure that you have the correct address and know how to get there to guard against becoming lost.

11. TUESDAY. Beneficial. A beneficial astral climate beams on Leos with a Virgo eclipsed New Moon in your solar house of values, possessions, and money. This is another positive period. The more time you spend on improving wealth and personal income, the more likely you are to see an increase. If you have been lax with organizing monetary affairs, put everything in order now. Keep a record of when bills are due to avoid bad checks and late payments.

There could be some issues with your mate or partner concerning the current state of your joint bank account. Arguing is likely to result in misunderstandings, so it would be wiser to kiss and make up and to promise better fiscal management in the future.

12. WEDNESDAY. Tricky. You might feel a little muddled. If you are out in public, guard your valuables. Don't leave them lying around where the unscrupulous can help themselves to your belongings. Coping with people in authority could be problematical because you are not seeing things with your usual clarity. An easygoing atmosphere between you and your colleagues might not exist either. Coworkers and customers might be more complex than usual, making it difficult for you to give in as much as you usually do. If feasible, lock yourself away in your own office, store room, or cubicle. You are better off working alone and will get much more done.

13. THURSDAY. Comforting. Look forward to a better day than yesterday. You will be on the move with more energy and enthusiasm. If you do need to concentrate on employment matters, steer clear of those who are inclined to delay you with numerous questions or idle gossip. Children's habits might come under scrutiny. It would be a good idea to monitor phone and computer use to ensure that there are no problems in these areas. Avoid promising more than you can deliver. This evening's entertainment should be extremely pleasant, with family members eager to please you.

14. FRIDAY. Communicative. The beginning of the day should be particularly rewarding. Attend to all important matters during the morning, then allow the afternoon to settle into more general or routine affairs. Relationships take on increased importance as you endeavor to channel your energy into this area. Although you need to be careful with what you say to your loved ones, open and honest communication could bring about a deeper level of support. Put off any legal proceedings unless you can act prior to midday. Romance is starred. Plans being made in this area could include impending nuptials or an engagement party.

15. SATURDAY. Distracting. This is not the best day to embark on a new project around your home. Too many distractions and upsets make the day a no starter. Instead, complete tasks already under way, or concentrate on routine housework. Over the next week vixen Venus challenges nebulous Neptune, increasing the potential for deceit and skulduggery. Don't become a victim. Be careful with all financial dealings, especially with friends, lover, and business partners. Defer going into joint ventures. Lavishing love and attention on loved ones will give you pleasure. If you don't have specific social engagements planned for this evening, do some home baking or make some ice cream.

16. SUNDAY. Practical. Take extra care if venturing out for a Sunday drive. Other drivers might not be as polite or safety conscious as you are. Move away from any volatile incident that threatens to escalate into road rage. Leos who are considering making home improvements could take the project one step further now. Draw up a rough sketch of what you hope your finished work will look like. It could be beneficial to engage the services of professionals or discuss the details with someone who can provide wisdom and experience. In this way pitfalls can be avoided. Devote time to a relationship that is ailing or failing.

17. MONDAY. Cautious. You are now entering a period where you may have or be involved in an accident or other mishap. Leo athletes should take more care than usual with warming up in advance. Also be sure to wear a mouth guard or helmet or other safety equipment. Be cautious of people who might try to profit at your expense. Don't announce any plans or goals prematurely. A reluctance to do what others tell you could cause upsets if you are not prepared to carry out orders. Social life is calling. A group activity should bring exciting contact, which will be a pleasurable way to spend your leisure time.

18. TUESDAY. Mixed. If you are seriously considering investing in brick and mortar, now is an excellent time to begin the process. Leos who combine imagination and creativity should enjoy success and increased popularity. There is a chance to clear the air with a friend you have been arguing with lately. Bring issues out into the open, forgive, forget, and move on. The energy needed to cope with necessary obligations should be plentiful, but don't overburden yourself. In your free time dream, meditate, or listen to soothing music. Leaving the humdrum world of reality even for a short time will induce deep relaxation.

19. WEDNESDAY. Demanding. Leos who are particularly talented in a creative field could consider putting on a display or show for colleagues and associates. You may create a sideline market that can put money in the bank. There are some hassles you can do without. Money, friends, and social activities are a potent mix that won't work well and should be avoided at this moment. Senior staff or management could be particularly tricky to handle, especially if there are high expectations of what you are supposed to achieve. Keep your cool in order to avoid a scene.

20. THURSDAY. Significant. It is time to take stock and make decisions regarding your personal and professional partnerships. If there are problems that need to come out in the open, there should be no holding back now. Deceit and trickery still surround you, but keep everything in proportion. Refrain from becoming involved in business deals. Continue to remember that if something is worth doing, it is worth doing well. Discussions at work regarding employment duties can be enlightening, producing some thought-provoking conclusions. A new relationship formed now could be a blissful affair for the unattached Leo.

21. FRIDAY. Challenging. This is another day when you will be in a hurry, with one eye on what you are doing and the other eye on the clock. If you are trying to meet a deadline, do your best but don't expect miracles. Overestimate the time that duties will take so you are not as stressed. Pay attention to health, and in particular to the amount of water you consume. To avert future problems, increase fluids if you are not drinking enough. Impulsive behavior by gambling or speculating will be very risky, so take care. There is a continued need to nurture an ongoing relationship. However, if it is not working out be realistic about it.

22. SATURDAY. Alert. Today will be extremely busy as people demand more and more of your time and energy. Fortunately you have plenty of zest to cope and to keep up with all the things you need to do. With so much happening recently, Leos in a loving relationship might have sadly missed out on quality couple time. Try to amend this tonight by staying home or going out as a twosome. Those who are inclined to be jealous or possessive might have difficulty controlling such behavior. Leo singles should steer clear of nightclubs and venues in known danger areas. Mix with a crowd, and take a taxi home.

23. SUNDAY. Enjoyable. The tempo of life picks up and more fun comes back into your life with the entry of the Sun into your Libra third house of interacting with others. Attention focuses on all forms of communicating, studies, and people who live nearby. Now is the time to organize short trips or a visit to relatives and to schedule important meetings, discussions, and workshops. Keep the pantry well stocked and your home spick-and-span since the number of visitors dropping by is likely to rise. Ideas, mental interests, and writing are all under favorable influences, and productivity should increase in these areas.

24. MONDAY. Favorable. Your magnetism will be very appealing. Creativity, ingenuity, and the ability to dig deep are evident today. Stockbrokers and all who are interested in trading shares should make excellent progress researching and studying the market. Lions who have free time would enjoy the challenge of an engrossing crossword puzzle or computer game. If you are interested in magazine competitions, you should do very well and might come out a winner. A school friend could turn up unexpectedly, bringing back pleasant memories of times gone by. You will enjoy the camaraderie, the gossip, and the chance to relax.

25. TUESDAY. Powerful. Share your skills. If you have expertise due to the personal experience of financial hardship or through training in economics, offer to assist other people to balance bank accounts and restore financial order. They will appreciate your efforts, and you will enjoy knowing that you have the wisdom to effectively provide help. Clean out closets and you are bound to find lost items and even money you had hidden and forgotten about. A past or a secret lover could consume your thoughts. Luckily this should only be a fleeting phase. Once you work out why you are fantasizing you can remedy the situation and move on.

26. WEDNESDAY. Changeable. Planning a short trip or a vacation overseas is likely to be difficult. If arrangements must be made today, the easiest method would be via the Internet. That way you won't have to stand in line for a travel agent or hold on the phone. Try hard to take interruptions and delays in stride. Someone you see on a daily basis is likely to get all worked up over trivial, petty issues. This evening's Full Moon in Aries heightens emotions and warns Leo people to take care when discussing serious issues. Don't enter into debates on delicate topics or challenge a self-anointed authority.

27. THURSDAY. Stimulating. You are likely to have a burning desire to learn. Travel might be high on your agenda for commercial reasons and as a pleasurable way to expand your vision of the world. Overseas or interstate contacts could be more significant now, providing you with increased assistance to achieve your personal aims and ambitions. Attending a conference or seminar can put you in touch with like-minded people and could also lead to a romantic encounter if you are currently single. Messenger Mercury moves into your Scorpio fourth sector, bringing increased attention to your living conditions, property, and family affairs. Buying or selling real estate could be a profitable venture now if you do ample research.

28. FRIDAY. Fruitful. Exploring different religions or philosophies as a way to learn and understand will appeal to you this morning. An early trip to the library might produce some interesting weekend reading. Problems involving a child could surface for Leo parents. Ask in-laws for advice, since they have been there before you. Mars, planet of drive and enthusiasm, enters your Cancer twelfth zone and stays there until the end of the year. Your energy might be lower than normal because this fiery planet is not happy in the watery depths of Cancer. Guard your health. It will be easier now to catch a virus or a plain cold.

29. SATURDAY. Diverse. Expect an up-and-down day, with some rough spots along the way. Be realistic about what you want out of life, and begin to take steps in this direction. The outlook is excellent for payments and collections, especially if related to property. Fiscal management remains a priority. Review insurance coverage on your living quarters, business equipment, vehicle, and any special luxury item. Ensure that loss from an accident or theft is well covered. Excellent ideas for landscaping and home decorating should flow easily if you are planning to renovate or refurbish. Write these down so you can develop a functional plan.

30. SUNDAY. Relaxing. This is a good day to wander through an old church or a gallery studying art, murals, stained glass windows, and paintings. If you prefer home pleasures, sorting through bits and pieces from your childhood or the more recent past can be an absorbing recreational pursuit. If you come across items that bring pain instead of pleasure, don't hold on to old hurts or past resentment. Doing so can halt your emotional growth. Let go so you can forgive and forget. Enjoy intimacy with your significant other, or gather with friends to share a leisurely meal and good conversation this evening.

OCTOBER

1. MONDAY. Changeable. The desire to learn and grow can be a driving force behind all of your decisions. You might sign up for a new class on impulse. Friends can be particularly annoying, dropping by unannounced and disturbing your thoughts. However, ideas that can come up during your conversations will give you plenty of food for thought. Flickering feelings of love for a person from another walk of life can upset your comfortable lifestyle, but the outcome can be enriching in the long run if you can let go of your inhibitions and preconceptions. A lot of changes are occurring all around you, so take time to digest and assimilate them into your everyday life.

2. TUESDAY. Constructive. Your overactive mind can make it hard to relax, keeping you on the move no matter how tired you become. Thoughts you put down on paper will be good reading in the future. If recuperating from an illness and feeling cooped up at home, take a walk outside, preferably not alone. This will get your circulation going and clear away the frustration of doing nothing. A neighbor or relative can be a great help if you are not too proud to accept an offer. A windfall may be coming your way, giving you just enough money to finance the purchase of a home or to do the renovations that you have been planning for a long time.

3. WEDNESDAY. Quiet. Take it easy and everything should fall into place without too much effort. A vacation may be due but your travel plans may no longer appeal. Don't worry about changing your itinerary at the last minute if you now feel like heading for a more secluded spot rather than a popular tourist destination. Peace and quiet are much more in keeping with your mood right now. A brother or sister may be looking for a job and ask you to put in a good word for them with a friend who can pull strings. If this puts you on the spot, you might suggest they take a course that will give them the skill and practice to get a job based on their own merits.

4. THURSDAY. Mixed. The infatuation may have gone out of a love affair, leaving you feeling flat and thinking about breaking it off. Don't be scared to make changes. The more you stay true to yourself, the freer and happier you will be. The day will get better as you go along. An invitation to work behind the scenes on a large project could be very lucrative for you. If a child is making a lot of demands on your time and energy, a play group could be of as much benefit to them as to yourself. Children of all ages, and adults too, need interaction with their own age group in order to experience the stimulation of the outside world.

5. FRIDAY. Stimulating. You will make a good impression everywhere you go. Your enthusiasm for interesting and creative ideas makes your conversation infectious. A family member may tell you something you don't want to hear. However, the sooner you listen and do something about it, the better you will feel. Plan an evening out with your mate or partner. If your life is so busy you hardly see each other, traveling will give you both a chance to have really good talks without interruptions. If you have to make a speech in front of a crowd or even to a table of friends, keep it short, simple, and from the heart.

6. SATURDAY. Auspicious. This is a day for meeting interesting new people, starting creative projects, and simply having fun. Leo singles might finally meet a very special person and experience a spiritual lift. Travel plans can be made in a hurry when a friend offers you tickets at a discounted price. If a friend or partner is having trouble with someone you like, talk to both of them and see if you can smooth things over. Just be careful not to reveal any confidences told only to you. Luck is on your side, making bargain hunting a breeze and a job interview successful. On the other hand, control your desire to overindulge, which could destroy all the hard work you have put into your health and fitness.

7. SUNDAY. Helpful. The needs of other people will be first and foremost in your mind. An elderly relative still living in their own home alone would appreciate some help to sort out their financial situation or to go shopping. If a nursing home is in their future, do ample research before you help them make a final decision, ensuring that it is the right move. Financial support for a personal project should be available. Don't let self-doubt hold you back from realizing your dreams. Although partnered Leos may want to get away alone, it is important to take the time to talk it over together before you make any definite plans. In that way you will avoid misunderstandings and hurt feelings.

8. MONDAY. Emotional. All sorts of surprises may come along, upsetting your normally rational mind. Try not to let emotions run away with you. Instead, put on your thinking cap and search for a solution to whatever problem is upsetting. The interest rate on your credit card could increase and make repayment almost impossible. It might be worthwhile to take out a personal loan with a modest interest rate and get rid of the card for good. Borrow a little extra so you can buy something you need, then work out a budget to suit those lower payments. News of a major lifestyle change can be exhilarating but at the same time vexing as far as your career plans go. Take each day as it comes and let Mother Nature do the rest.

9. TUESDAY. Courageous. Hard work and courage are your best friends at the moment. Don't let new ideas keep you from finishing projects you are working on. Instead, incorporate new ideas into what you are doing. The results may be startling. If a brother or sister is arriving home after a trip, organize a welcoming party by writing one e-mail to everyone instead of spending the whole day on the phone. One unpleasant neighbor in the past might have put you off socializing locally, but you will be surprised at the variety of people and amusements on your own block. Go out for a walk and find out what's going on.

10. WEDNESDAY. Opportune. Sacrifices for what you deem a worthy cause will be easy to make. Dedication to your particular interests can be so strong that you sign up for a course which will take away much of your free time. Your mate or partner may appear to be interested in your projects, but if you have a heart-to-heart you might hear a different story. Add balance to your life by honoring all aspects. You will then be a happier person. A business contract may seem to have covered all bases, but if you read the fine print you might detect one important point that has been skipped over in your negotiations. Don't sign anything without a thorough reading. Also be very wary of guaranteeing a loan even for a family member.

11. THURSDAY. Sociable. The New Moon in Libra bodes well for beginning new projects and also for starting assignments. Leo students will find a new subject inspiring and could even change their major to specialize in this particular area. Some Leo students may decide to apply to be an exchange student. The experience is sure to broaden your horizons and add to your knowledge of a foreign language and culture. Social contacts through a class, personal interests, or community projects are likely to increase, adding to your personal popularity. A heart-to-heart talk with one of your close friends could uncover a secret which will explain a lot about their recent behavior.

12. FRIDAY. Distracting. Mercury, the planet that rules communication and short-distance travel, starts to move backward today and will continue to do so for the next three weeks days. This indicates that your thinking is likely to turn inward more often and making decisions, finalizing contracts, or maintaining concentration will all be harder. Car trouble is another manifestation of this transit. A financial burden may now be lifted, giving you the chance to focus on the things you love most. A creative project should seem possible, and the prospects of a successful new business venture are good. You have solid, reliable people backing you, so don't wait any longer.

13. SATURDAY. Complex. Other people's easygoing exterior can mask quite the opposite. There is a feeling of selfishness in the air. Consider your own underlying motives when you offer to give up some of your own valuable time to help another person. If you are honest and your conscience is clear, you have nothing to worry about. A relationship may have reached a point where you are ready to start planning your future together. However, all sorts of problems have to be sorted out and worked through before you can do so. This process will actually turn out to be invaluable, so be patient with your partner and ready to learn something basic about yourself.

14. SUNDAY. Misleading. Relying on other people could be a drawback. They are likely to have problems of their own to deal with and may leave you to resolve yours on your own. If thinking about investing in a work of art or piece of real estate, enjoy looking at all options available to you. Writing down your thoughts after viewing each one will help you evaluate what is your best bet. A large social event might have to be missed due to family demands. For Leos, blood is thicker than water and therefore more important in the overall scheme of things. Your determination to do what is right won't let you down, no matter what other people say or demand.

15. MONDAY. Promising. Take a broad-minded approach and you will be able to handle whatever comes your way. The need for reform or a radical change may become obvious, turning your thoughts in an entirely new direction. A natural talent could be developed into a profitable business teaching your skills. Don't hesitate to start the training that will help you realize your ambitions. Even at a mature age you are never too old to follow your dreams.

An older person may ask you out, sweeping you off your feet with a very romantic approach to courtship. You might be ready to purchase a ticket to travel to another country and start saying your goodbyes.

16. TUESDAY. Passionate. Acting on impulse is the order of the day. Don't expect other people to do what is expected. They might do so, but then again they might not. Leo students will find this a perfect time for study and research. Insight gained can turn a boring subject into a fascinating one. A creative project can consume hours of your time as you become totally absorbed in what you are doing. Set an alarm to make sure you don't miss an important appointment. Lovers should skip a lunchtime rendezvous and plan an evening together so that you don't risk being late getting back to work and annoy the boss.

17. WEDNESDAY. Competitive. Give special attention to what you wear today. First impressions are often the strongest. If you are applying for a job or are going on any important interview, you need to give yourself a running start. Be thorough in all endeavors. There is a strong likelihood that someone is ready and waiting and all too willing to find fault with your work. You may put your own feelings aside in an effort to deal with immediate necessities, but don't ignore them all together. Do your work and then allow some time to focus on your feelings and act in a consistent way. Repressing your own feelings too much can lead to illness and depression.

18. THURSDAY. Satisfactory. Business negotiations may take an unexpected twist and demand your full concentration. In the end your extra effort should pay worthwhile dividends. Hard work and an earnest approach will win the day in any endeavor and will give your self-esteem a lift at the same time. You have more pull through your contacts than you might realize. A run-in with a government official can be resolved in your favor if you know who to call. Leo weight watchers might have trouble finding a diet that works. Instead of a set-in-stone diet, try just eliminating fast foods and alcohol from your diet. This coupled with exercise should soon see you thinner and glowing with good health.

19. FRIDAY. Uncertain. Pressure from all sides can make it hard to come up with any rational decisions. Before you know it, you could explode from frustration. If you talk about your feelings and acknowledge your shortcomings before you reach the breaking point, a compromise can be worked out. No matter how much research you do on an investment or gamble, you won't be able to rule out the element of risk. Let your good Leo intuition be your guide. Secrets have a way of being revealed, and an old one could suddenly become public knowledge. This will leave you feeling relieved and glad to be alive. Turn down a dinner date in favor of an early night and peace of mind.

20. SATURDAY. Easygoing. Good friends make this a day to remember. Listening to music, watching a mystery or romance movie, or telling stories with a party of friends can be good ways to enjoy yourself. If your mate is not feeling well, a relaxing day of fun and laughter would be good medicine. Alcohol should only be used in moderation. Otherwise you might find that your interpretation of events is distorted and you experience illusion instead of illumination. A chance to go sailing or to walk on the beach would be a perfect way to spend the day. Tonight let your hair down and go out dancing or enjoying karaoke.

21. SUNDAY. Happy. Agreement and enjoyment should accompany all of your activities. You will experience added vitality and a zest for life. Creative pursuits can attract the whole family. Romantic couples will be more interested in sensual rather than mental communication. A change from your usual routine may suit you perfectly. Experimentation can take you to all sorts of exciting offbeat places. The urge to beautify your environment could send you shopping and adding to your credit card debt. Major decisions should be put off for another time because your practical nature may elude you now. Flirting might be hard to resist since your sense of adventure is strong.

22. MONDAY. Significant. Upsetting circumstances can prove fortunate once the initial shock wears off. Keep in mind that anything can happen and probably will. Don't rush, even if you are running behind, or you risk causing an accident. Emotions will be up and down. There are sure to be a few frazzled tempers to watch out for at work. Concentrate on your breathing if you feel you are going to lose your cool. An introduction to someone who is well known could leave you at a loss for words. Tell them how you feel and see what happens after that. A dreaded bill can arrive but be less than expected, leaving you with enough cash to take your mate or partner out for dinner.

23. TUESDAY. Chancy. You may feel pressured by friends or relatives to put your money into a joint venture that you instinctively feel is a bad investment. Even if it is real estate, the property might be in the wrong position or the market could be weak. Voice your doubts and you might save everyone from losing money. You or your partner may have the chance for a promotion by moving. Talk honestly about the change and the impact on each of your lives before making a final decision. Sometimes money is not the most important thing in life. A family dispute might have involved you regardless of your point of view. Try to stay impartial and help diffuse the situation, not make it worse.

24. WEDNESDAY. Optimistic. Political views can interfere when it comes to socializing. Let other people have their say but don't allow a difference of opinion to escalate into an argument. Otherwise you might lose valuable prestige and clout with your group of friends. This is a fortuitous time to look into higher education, if not for yourself maybe for your children. The Internet is a great way to find courses of interest, but then visit in person and get a feel for each school and its students and teachers. If you have to attend a conference or meeting that is out of town, try to arrange a carpool. You might meet someone to pass the time with while cutting costs.

25. THURSDAY. Insightful. Young Leos may find that plans for travel and adventure lead to parental disapproval. Contact an older relative who traveled in their youth and ask for support. At the same time you might pick up a few handy hints. A restless spirit can be the result of an inquiring mind. The study of science and religion can be akin to travel as you investigate the different worlds of physics and the spirit. Be adventurous. Don't let a lack of education in one area put you off aiming for your dreams. Anything is possible with the right approach. Join a group, such as a debating team, and test yourself against other inquiring minds. You may surprise yourself.

26. FRIDAY. Bountiful. A new job opportunity might lead you to a new social set and the chance to move up in the world. You may have to outmaneuver your peers to get ahead, but if you are neither dishonest nor underhanded you won't have to feel guilty. A risky investment can pay off with a surprise win. A gamble could put extra dollars in your wallet and allow you to treat your family to something special such as a big-screen TV. You may be losing your enthusiasm for a competitive sport that you have always played. Instead of giving up completely, think about becoming a referee or coach so that you can still enjoy the physical exercise without having to beat anyone.

27. SATURDAY. Prosperous. Recognition for your achievements can give your self-esteem and confidence a huge lift. You may be asked to stand up in front of a crowd and accept an award or say a few words of encouragement for others. No matter how shy you feel, you will be equal to the task. Entertaining at home will appeal this weekend. Some guests from out of town could pick up the pace. With an eclectic guest list of neighbors, friends, and family members, the fun and games should last into the wee hours of the morning. An interest in the arts may lead to experimenting with all sorts of different mediums. As a Leo you are a natural performer and artisan, so you may end up with a fascinating new career.

28. SUNDAY. Healing. Regardless of the problems that have gone before, a relationship can be reclaimed and renewed with trust and honesty. It is all too easy to become complacent and end up telling little white lies to keep the peace. Eventually these can add up to one huge deception. In the face of adversity, an honest confession is worth more than your pride. Be particularly astute when handling partnership or group funds. You may be held responsible for any cash that goes missing. Getting out of the house and playing with youngsters will give you the chance to talk about anything and everything and will give them the opportunity to get any problems off their chest.

29. MONDAY. Sensitive. Returning from a trip overseas can leave you feeling like a stranger in a strange land. Or friends from the past may have moved on. Your hometown may no longer be recognizable. Relationship difficulties may have reached a point where you feel you must either make a lifetime commitment or walk away forever. This very fatalistic approach might simply reflect your current mood, so go out for some fun. Wait until tomorrow before making any major decision. A personality clash could be the reason for trouble within a group. Face differences that exist rather than trying to make it all seem the other person's fault.

30. TUESDAY. Relaxing. Turn your attention to yourself and make some pleasing changes to your environment. The happier you feel, the better your whole life will be. A physical fitness program might stimulate your enthusiasm. If you take up jogging as a way to stay fit you will have some time to think at the same time. If suffering from insomnia, look into learning meditation to help still your mind and aid in relaxation. Your humanitarian spirit is strong, and donating your time to those in need will be very rewarding. You may be able to teach a class in a creative subject and pass on the joy you feel in your art to others.

31. WEDNESDAY. Useful. Take advantage of the slow start to the day to attack your pile of paperwork. Sort through and pay bills. Clear away all clutter. Spend time on the Internet, and be sure to update your virus protection and safeguard your hard drive. You may be in touch with somebody over the Net who lives in a foreign land and shares thoughts and feelings with you. This virtual reality can be more pleasing than real life because it takes the risk of spontaneity out of communication. Consider what you want from life and what you appreciate most. You might reach a conclusion that offers you a new and far more promising course of action than the current one.

NOVEMBER

1. THURSDAY. Creative. The Moon in your sign of Leo today and tomorrow signals the start of a new lunar cycle for you. Although you may feel that a project on the drawing board is not yet ready to go, start setting the scene. A confrontation can hurt your feelings and pride, but when you think about what was actually said you might recognize some very constructive criticism. You have to spend money to make money. Even though you may be reluctant to fork out extra bucks on new equipment, it will pay for itself in no time. As a Leo you like to look good. Spend a little extra on your wardrobe and toiletries and there won't be a person who doesn't notice you when you enter a room.

2. FRIDAY. Positive. Romance can put a spring in your step and add flair to your style. There is nothing better than the sense of a bright new beginning. Whether you are off on a trip, stepping out with someone new, or simply making the most of the daily grind, your optimism and upbeat attitude will make the smallest of tasks enjoyable. Overcommitting yourself is a danger. Don't make promises you don't intend to keep, and then you won't have to avoid your friends and neighbors in the future. Your creativity is at an all-time high. Ideas for renovations, entertainment, and even gourmet dinners will keep you busy. Leo students should do well on exams but be sure to read the questions thoroughly.

3. SATURDAY. Cautious. Your need to feel in control is stronger than usual. You will be more exacting when it comes to spending money. A feeling of obligation can be allayed by buying a gift to express your gratitude, although finding the right gift might take all day. Purchasing an expensive item could take a lot longer than expected as you peruse sale flyers and visit department stores and discount outlets looking for the best bargain. Your diligence should pay off in the end, but a shopping escapade today is likely to be fruitless. Even if a business proposition sounds good, take time to do your homework before giving a definite answer.

4. SUNDAY. Impulsive. A sudden hunch may be all you need to rush off on a new adventure. After yesterday's thorough approach to everything, you can now throw caution to the wind. Your mate or partner might not be in a great mood, finding fault with all that you do. Jumping down their throat won't make things any better. It is in your best interests to be forgiving and find out what the problem is. They may just need to get a lot of frustrations off their chest, and who better than you to listen and sympathize. Dinner can turn into a heated debate and, if you are not careful, a full-scale war. Be diplomatic and you should be able to calm troubled waters.

5. MONDAY. Pressured. Someone who is close to you may try to bulldoze you into something you don't want, but at the same time you want to please this person. You might be tempted to slip out the side door and avoid the situation altogether, which might be the best approach. Your efforts to control finances can be upset by unforeseen expenses. Lighten up a bit. Factor fun and entertainment into your budget, and be happy to save a little less. A sense of fate can impact an experience with your mate or partner. Don't let the moment go unacknowledged. Conditions are starred for deep, meaningful communication, and you may share something together that is priceless.

6. TUESDAY. Sensitive. Unconscious attitudes can surface, peppering a casual conversation with mixed innuendos. Be careful about sharing how you feel. Quiet reflection regarding your emotional responses could be very enlightening for your self-understanding. A handsome insurance payout can relieve a sense of loss and turn your thoughts toward replacements that are far better than the originals. Leo students should consider purchasing a new computer program to aid research projects. This will allow you to do more work alone in the comfort of your own home. Clear up paperwork and check all messages to make sure you haven't missed anything important.

7. WEDNESDAY. Hectic. This is likely to be a very busy day filled with problems that keep you thinking at high speed. Pay extra attention to your diet. Be sure to take vitamins to protect your nervous system. Leo writers will find that words flow and imagination never runs dry. The temptation to exaggerate to a new acquaintance could be hard to resist, but then comes the pressure to live up to all your promises and tales. If you are searching for possible investors for one of your original ideas, your witty conversation will be an asset along with your self-confident demeanor. Just avoid overkill with a hard sell. Focus on the positive but recognize whatever has negative implications.

8. THURSDAY. Enjoyable. Domestic pursuits and visiting family members will give you plenty of satisfaction. If you recently moved you may still have a lot of unpacking and rearranging to do to suit your needs and comfort. An elderly relative might need your support to move or to plan a move. The arrangements can make them feel insecure, so try to arrange to have all their personal possessions around until close to moving day. Disbanding a home and all of its memories, plus the feelings of loss, can be very hard for you to deal with as well as the person directly involved. Expect a problem with the authorities over a development application, and be prepared for a fight.

9. FRIDAY. Easygoing. Venus, the planet of love and beauty, moving into Libra today highlights your everyday surroundings and activities with easygoing pleasure and enjoyment. You may be inspired to beautify your home. With the New Moon in Scorpio and your home sector, this is a favorable time to look for a new apartment or start home renovations. A surprise visit from a family member can lead to entertaining and cooking something special, perhaps resurrecting an old family recipe. An offer can come through the mail and give you the impetus to make the changes you have long wanted. Socializing with friends and neighbors can be fun, but set aside some time to let your mate or partner know they are most important in your life.

10. SATURDAY. Comforting. This is one of those days when you don't have to do anything in particular. You can just stay home and try out a few ideas, watch a movie, and eat snacks to your heart's content. If you have an important guest coming for dinner, you may spend the whole day preparing to ensure making a great impression, which you will definitely do. A new project can be started, but first spend time organizing your tools and equipment. This will free you from interruptions that could hold up your progress. If your mate or partner is not feeling up to par, keep them warm and shower them with nurturing to guarantee a speedy recovery.

11. SUNDAY. Challenging. A social engagement might be set to cost more than you can afford. Be enterprising and you should be able to juggle enough obligations to get the necessary cash that will enable you to take part. An enterprising spirit is called for. You can make some very interesting and fortunate contacts if you put yourself forward in today's challenging atmosphere. An elderly relative may decide to give you some long-winded words of wisdom, but don't switch off because there will be some valuable information that will work to your advantage if heeded. You may have to act as mediator between friends and the experience will teach you a thing or two as well.

12. MONDAY. Optimistic. You stand to make a modest gain speculating on a risky venture, but don't go all out or you might lose everything. Luck will come from an honest approach and from being true to your ideals. Outside influences play a large part in all of your activities today. Make plans, but if you try to stick to them too rigidly you will be open for disappointment. Don't believe all you see and hear via the media. The ratings game means the truth can be distorted for the sake of attracting attention. Business news can be corrupted by private interests in an attempt to influence market prices. A love affair that has become stale can be renewed with a playful and loving approach.

13. TUESDAY. Relaxing. All your plans should go like clockwork. Halfway through the day you are apt to be well ahead of time for a change. Don't allow your emotions to take over, however, or you could ruin your schedule with a long lunch. Overindulgence is your biggest enemy. Leo dieters could destroy weeks of good work in one big orgy of excess. Love is in the air, and if you get all your work finished early you can enjoy a long, romantic evening with that special person in your life. Advancement at work can mean more money in your wallet and a chance to get on top of bills. Friends may drop by this evening, perhaps bringing food to make a delicious dinner for hardly any cost to any one person.

14. WEDNESDAY. Exhilarating. Charity work can stretch your resources to the limit but give you the satisfaction of a job well done at the end of the day. You are very dedicated to your favorite cause now and will enjoy any challenges that come your way as a test of your abilities. If you feel run-down from burning the candle at both ends, consider starting on a diet to give your body and organs a rest from fast and processed foods. Combine this with plenty of rest and in a short time you will feel like a new person. This also is a good time to consider counseling. Insight into your inner motivation and desires is sure to be enlightening.

15. THURSDAY. Changeable. Get up early and focus on completing your chores. You are likely to be sidetracked later in the day from your intended timetable. Your workplace may be in for a surprise audit or inspection, and you will look good being up to date. Dissatisfaction on the home front could be an underlying distraction. If you are having trouble with your lease or mortgage, try to sort it out once and for all. Hire a lawyer if you must, just to put closure to the matter. If there is an unspoken disagreement between you and your mate or partner, bring it out into the open so you can mull it over together. With a little extra give-and-take you can resolve any and all differences.

16. FRIDAY. Distracting. Expect a few delays and minor disagreements, but nothing really important. There will just be minor irritations that take your attention away from what you would prefer to be doing. An attraction to a neighbor could make your mate or partner jealous and leave you feeling upset. Work it out without involving the neighbor. A legal contract could be held up due to a minor disagreement. Rethinking what you are doing could be a blessing in disguise, giving you a way out at the last minute. You may not want to be alone today, although it would provide a chance to better understand your feelings. Balance out your day with some solitude and some socializing.

17. SATURDAY. Opportune. Your energy level may be low, and getting yourself up and going this morning might take a little longer than usual. Have a nourishing breakfast to energize you. Write a list of what has to be done so that you don't forget something important. Emotional desire might overpower your practical nature. You may decide to get away with your lover, then spend hours poring over travel pamphlets looking for a romantic hideaway. Your charisma is strong. You could be voted in as a representative, forcing you into the limelight. You may feel uncomfortable about this, but eventually public recognition will come naturally and you will be in your element.

18. SUNDAY. Mixed. Money matters come under the microscope today. This is a very good time for sorting out financial problems and getting everything back on the right track. Turn to a financial adviser if you are unsure, so that you can make decisions and finalize a budget once and for all. A clash of egos can undermine your authority, especially if you are up against someone who is older or more powerful. Treat this as a test rather than becoming defensive. Confrontation happens all through life, so be honest and true to yourself. Make sure you know what you are talking about and you won't have any worries. Tonight promises excitement and the chance for romance.

19. MONDAY. Dynamic. A business transaction takes a positive twist, putting you in the driver's seat. This will enable you to propose the changes you want and probably achieve them. Travel is indicated. You might take off on the spur of the moment when opportunity arises. Leo singles are likely to be pursued by someone very attractive and fun loving. This new relationship can take you into a new group of friends and contacts as well as broaden your romantic horizons. A personal project can get a needed push when a family friend hooks you up with some great connections. Avoid overindulging in food or drink and the day should be very successful.

20. TUESDAY. Pleasurable. Investigating a new topic of interest can take you where you never intended to go. You may look into a new health regime and the philosophical concepts behind it. As you delve further into this topic, it is likely to affect your way of thinking about the world and your place in it. The comforts of home hold special appeal. Through your research you can travel far and wide without ever leaving your easy chair. Home renovations may take you out of your neighborhood looking for the right materials to fit the decor of your home. Don't be afraid to bargain about the price. You could come home with a real treasure. In-laws can be surprisingly helpful.

21. WEDNESDAY. Stimulating. Travel and education are highlighted. You and your mate or partner may be tempted to sign up for a workshop to explore the bonds within your relationship. An interest in different philosophies can give you the impetus to travel and to study various lifestyles. Check the Internet for some good ideas about the best places to visit away from the usual tourist routes. A sister or female friend could be relying on you for company more than you like. The only fair way to deal with this situation it is to be upfront and honest. You don't have to hurt anyone's feelings, and your decision will probably be in their best interest also.

22. THURSDAY. Rewarding. Your creative Leo flair will be on show for all to see. Your family is likely to be especially impressed. This is a favorable time for Leo entrepreneurs to think about setting up a business. You should be able to get the backers you need to get off the ground smoothly. Be aware of the competition, which will pull out all the stops and play the game to win. You may be at the forefront of a sport and could be rewarded for your achievements. This might be just what you need to establish a career as a coach in the future. Making the right decisions comes easily now, so take advantage of your good fortune. Enjoy the company of young and old relatives.

23. FRIDAY. Inquisitive. Your inquiring mind can get you in trouble if you are not careful. Your tendency to talk too much and ask questions at the wrong time could put you at odds with your colleagues and undo all your points with the boss. Balancing your home life with your career means keeping your mate or partner happy. Surprise your loved one with a romantic dinner date out on the town, or take all the trappings home for a romantic dinner. There may be something deceitful going on among your friends. If you get involved it will only bring you down, so keep your distance. Just be sure to keep an eye on what is going on in case it gets out of hand and somebody gets hurt.

24. SATURDAY. Renewing. Today's Full Moon in Gemini puts the focus on your social life and expectations. Your need for social contact can take you to places you would not normally frequent and put you in touch with people you would rather avoid. If you are at loose ends, go to a sports event and mingle with the crowd, letting out pent-up frustration by cheering for your team. A day at the races could be fun, and a small gamble might prove profitable. Long-ago friends could call on their way through town and give you a house full of guests to enjoy and reminisce with. Get out the cards and play for fun, not money, while you talk into the wee hours.

25. SUNDAY. Spirited. If the special person in your life has a child from a previous relationship, you may fall into the trap of competing for attention. Pull back and you will recognize that there are two different relationships going on. Rather than compete you need to co-exist. Work on finding the balance and then the dynamics will become positive. The child might even start to enjoy your company or look to you for guidance. Get outside for fun and fresh air. You might go walking and window-shopping, or you could take your bikes and explore locally. A community gathering could offer pleasant entertainment this evening.

26. MONDAY. Relaxing. You have been under a lot of pressure lately, and today is a good time to slow down and take it easy. If possible, take the day off if you feel everything is getting to be too much for you and your emotions are all wound up. This is an excellent day for working behind the scenes or doing research on a pet project. You could spot a few bargains if you go out shopping. Consider buying a book on investing in the stock market to learn about different companies and world markets. You might gather some interesting information from people you know who are in business. As a Leo you have a natural flair for speculation.

27. TUESDAY. Refreshing. Concentrate on your health. Study diets that pick you up and fortify your immune system. The Internet is a wealth of information, and you might end up learning more about all sorts of topics that come under the umbrella of health. You might even be intrigued by laughter therapy and purchase old movies to keep you laughing day after day. Keep to yourself as much as possible since you are apt to pick up on other people's feelings and emotions and end up losing touch with your own. Working for a charitable organization might suit you, giving you the chance to help other people without taking their woes home with you. Be extra kind to the one you love tonight.

28. WEDNESDAY. Buoyant. The Moon moves into your own sign of Leo today, where it will stay for two days. This is a favorable time to focus on your personal goals for the next month. Emotions are apt to fluctuate. If you feel that your mate or partner is being unreasonable, take a look at yourself before you react. No obstacles will be too big for you. Leo confidence is high right now. The desire to brighten up your surroundings might include an entertainment area and game room. Adding such things as a pool table or big-screen television will give you hours of fun and attract friends over to visit you. New friendships with talented and interesting people are on the horizon.

29. THURSDAY. Mixed. A spur-of-the-moment extravagance can deplete your savings if you are not careful. Misunderstandings are scattered throughout the day and may be caused by unclear intentions. Double-check what you are hearing before you jump to any conclusions. A business partnership should be avoided until and unless you have all aspects checked out by a reputable lawyer. Even then make sure you read the fine print for yourself. Leos who are organizing a wedding or other celebration should make sure all details are covered to eliminate the risk of confusion and glitches. New hires may be about to receive a posting, perhaps far from home and family.

30. FRIDAY. Stimulating. A passionate approach to life will provide rich and rewarding experiences. A powerful and intimate atmosphere between you and your mate or partner starts the day on a high note and sets the scene for success. You will not want the company of superficial people, and neither will anyone put up with you being less than honest. Business dealings should turn a profit if you are prepared to put in hard work and research. Once you know what you are working with, attracting interested investors will be a satisfying challenge. A course at your local gym is likely to benefit you mentally as well as physically.

DECEMBER

1. SATURDAY. Cautious. Money worries could cause you to take a closer look at your lifestyle and spending habits in an attempt to cut costs. Just be careful that you don't go too far the other way, coming up with a very lean budget that will be too hard to maintain. Curb your excesses and you will find a healthy balance that allows you to have fun while you are saving. Children may be rebellious and need some discipline, but don't stifle their creativity. A risky business venture can attract not only your interest but many other people's as well. Don't let your competitive spirit take you past the point of no return. If you miss out, take it as an omen that the deal wasn't right for you.

2. SUNDAY. Significant. A misunderstanding with your intimate partner may cause you to reassess your values. You might feel you are being confronted from all angles. Instead of casting blame, take a long, hard look at yourself. Social aspirations and a desire to bring about improvements can push you to take a public position and then actually do something about it. Joint assets may become a bone of contention between you and your mate or partner, whether loving or business. The only way around the problem is for both of you to give a little and find a workable compromise. Leo gamblers could make a million or lose a million, so watch out.

3. MONDAY. Hectic. A busy schedule could give you reason to rush, but the faster you go the more mistakes you may make. Remember that the race is not always to the swift. If you are going to be in the car a lot, take along a bottle of water as well as good music to calm your nerves and help pass the time. A rift between you and your lover can be healed now. You might want to plan to get away for a romantic break that will further rejuvenate the loving relationship between you. You are likely to be the life of any party and will have enough invitations to keep you out every night for the next month. However, keep tabs on your energy level right now, aiming to maintain a balance for your own well-being.

4. TUESDAY. Motivating. Start the day with a thorough review of paperwork. Clutter will result in important letters, reports, or phone numbers being lost and time-consuming searches for them later on. Once you have cleared the decks, everything else will fall easily into place. You might even discover a bill that is due, allowing you to pay it before late fees accumulate. A fascination for mysticism could lead you to start a course in esoteric arts. Your mind will be easily sidetracked, so keep a list of all that you have to do and you should manage to get most of them done. A dance class could be just the thing to get you and your partner out in the evening, sharing the movement and rhythm.

5. WEDNESDAY. Loving. Venus, the planet that rules love and indulgence, moves into Scorpio and your sector of home and family today. As a result you will want to beautify your home and delight your loved ones. Harmony will only be gained by give-and-take. Negotiations to find that fine line of domestic bliss should go smoothly. Just be careful to avoid overindulgence. It is fine to enjoy life's pleasures, but too much will make you soft as well as adding to your outstanding debts. Make this 25-day period a happy one but don't let it leave you broke at the end of it. A friend may ask you to go into partnership as a way of raising investment cash, and it may be the best move you ever make. Think long-term.

6. THURSDAY. Active. Memories of festive family traditions playing in you head, you may be inspired to change plans for this year's celebrations. You may have to accommodate the customs of a foreign culture due to someone new in the family. This will call for compromise on both sides. Renovators in the middle of a major job might start to worry whether the job will ever be finished and whether it will suit your timetable. Ask a friend who has had similar experience for advice on how to hurry them up without making them go slower, which unfortunately can happen. If you receive an offer for a preapproved credit card in the mail, do not accept it just to enable you to go over budget on presents that you really can't afford. Eventually you will have to pay in full.

7. FRIDAY. Average. Waking up with a headache can make you regret excesses of last night. Although it may be hard to get out of bed, the day calls. Once you have had a shower and a cup of coffee you will be back in the land of the living. If a business deal developed complications over the last week or so, contact a legal adviser to ascertain your best course of action. There may be a hidden agenda that only a trained eye will pick up. A love affair can start to deepen even if you are unsure of your partner's level of commitment. The problem lies in the area of trust, and as a Leo you need to work on your own ability to trust. In return, your potential partner needs to learn to trust you.

8. SATURDAY. Expressive. Today the Moon joins the Sun, Mercury, Jupiter, and Pluto in Sagittarius, all in your sector of fun and creativity. Friends are a very important part of your life at the moment. You could be involved in organizing a large bon voyage party, a wedding gathering, or a child's end-of-year concert. An intrigue among friends might be the hot topic, with the gossip starting to take on a life of its own. Your enjoyment of pranks could get you in trouble if you don't tone them down. You could even be forced to pay a fine that will lighten your wallet just when you need every cent. Start planning your next vacation now so that you have plenty of time to pay for it.

9. SUNDAY. Optimistic. The New Moon in Sagittarius starts a new monthly cycle, making this a positive time to start a personal project, sign up for a course of study, or begin wedding plans. Leos who are feeling ready to start a family should not hesitate. An urge to cut loose and get out of a rut could make you think about changing your current job or profession. This is an excellent time to get out to the mall and finish your Christmas shopping before everything gets picked over. You could be the lucky shopper who gets a very special bargain. You may feel a little jealous of a friend or lover, but the feeling is unfounded and won't last long.

10. MONDAY. Sensitive. If Leo pride gets the better of you, you might end up taking on more than you can possibly manage. Stop playing games with yourself and ask a friend or family member to give you a hand. Before you know it, you will be enjoying yourself again. You may do better working behind the scenes, giving you space to think about your feelings without being influenced by other people. Stay off the roads as much as possible. Road rage and speeding are a high probability, causing danger to all. An early morning argument with your lover can bother you all day unless you send a message of reconciliation, making the rest of the day bright and sunny for both of you.

11. TUESDAY. Opportune. A sideline business operated from your home might start to look like becoming your main job. While you are still balancing two jobs, it would be wise to see an accountant and find out how you can limit your taxes. Also ask about the pros and cons of incorporating your business. An accident or a close call can make you think more about your future and change the way you look at your everyday habits. Leo smokers or drinkers might decide to give up and go on a health kick. This is a good day for cleaning out closets and drawers and getting rid of old junk. Or you may focus on handicrafts and create interesting and inexpensive presents.

12. WEDNESDAY. Cautious. Welcome news of a lover or relative who is far from home will cheer up your day and vanquish doubts that were lurking in the back of your head. People around you are likely to seem more reserved, leaving you unsure of exactly what you should be doing. Your boss might be overly critical and stifle your initiative as a result. However, if you take things slow and steady you should come out all right. Work on upgrading your home security in preparation for the holiday period. It will put your mind to rest knowing that your valuables are safe, wherever you are. The same goes for your pet. Forget the cost of boarding since you would not be able to relax unless you know the dear animal is being well looked after.

13. THURSDAY. Hectic. The pace is always busy at this time of year, but today there are all sorts of controversies that complicate even the simplest tasks. Gaining cooperation from those around you might be almost impossible. You will probably have to take matters into your own hands to get anything done. Organizing a social function can become harder when you are confronted with rules and regulations on the use of alcohol, time limits on noise, and so on. Check these out before picking the venue. Rivalry between you and a friend over a potential lover could get so underhanded that you decide to drop out of the contest. You might be surprised at the outcome once you no longer wish to play.

14. FRIDAY. Tantalizing. Dreams and fantasies can interrupt your night's sleep and leave you feeling dazed and confused at daybreak. A leisurely shower or bath and then a strong cup of coffee should have you feeling fresh as a daisy. However the fantasies are likely to linger all day, coming to mind in the most stressful situations. Be very careful if you are tempted to start stretching the truth. You may be caught in a little lie and left with egg on your face. Negotiations and contracts could be put on hold and start to look like they may collapse altogether unless you act quickly. You and your mate or partner could end up in an argument if you drink too much tonight, so try to be moderate.

15. SATURDAY. Stimulating. A group of friends may invite you to join in a risky investment that has the potential to be very profitable if all goes well. Do your own homework on the deal before making a decision. Go with your good Leo instincts rather than what others tell you. Then you won't end up feeling railroaded if things don't work out. A love affair might be so intense that you struggle with feelings of possessiveness when you are out together with friends. If you find yourself wanting to stay home more and more to avoid these situations, examine your ability and willingness to trust others. Talk to your mate or partner honestly and they are likely to put your mind and heart at ease.

16. SUNDAY. Exciting. A family member may be about to receive a windfall that will enable you to invest in a home of your own. When you shop around for the best offers in mortgages, you might find that the best deal isn't with a bank. Your mother or aunt has some good advice for you if you take the time to listen. However, you could be so excited about a social event that you don't have time to listen to anyone. Be careful not to become dogmatic, closing your mind to the many opportunities available in the present climate. A meeting with a stranger can set the sparks flying for a night of passion, but be prepared for the possibility that the affair may end as suddenly and quickly as it starts.

17. MONDAY. Extraordinary. The atmosphere surrounding you may seem quite unstable, with all sorts of changes going on around you. Fortunately once you start to accommodate these changes some extraordinary things will happen. Missing someone close can be very painful, but there is the likelihood that this will cause your latent psychic abilities to make themselves known to you. It is a good time to look inward for guidance from your higher self. Meditation will help open the channels. If you just ask yourself a question before going to bed, in the morning the answer should become clear. You can rely on your good Leo intuition.

18. TUESDAY. Fruitful. A contract could come through and give you cause for celebrating. Your mate or partner may book a suite in a luxury resort as a way of making this time special in your hall of memories. Leo students and parents of students may attend an award night and be proud of the recognition for excellence. Living with a roommate makes a lot of sense on a financial level, but when it comes down to living with another human being there can be a lot to get annoyed about. Treat it as a lesson in tolerance and you should survive the experience unscathed. A company conference may mean spending a couple of days out of state. Take along your loved one and enjoy exploring the main attractions.

19. WEDNESDAY. Expansive. Leos should be on the job today with lots of enthusiasm and an eye to fulfilling a dream. If opportunities open up for a promotion within your company, do not hesitate to put your name in for it. Unless you aim high you won't get there. A position of team leader could come your way and suit you perfectly. Don't let shyness or lack of confidence hold you back. Partnered Leos may have a problem at home due to being absent often. You might be turning into a workaholic, so try to add balance to your life. Travel for work is also indicated. You might even be sent overseas to take charge of a distant branch office.

20. THURSDAY. Intense. Providing you really get involved in whatever you are doing, the results should be quite powerful. You may be repairing something that has broken down, such as an automobile or appliance, or it can be a situation which has broken down and needs a radical overhaul if it is to be salvaged. Other people can seem unreasonable, putting you in a position where you have to defend your right to be an individual. Colleagues at work can be very supportive, however. Leos who are in a leadership position might be voted the favorite boss in the workplace. This will give you an edge with your employer and maybe even lead to a raise or a promotion.

21. FRIDAY. Strenuous. Getting a block of time to yourself may be nearly impossible right now. Social engagements, overtime at work, doctors or dentist's appointments, and sport commitments might take up all of your time, leaving hardly any for eating and sleeping. If you put a time management plan into action, you will be surprised how the wasted minutes can add up to hours. Do this and you can finally get on top of everything. A loved one is depending on you to help them, so make sure not to overlook this commitment in your rush to get everything done. Traffic is likely to be backed up. Give yourself plenty of time to get to your destination and you won't be late. Take home a bottle of champagne to celebrate the end of the work week.

22. SATURDAY. Constructive. From now until January 20 next year the Sun will be visiting Capricorn and will shine its light on your solar sixth house, which rules work and health. The Sun in this position gives you added strength, so your energy level should be high. Leos who have been ill should start to recuperate now. If outside commitments are infringing on your time with the people you love, especially your lover, put your foot down and make changes so that you do not miss out on close and loving relationships. You and your mate or partner should focus on a common interest such as a sport that you can play together, obtaining outside stimulation from friendships and shared interests without having to be apart.

23. SUNDAY. Confrontational. Group projects will be a challenge. If you are trying to collaborate with a group of friends, the best you are likely to achieve is an agreement to disagree. A farewell can turn into an emotional scene as a sense of an ending exaggerates the drama. A personal project could take up a lot of your time and give you much enjoyment in return. If planning a surprise for a child, the fun and expectation can be very uplifting. Because your optimism knows no bounds, plans can escalate out of control and become impractical. Don't let your generous heart rule your logical side. Giving your time or money to a charitable enterprise can be very rewarding.

24. MONDAY. Reassuring. A gift of money may arrive early and make your day. Enjoy some private time at home alone. If possible, get up early in order to finish off small details and last-minute duties in preparation for tomorrow. Friends are likely to drop by and hold you back, but this is a time for sharing and support. One friend in particular may need a heaping measure of help. Leos who are involved in helping those less fortunate might visit the local hospital to talk with people who are alone. Carols by candlelight can be a treat for the whole family, bringing a tear to your eye and a smile to your heart.

25. TUESDAY. Merry Christmas! If entertaining at home you will have no trouble enjoying the company of family members and close friends. No matter how much you love to impress guests with your organization and cooking skill, you might be working so hard all day long that you miss the opening of presents and other moments that can never be repeated. Relax and get everyone to help set the table and serve the meal. Even if it isn't done the way you would prefer, you will be sharing. Take lots of photos to add to your album. The evening should be a time for you to relax. Postpone cleaning up and go out for some fun. A nightclub or casino could bring you luck in money and love.

26. WEDNESDAY. Enterprising. A job behind the scenes may not be what you are looking for but could prove very lucrative. Leos who are involved in volunteer work should find that giving up time to help other people provides a better feeling than anything else you could do. This is a good day to start a personal project. Your creativity is at a peak, and your ability to refine your techniques and procedures is an added extra. If off on a vacation you may spend today shopping and visiting. Set the evening aside for some uninterrupted time with your mate or partner, or maybe catch up on all the news with an old friend via a long-distance phone call.

27. THURSDAY. Surprising. Someone from your past may come back into your life and rekindle your romance. However, you will have to find forgiveness in your heart if your love is going to grow into a meaningful relationship now. Financial matters should be smooth. This is a starred time to work out your budget for the New Year ahead. Staying on top of your current income and expenses will bode well for future savings. Extra hours at work should pay well and will be welcomed as a chance to get ahead after the expense of Christmas. Just don't neglect your love life. Tonight the unattached Leo might meet an attractive stranger who sweeps you off your feet and makes you feel like a million dollars.

28. FRIDAY. Productive. Rewards for your efforts are sure to come your way, boosting your self-worth and net worth. Your responsible and hardworking attitude will be appreciated by all, especially your employer who might be tempted to award you a bonus. This is a favorable time to start a new diet and exercise regime. You are likely to stick to it and achieve good results. A nutritionist can provide advice on what to eat and what not to eat for your particular metabolism and help you maintain a good energy level as well. A business deal can spring a surprise on you, putting you in a position of having to talk fast. If you know the figures and the product you should be well satisfied with the outcome.

29. SATURDAY. Upsetting. You might wake up feeling annoyed and stressed this morning and find the rest of the day follows suit. Double-check all figures regarding a business deal or negotiations of any sort. When you know that your facts and figures are correct, you will have extra confidence if anyone tries to obtain a discount or better terms. You may be so broke after the festive period that you are forced to visit the pawnbroker to cash in one of your valued possessions. Just be sure to think about what you are doing before you let the item go, maybe for good. An encounter with an ex-lover could leave you dazed and confused, which is probably why you are not still an item.

30. SUNDAY. Vibrant. Venus, the planet that rules love and beauty, moves into Sagittarius and your solar house of fun, lovers, and children. This puts you in your element as Venus adds her charisma and attractiveness to your personality. More than one lover could be knocking on your door, and you are likely to be the center of attention wherever you go. Creative projects can get off the ground now. Your interest in a new hobby or project is apt to bring out a hidden talent that you never knew you had. You will enjoy pleasing yourself talking on the phone, surfing the Internet, playing the dating game, or updating your diary about your most recent escapades.

31. MONDAY. Reflective. There is a lot going on today, and different New Year's celebrations for you to choose from. You might prefer to keep to yourself for much of the day. Local entertainment with friends and neighbors can appeal more than the pushing and shoving of a large crowd. If you have to go to work, idle chatter or gossip is the last thing you will feel like listening to. Take your headphones and tune out if you can. Surprisingly, Leos who are telephone salespeople might have a great day, raking in the commissions. This is because your ability to tune into the voice on the other end of the line enables you to strike a chord with their emotions. After a couple of false starts your New Year's celebration should be a big hit.

LEO
NOVEMBER–DECEMBER 2006

November 2006

1. WEDNESDAY. Eventful. Do something out of the ordinary today rather than proceed with the normal everyday routine. Choose an activity that is different, stimulating, and provides a change of pace. Interesting encounters could prove eventful. Leo singles are likely to fall in love, then out of love just as quickly. Systems and methods that have worked well in the past could be outdated and in need of a thorough overhauling. A clash of social plans between you and your mate or partner means that someone may miss out. If you want to keep the domestic peace, you might have to apologize and explain why you are making a certain choice.

2. THURSDAY. Fine. This is a time to forge ahead with all of your dreams and desires. Formulate plans that will be ready for implementation when Mercury moves forward later this month. Furthering your education may be important for Leos seeking to improve career potential. Gaining a formal degree will also increase your worldly knowledge and awareness. Try to steer clear of other people as much as possible. Cooperation is apt to be lacking. If there is any lingering tension with a friend, now is the time to clear the air. Send a casual, humorous e-mail attached with an invitation to share lunch or to go for a drink after work.

3. FRIDAY. Satisfying. Let other people have the benefit of your knowledge and wisdom. Hold a training seminar, workshop, or short-term class. Travel might be on the agenda, perhaps for business or commercial purposes. This should prove worthwhile in terms of profit and pleasure as well as providing a welcome change of scenery and routine. Inspirational people could attract your attention. Just remember that at times first appearances can be deceptive, so proceed with caution. There is a probability that someone may drain your mental and physical energy unless you are discerning with your choice of companions.

4. SATURDAY. Harmonious. Make the most of today's happy atmosphere. This is a favorable time to invite the boss or a close business associate home for dinner or to entertain a small group of interesting people. Be prepared for a couple of minor incidents or mishaps to occur, although this is unlikely to dampen the party spirit. With your creativity enhanced, put this energy to good use by participating in activities that utilize your talents extensively. Relationships could gain a significantly meaningful boost. Leo singles should go out and have fun this evening. Do not be too concerned about finding a potential mate; this person will eventually come to you.

5. SUNDAY. Sensitive. As a Leo you thrive on drama, and that could be the theme of the day. With the Taurus Full Moon occurring in the career sector of your solar chart, an intensity surrounds you that is not usually present. This relates to family matters as well as to employment concerns. Once again don't expect too much cooperation from anyone in your inner circle. If conflict does arise, try to keep detached so that tension evaporates quickly. If you happen to be drawn into the fray, disharmony is likely to be prolonged. An increase in your workload over the next few weeks is probable, but you have the perseverance and tenacity to get through it.

6. MONDAY. Mixed. You could receive disappointing news regarding a social event you have been organizing. There is a possibility that you have overlooked some costs and will now need to scale down decoration or entertainment plans. You need to continually fine-tune your creative and artistic skills. Find a nonphysical pastime or hobby that enables you to use these talents while also promoting relaxation. Adapting new attitudes and approaches to long-term professional goals may be necessary. With yesterday's Full Moon still affecting your emotional responses, possible resistance from colleagues in your work environment can be expected.

7. TUESDAY. Variable. A power struggle or a need to control other people could become a problem for you. If this is occurring quite frequently, consider the underlying cause of your behavior so that changes can be implemented allowing you to handle a similar situation in a different manner in the future. Group interests are preferred, and happy times can be shared. Take a photo of everyone together, then give a copy to each person the next time you meet. Romance is likely to be passionate and fulfilling. Soft lights, gentle music, and a dinner for two can make this evening a pleasurable end to the working day.

8. WEDNESDAY. Profitable. With the festive season fast approaching, now is the time to begin activities that involve self-nurturing. Look after your personal health, hygiene, and physical well-being. Join a fitness club, begin a sensible diet, or increase your daily vitamin intake. Keeping items that are no longer useful is unproductive and encourages excessive clutter. Plan a garage sale to sell all that you can, then donate the rest to a worthwhile charity. Anything worn beyond repair should be discarded. You may need to make some adjustments to your socializing approach so that you are on the same wavelength as a newcomer you recently met.

9. THURSDAY. Imaginative. Retreating behind close doors could appeal to the overly sensitive Leo. Connecting with your imagination aids in bringing creative ideas to a constructive form. If you forget to do something, don't try to cover your tracks. Your forgetfulness will be forgiven quicker if you own up and accept responsibility. Taking orders from other people, especially if you consider them less experienced than you, might be challenging. Don't let this upset you, just do as requested and get the job completed with a minimum of fuss.

10. FRIDAY. Active. Because it is Friday there could be the usual problems as well as additional ones that increase your workload even more. Stay alert if on the road. Lack of concentration by you or another person could result in an accident. New insight into your own emotions, family patterns, and social conditioning can assist in removing negative behavior that no longer fits your lifestyle. This is an opportune time to reveal the outgoing and generous side of your Leo nature. Later in the day pay special attention to personal desires even if this means that family matters have to be put aside for a short period.

11. SATURDAY. Complex. Heed the warning from yesterday concerning road safety. Take care if running errands or driving on the roads. Speeding or parking illegally could be costly. Slowing down and obeying the law will save you money and stress. This is a good time to spend on self-improvement before the social season gets into full swing later this month. New skin care products, a designer outfit, or trendy accessories should lift your spirits. If these types of purchases would lighten the wallet too much, opt for a change of hair color or style to provide a boost. Avoiding emotional intimacy could cause relationship issues.

12. SUNDAY. Subdued. Treat yourself kindly. It may be difficult to bring up any relationship matters with your mate or partner, but make a concentrated effort. Issues troubling you need to be brought out into the open and discussed. If your loved one is unaware of your concerns, behavior patterns will most likely remain the same. With the current celestial energies creating a more somber atmosphere, seek advice from an older person or attend a counseling session with a qualified professional if feeling depressed or unhappy. Help erase negative thoughts by venturing out and having fun at the movies or a live concert.

13. MONDAY. Constructive. Check the mail early today since it might contain a welcome boost to your finances. A realistic, no-nonsense attitude will assist productivity and efficiency. Take charge of a problem or pet project that other people have been unable to resolve or complete. Your ability to use original or uncommon methods to find a solution will certainly be appreciated. Attempt to be open to the views expressed by others, even if you don't understand their reasons. For Leos requiring specific guidance, a counseling session could put you back on the right path.

14. TUESDAY. Distracting. Unexpected events could cause frustrating disruptions. Your dwindling bank account might also be presenting difficulties, especially if money that was earmarked for joint debts or the household account is no longer available. If you exceeded the budget, confess and make arrangements to get money from a new source. Don't risk a negative impact on your excellent reputation and high-class integrity. If you made a promise, stick to your word. Opt for a quiet night at home to release stress and revitalize your body and soul. A long soak in the hot tub should prove invigorating.

15. WEDNESDAY. Buoyant. Your social and diplomatic skills shine under today's lunar influence. If a relative intends to return to school or attend a training course to improve job prospects, offer support and whatever financial assistance you can afford. This is an excellent time to make friendly overtures, forgive past grievances, and make an effort to visit someone who will appreciate your cheery disposition. Be a team player. People are prepared to cooperate and show a united front with you. A cultural event could provide a pleasant distraction from your typical recreational pursuits.

16. THURSDAY. Troubling. Your energy level remains low. No matter how much effort you apply, you could be harboring doubts in the back of your mind about whether people appreciate your work. It might be better to keep these feelings to yourself because colleagues could brand you churlish if you reveal your thoughts to them. Feelings of emotional isolation could limit how you respond to those in your immediate environment. Retaining a sense of humor and continuing to smile will be important. Put up a good front.

Organizing family correspondence should be a high priority. Make plans to purchase suitable equipment for a home office. Once Mercury moves forward tomorrow, you can act on these plans without delay.

17. FRIDAY. Pressured. It may be the end of the week but pressure is still mounting. In a desire to complete more tasks than usual, there is a risk of taxing your physical energy. The love planet Venus now moves into the optimistic sign of Sagittarius and your fifth house of leisure pursuits and romantic adventures. This movement brings lightness to the energy previously surrounding you, especially in the romantic area of your life. Later in the day Mercury goes in direct motion, bringing an end to possible annoying delays or problems associated with all functions of communication.

18. SATURDAY. Cooperative. The Moon enters Scorpio, joining four other planets there in your fourth house. As a result, affairs relating to your domestic environment take on more importance. Communication flows well throughout the morning. If you need to resolve differences or ask favors of a housemate, this is your opportunity to receive a positive response. There is also the likelihood that major changes could occur at home or to the number of people currently living with you. If someone is preparing to move from your home, advertising that you have a room available should lead to a good selection of suitable occupants. Singles in the right place at the right time attract a promising romantic partner.

19. SUNDAY. Favorable. This is not the best time to follow any of your hunches. It would be far better to make decisions or choices based on confirmed facts. Indulge yourself just a little today. Spend time with your family or other people who make you happy. Uranus, the planet related to chaos and the unexpected, is now moving forward in the zodiac. Although you are unlikely to experience this influence on a deep personal level, areas of your life that may have been in low gear could now begin to move forward. Joint business or private financial dealings that were going nowhere may suddenly take off.

20. MONDAY. Successful. Today's New Moon in Scorpio in your fourth house encourages further attention on your home and living conditions. This is an opportune time for Leo home owners or business operators to list a property for sale. New enterprises, especially renovations, begun under this lunar influence are less likely to run into any major difficulties. Your Leo leadership abilities could come to the fore more than usual. This may lead to being promoted to a higher paid position. A boost in status and prestige is another possibility. An honor or recognition from your peers could also be forthcoming. Do what you know is right despite the ease of a shortcut.

21. TUESDAY. Changeable. Many Lions crave excitement today. Add variety to your normal activities to avoid monotony. Running errands, attending meetings, or hosting a gathering could make this a very hectic day. Changes in your home environment require immediate attention to reduce a possible negative impact. A roundtable conference could bring troublesome issues to the surface. Leo parents could find children more bothersome or more untidy than usual. Be proactive and introduce a system where youngsters are rewarded each time you receive help or cooperation from them.

22. WEDNESDAY. Promising. Your nervous temperament could be troubling today. To assist in reducing nerves or restlessness, begin a project that you can work on until it is satisfactorily completed. Guard against taking unnecessary risks that could cause future problems. The Sun is now entering the independent sign of Sagittarius, which is your solar fifth house of romance, children, recreational pursuits, and creative expression. Your ruler, the Sun, is very happy in this particular position, so expect the pace of life to increase. There will be numerous parties and other social occasions to attend over the next few weeks.

23. THURSDAY. Fruitful. Do some serious thinking on this holiday. Consider the benefits of increasing your employment skills through extra training. Sufficient multitasking skills can lead to moving up the corporate ladder and can also provide confidence to strike out in your own business. You will want to be seen and noticed by your friends and family members. If the day is well organized and efficient, you will receive well-deserved compliments. Any tension experienced on the home front could arise from the conflict of career and personal demands, necessitating an adjustment, compromise, or possibly both. Someone you meet for the first time may spark a romantic vibe.

24. FRIDAY. Fortunate. Jupiter, the big planet of good fortune, has now begun a new twelve-month cycle residing in its own sign of Sagittarius in your fifth house of love, fun, and good times. Over the next year even the most serious Leo will want to play more and experience an abundance of pleasurable activities. This planetary energy also enhances your artistic skills and brings out your inner creativity. Promoting your personal interests, participating in special endeavors, and improving the romantic area of life are areas where you should be touched by the luck promised by this exciting new phase.

25. SATURDAY. Spirited. Some Leos may be preparing to walk down the aisle while others could be leaving on a honeymoon or holiday break. Sudden infatuation is possible now. If you are unattached, enjoy the romance but wait awhile before deciding to make a permanent commitment. Bargain hunting should be an enjoyable experience. Begin to plan your purchases for the month ahead. Entertaining situations and developments will be possible, bringing enjoyment and delight. A lunch date with friends or your lover should be pleasant providing that you don't overindulge. A gift or present might be forthcoming.

26. SUNDAY. Exciting. Home and family life should be fairly smooth throughout the day. You are likely to be busy organizing an upcoming social function and activities for family participation. Preparing a candlelight dinner for two is also a favored activity. Go all out this evening to show your mate or partner how good your culinary skills are as well as how much you enjoy putting them on display. A surprise or sudden event could have you jumping for joy, barely able to contain your excitement. A domestic disagreement could occur around lunchtime if you or a family member is unwilling to compromise.

27. MONDAY. Invigorating. You may wake up this morning feeling slightly under par, not ready to face the new working week. If home duties and responsibilities are becoming too much to manage alone, perhaps it is time to organize a duty roster for specific tasks. Leo parents should make sure even the youngest member is given a chore to perform. A bonus or overtime payment is likely to increase joint funds, allowing for a few extra treats. This is a favorable period to ratify or negotiate a contract that will improve the quality of your lifestyle. A special school function could be enjoyable for the entire family.

28. TUESDAY. Unsettling. Take extra care with all communications. It may not be what you say but the tone of your voice that causes confusion. Leos employed as telemarketers or at a collection agency should achieve better results during the morning hours. Later in the day you will need to exert greater effort to obtain the same outcome. If you don't have a budget or savings plan, a lot of time may be wasted trying to find out where your monthly wages go and why you are in the hole. Implement a financial strategy so you can track spending and prevent overextending yourself.

29. WEDNESDAY. Empowering. Be careful with your romantic desires. You could be attracted to or become interested in someone who is not right for you. Financial matters might be causing concern regarding your long-term security. Problems relating to insurance, taxation, or a pension might require urgent input. If you recently made a large expensive purchase, this is a favorable time to obtain comparison quotes for insurance coverage. If you are considering applying for a bank loan, waiting until afternoon should lead to a more favorable response. You could be given more responsibility handling company finances or petty cash.

30. THURSDAY. Auspicious. Trying to control boredom or agitation could test your patience. Live in the moment. This is a good time to actively gather information and facts. This is also a promising period to host a party providing that you don't go overboard with a theme or with catering requirements. You could be fortunate enough to rub shoulders with an important person or with someone who can assist you in achieving personal aspirations. Smooth over any minor disputes with loved ones, and be careful not to make too many new demands. Relax with your significant other this evening and enjoy the romantic vibes.

December 2006

1. FRIDAY. Stimulating. This will be a stimulating day if you venture out and embrace new experiences. Meet up with people who have different point of views or research spiritual philosophies of the sages. A flurry of activity around the home front is likely for Leos who are expecting an influx of weekend guests or casual drop-in visitors. Be cautious about overextending yourself in areas where your efforts may not be fully appreciated. If you are given a supervisory role or position of authority, proceed slowly. Endeavoring to bring about immediate changes could alienate coworkers and associates. A favorite hobby could appeal this evening.

2. SATURDAY. Refreshing. As a Leo you are renowned for original flair, creative talents, and leadership abilities. Expect family members to ask you to take charge of a special upcoming event or gathering. Use the wonderful celestial influences currently prevailing to decide on a theme, decorations, or a menu that will surpass anything you have previously done. This will bring the recognition you deserve. Reading, thinking, and learning about how to improve your work flow should be a priority if you are aiming for praise or a promotion. A reunion with a friend who had faded from your social scene will be exciting, stirring up happy memories from the past.

3. SUNDAY. Guarded. During the next week watch carefully to avoid being drawn into anyone's power play or mind games. Communication with family members and loved ones might be tense and full of misunderstandings. Be careful not to go off on a tangent, which could make the day unproductive and unrewarding. Matters concerning real estate or rental property could require attention. If the lack of personal references is a problem, a friend should be able to provide assistance. Seek the company of people who don't often cross your path but are known to provide stimulating topics of conversation or debate.

4. MONDAY. Complex. Today's Gemini Full Moon accentuates your eleventh house, which is the area of your solar chart that deals with long-term hopes and future aims. Complex issues could evolve, with some of your professional goals requiring immediate attention. There may also be a focus on delegating power, obligations, or authority. Applying concentrated effort can lead to a beneficial change that helps you achieve long-desired aspirations and ambitions. Communication with other people might be more serious and ponderous. Try to keep your thoughts, imagination, and ideas positive. These ought to be creative, finding a new approach to personal relations and work.

5. TUESDAY. Dynamic. There will be an occasion today when you need to be discreet. However, if whatever you see as a problem is not illegal and doesn't harm you personally, it might be best to keep quiet. You are apt to be more sensitive to remarks made by those within your inner circle. Perhaps you are reading more into their comments than what was intended. Just before midnight Mars, the planet of passion and action, moves into freedom-loving Sagittarius, emphasizing love, children, and all activities that you hold dear to your heart. This marks the beginning of a dynamic period when activity and energy can be expanded in the pursuit of love, amusement, or speculative interests.

6. WEDNESDAY. Inspirational. Be prepared to do some basic reevaluation of the important things now happening in your life. This can help you to remove realistic or imagined obstacles that could be hindering your progress. Find a quiet spot where you can read a good novel, concentrate on upcoming events, or just reflect on essential matters concerning your general well-being. A project that is awaiting your creative finishing touch can be completed successfully with a minimum fuss. Your dreams may be trying to get a message through to you, so try to pay attention and write down as much as you remember.

7. THURSDAY. Exhilarating. You are likely to attract more interest from those around you. Go all out to display your abilities, expertise, and strengths. Follow your visions. Leo imagination and inspirational ideas are heightened. Artistic themes should appeal during this period. Set aside time to visit an art gallery or a museum to view the works of the masters. Bright, exuberant colors will fascinate and excite talented Leos employed in a creative field. Uplifting romantic experience is likely, including the possibility of a declaration of love or a marriage proposal. Unusual recreational pursuits could appeal, but do not put yourself in physical jeopardy.

8. FRIDAY. Fulfilling. The emphasis continues to be on creative expression, leisure time, and romance as mischievous Mercury moves into Sagittarius and your fifth house. Optimism is high. The love you shower on other people will come back to you in equal measure. A positive relationship cycle has begun. Communicating to your intimate partner on a deep level should be easier. Activities and endeavors that allow a free expression of your creative flair are favored. As a Leo you know how to party and have a fun time. Over the next few weeks do not turn away from your desire to enjoy yourself in the company of loved ones.

9. SATURDAY. Buoyant. Leo's love of romance is well known, and this is likely to be displayed prominently at this time. Whatever you do or say, do it in the right way. There is never a second chance to make a lasting first impression. Take advantage of any opportunity to become reacquainted with an old hobby or pastime by adopting a fresh approach. Other than some minor snags early this morning or later in the afternoon, relations with your mate or partner should be harmonious and uplifting. If conflict does arise, you can expect an easy resolution without having to make any significant compromises. Social gatherings provide enjoyment.

10. SUNDAY. Invigorating. A new love interest could appear on the scene, but tread carefully. Displaying a pushy or possessive attitude could be a deterrent to just the person you hope to impress. As a Leo you have the ability to see the larger vision in anything planned or attempted today. This is the time to organize upcoming seasonal social functions, birthday parties, or family get-togethers. Even though a special family commitment could be hard work and tricky to arrange, you should be able to overcome any obstacles with ease. Keep menu requirements within the budget and don't forget to cater to the special needs of the older generation.

11. MONDAY. Cautious. Take care if mixing money with friendships. Problems could lead to contentious issues that do not have a quick or easy solution. Also be wary if you intend to borrow or lend any personal possessions. Venus, goddess of love, money, and values, now moves into the dependable and loyal sign of Capricorn and your sixth house. This sector of your solar horoscope deals with employment conditions, work and coworkers, routine, health, service, and harvest. A positive change of attitude toward your health is just what the doctor ordered.

12. TUESDAY. Easygoing. Focus much of your attention on financial matters and the lack of available funds. Even though it is the season to be jolly, you may need to search out less expansive ways to seek pleasure and fun. If celebrating with friends today, split the bill equally. Don't be tempted to generously offer to pay the whole amount since a subsequent shortage of funds could cause embarrassment. During this festive season try not to spend more than you earn. A promised pay increase may be rescinded or may not arrive as quickly as you hoped. If you are owed money, request immediate repayment.

13. WEDNESDAY. Useful. Correspondence and communication may have you overloaded and sinking beneath a pile of paperwork. You might need to put some of your social plans on hold so that you can clear up the backlog before the festive celebrations start in earnest. Try not to intervene in a clash of wills between colleagues. A solution should be found fairly quickly without you being involved. If you haven't organized the annual tasks of sending greeting cards and arranging decorations, now is the time to do so. Don't be tempted to spend too much to entertain a special friend or relative who is visiting from another city.

14. THURSDAY. Relaxing. The day should flow extremely well. New investment chances look worthwhile, possibly producing significant financial gains. Even a speculative venture that you previously doubted could now begin to turn a profit. However, don't be too unrealistic. Keep in mind that small gains are better than none at all. Love and laughter surround you as you roar headlong into the upcoming holiday season. Your creativity is enhanced and can be used to add special touches to party or other festive arrangements. If you are part of a couple, plan a very romantic evening with your significant other.

15. FRIDAY. Successful. Pay close attention to incoming e-mails, phone calls, or messages. Keep a list or you could overlook or misplace something that is important. Other people could act erratically or in a way not expected. This is a favorable period for Leos who are involved in sales or public relations. Organization, negotiation, and discussion should bring beneficial agreements for business or commercial interests. A tricky decision could be necessary this morning regarding finances shared with someone close to you. If you disagree with allocation of joint money, speak up and your point of view will be respected.

16. SATURDAY. Constructive. Hassles on the home front are likely. Waiting for an expected delivery or for guests who fail to show up at the set time will be frustrating, and even more so if no one bothers to contact you with a plausible explanation. You could come across just the right gift or bargain you have been searching for, or an item you never thought you would find. If you are going away over the Christmas break and haven't finalized holiday plans, do so now. An increase of household chores means that you need to handle these quickly and efficiently so that your efforts are not too stressful.

17. SUNDAY. Positive. An enthusiastic and optimistic atmosphere prevails. Aim to get as much holiday preparation done as possible to avoid a last-minute rush out among the festive crowds. A practical approach to gift purchases for coworkers and business associates should produce the best results. Over-the-top presents or funky gadgets may not be appropriate or appreciated. Your home and family take on more importance as you devote time and energy to entertaining loved ones. A gathering of extended family members or an overdue get-together with friends could be a highlight of your festive celebrations.

18. MONDAY. Intense. Emotions are deep and powerful, propelling you to a great deal of passion and intensity. Just try to keep composed throughout the day. A conversation that starts out as an innocent or simple discussion may soon have you all stirred up and emotional. Steer clear of dangerous areas and of people who do not have high moral standards. Repairs and maintenance around the home or office can be successfully carried out. If tasks are complicated, contact a professional rather than attempting to do them yourself. A pastime that offers a stimulating mental challenge is the most suitable activity this evening.

19. TUESDAY. Optimistic. Look forward to a pleasant day with positive experiences and outcomes. This is a perfect time to socialize and to host a gathering. Get on the phone or Internet and invite your favorite companions for an enjoyable evening at your place. If children will be attending, make sure the pantry is well stocked with interesting snacks and healthy goodies. It would be a good idea to have plenty of activities to keep youngsters occupied and under control. The news that a couple who previously split up has reconciled is sure to bring happiness and a sense of relief to many. A promising romantic potential exists for Leo singles.

20. WEDNESDAY. Sparkling. The Sagittarius New Moon this morning in your fifth house brings excellent trends for intimate relationships and love affairs. An improvement in your love life will be a welcome pleasure. Your creative talents and skills are also accentuated. Act on a sense of freedom and adventure to learn, experiment, and explore the unknown. Taking the initiative on the job can display your many capabilities. However, don't allow anyone to pile work on you that is not your area of responsibility. A door that you thought had been closed could now open, offering potential opportunities and future gains.

21. THURSDAY. Distracting. Today's restless atmosphere makes concentrating difficult. To add to the stress and pressure, there may be some unsettling problems at work that require an immediate solution. Discussions with colleagues, employees, or your employer could be productive, leading to positive changes. Leos starting a new exercise program should plan on progressing slowly. It is now too late to lose those extra pounds in time for the festive season, so take a sensible approach. If you are involved in a physical contest or activity, make sure you respect your limits so that you avoid overexertion that would result in strain or muscle injury.

22. FRIDAY. Interesting. The Sun, the ruler of your sign, has now moved into ambitious Capricorn and your sixth house of employment aims and health interests. As a result a more serious attitude will begin to envelop Leos. Expect trust and loyalty from your colleagues and associates. You are now more determined than ever to resolve ongoing problems in the work environment. Taking care of yourself and loved ones could keep you busier than usual. Resume your exercise program, perhaps by renewing an expired gym membership. An emergency on the job could necessitate changing evening social arrangements at the last minute.

23. SATURDAY. Exciting. With so much excess energy, you are in danger of going to extremes and causing yourself injury. Maintain your normal exercise program and limit strenuous physical activities. Devote time and effort to last-minute festive preparations. Although it may prove challenging to please everyone in the family, you will have fun trying to do so. Just don't run yourself ragged. Loved ones and friends will have to become reconciled to the fact that you cannot do everything that is asked of you now. An invitation to attend an exclusive party or dinner at a fancy restaurant will lead to a flurry of activity as you decide what outfit will suit the occasion and especially what jewelry to wear.

24. SUNDAY. Satisfactory. This morning is not a good time to work with other people. If doing so is unavoidable, at least try to stay out of disputes. By the afternoon negative influences should have passed and you can throw yourself into ongoing activities. If you are playing host tomorrow, take extra care to ensure that you have all you need for catering purposes. Going out this evening with loved ones should give a special meaning to the festive season. The current influences warn you not to take risks. You are in an accident-prone phase, so walk but don't run, especially if out in wet or icy weather.

25. MONDAY. Merry Christmas! Intense communications with loved ones early in the day include a wide range of emotions, from passion to anger or frustration. Whatever you are feeling will be released, whether negative or positive. This special day is not a good time to bring any disputes out into the open. An argument could erupt, or you might hear things that are not to your liking. By this evening you will be tired and exhausted from all the hustle and bustle of organizing the festive celebrations. It is time to relax and enjoy yourself. Your hard work will pay off, and everyone should experience a joyful and happy occasion.

26. TUESDAY. Manageable. The festive atmosphere continues throughout the morning. While everyone remains in good humor, this is the time to ask for help in clearing away the remnants of yesterday's activities. Don't be a martyr and do it all alone. Later in the day when tiredness descends, irritability and grumpiness might surface. Realizing how much money you have actually spent on gifts, socializing, and catering could cause concern with the person who shares your finances. If you are intent on venturing out this evening, it would be advisable to take it easy and not get caught up with the holiday crowds.

27. WEDNESDAY. Constructive. After a month of romance and increased artistic expression, the energy is now undergoing a change. With Mercury moving into practical Capricorn and your sixth house of employment conditions, you should now begin to work longer and harder. This will bring you closer to cherished goals. An opportunity now exists to review an old practice, pattern of behavior, or negative attitude. Once you realize how easy it is to slip back into former habits, you can work on bringing about positive changes. Someone is unlikely to see your point of view, which could be a clash of egos. You may just have to agree to disagree.

28. THURSDAY. Spirited. If still on a holiday break you could decide to look for a stimulating new pastime to occupy your time and offer relaxation. Metaphysical studies or alternative therapies may be topics of interest if you are seeking to increase or gain knowledge or wisdom. Organizing a future travel itinerary or searching the Web for interesting vacation destinations could appeal to Leos who are considering an overseas journey. An unusual development or situation could call for a quick change of plans. A social invitation received now may be too good to refuse. Someone from a distance might attract the attention of the unattached tonight.

29. FRIDAY. Accomplished. Even though it is the last day of the working week for many Leos, business and professional interests take on increased importance. Adopt a practical approach if asked to take part in a new business idea or venture. Check all the accounts and seek outside advice to ensure that it is a viable proposition. An interview for a promotion or new position within your company should proceed well for the career-minded Leo. Something quite unexpected could delight you and also bring financial rewards. Give yourself a special treat, or take the family out to a favorite restaurant so you can have a night off from chores.

30. SATURDAY. Confusing. Mixed trends exist throughout most of the day. The current confusing influences warn against making important decisions or choices. Your judgment may be clouded. If you tend to daydream, use this energy creatively. Dream up a fantasy theme or make unusual decorations for your New Year's celebration. An older person may be feeling left out of social activities or could be in a despondent mood. Do your best to cheer them up by involving them in your plans. Be firm when dealing with a teenager. Giving into a youngster's whim now might lead to more problems at a later date.

31. SUNDAY. Encouraging. Misunderstandings are foreseen with a friend or someone else you usually agree with. If it is not a major concern it may be better to overlook the dispute and move on. If you are booked for a heavy social night, try to rest this afternoon to restore your vitality. Then you should have plenty of energy for this evening's busy social agenda. This is an opportune day to set your sights high. Concentrate on hopes, wishes, and future goals. If you haven't made New Year's resolutions, give some thought to what you hope to achieve in 2007. Arrange transportation to and from your destination so you can relax and have a good time late into the evening.

LIVE PSYCHICS on Your Cell Phone!!!!

Find Your True Love, Romance, Happiness!

Is there money in your future?

Get all of you questions answered NOW!

Your FUTURE could be only a Text Message away!

Text PATH to 27777

Text: PATH to 27777
From your Cell Phone
.99 - $1.99 per message received 18+

Join The Party, It Never Ends!
See what's happenin' with the GIRLS
And maybe meet some guys TOO!

1-900-288-GIRL
4 4 7 5

$3.49/min 18+

WHAT DOES YOUR FUTURE HOLD?

DISCOVER IT IN *ASTROANALYSIS*—

COMPLETELY REVISED THROUGH THE YEAR 2015, THESE GUIDES INCLUDE COLOR-CODED CHARTS FOR TOTAL ASTROLOGICAL EVALUATION, PLANET TABLES AND CUSP CHARTS, AND STREAMLINED INFORMATION.

ARIES	0-425-17558-8
TAURUS	0-425-17559-6
GEMINI	0-425-17560-X
CANCER	0-425-17561-8
LEO	0-425-17562-6
VIRGO	0-425-17563-4
LIBRA	0-425-17564-2
SCORPIO	0-425-17565-0
SAGITTARIUS	0-425-17566-9
CAPRICORN	0-425-17567-7
AQUARIUS	0-425-17568-5
PISCES	0-425-17569-3

Available wherever books are sold or at penguin.com

FREE PARTY LINE

Make new friends, have fun, share idea's never be bored this party never stops! And best of all it's FREE!

775-533-6900

Never Any Charges! Call Now!

Only Regular Low Long Distance rates apply where applicable

Text Chat Party

Just text the word JOY to 85000 from your cell phone, and connect with new friends instantly!

Pro Chatters Inc. .99 - $1.99 per message received 18+

Star of Animal Planet's "Pet Psychic"

SONYA FITZPATRICK THE PET PSYCHIC

She can talk to the animals.
Read their minds.
Diagnose their problems.
Heal their illnesses.
Find them when they're lost.
And offer comfort from
beyond the grave.
This is her story—and the remarkable
success stories of her "clients."

*Includes Sonya's 7 simple steps to
communicating with pets
Plus—practical information on care and
feeding, emergency preparedness, illness, moving,
and introducing new pets into the household.*

0-425-19414-0

Available wherever books are sold or at
penguin.com

B096

HOROSCOPE DATING

Let the stars help you find the perfect MATCH

CAPRICORN

Characteristics building, using, organizing, achieving, ordering, climbing

Dec. 22 to Jan. 19

TEXT 'MATCH CAPRICORN' to number '46898'

AQUARIUS

Characteristics liberating, knowing, reforming, innovating, researching

Jan. 20 to Feb. 18

TEXT 'MATCH AQUARIUS' to number '46898'

PISCES

Characteristics accepting, inspiring, loving, fantasizing, visualizing

Feb. 19 to Mar. 20

TEXT 'MATCH PISCES' to number '46898'

ARIES
Characteristics independence, pioneering, fighting, acting, leading

Mar. 21 to Apr. 19

TEXT 'MATCH ARIES' to number '46898'

TAURUS

Characteristics producing, possessing, enjoying, having, maintaining

Apr. 20 to May. 20

TEXT 'MATCH TAURUS' to number '46898'

GEMINI

Characteristics thinking, communicating, learning, amusing, trading

May 21 to Jun. 21

TEXT 'MATCH GEMINI' to number '46898'

CANCER

Characteristics protecting, feeling, dreaming, securing, responding

Jun. 22 to Jul. 22

TEXT 'MATCH CANCER' to number '46898'

LEO

Characteristics ruling, respecting, teaching, playing, giving

Jul. 23 to Aug. 22

TEXT 'MATCH LEO' to number '46898'

VIRGO

Characteristics improving, working, serving, cleaning, studying

Aug. 23 to Sept. 22

TEXT 'MATCH VIRGO' to number '46898'

LIBRA

Characteristics pleasing, socializing, balancing, relating

Sept. 23 to Oct. 23

TEXT 'MATCH LIBRA' to number '46898'

SCORPIO

Characteristics concealing, controlling, influencing, transforming, dealing

Oct. 24 to Nov. 21

TEXT 'MATCH SCORPIO' to number '46898'

SAGITTARIUS

Characteristics seeking, exploring, travelling, understanding, believing

Nov. 22 to Dec. 21

TEXT 'MATCH SAGITTARIUS' to number '46898'

HOW HOROSCOPE DATING WORKS
TEXT: MATCH + YOUR SIGN to 46898
and the database using both Western and Chinese astrology will find and connect you to your best Match.
71% MATCH RESULT GUARANTEED!!!

By using this text chat service, you confirm you are 18 years of age or older and accept the terms of use at http://mobdesk.com. You are billed at **0.99** per message received (+ default wireless charges). To opt-out of the service send **STOP** to 46898.

Now in paperback from Berkley

Beyond These Four Walls
Diary of a Psychic Medium
by MaryRose Occhino

The extraordinary memoir from the "remarkably gifted medium"* who has helped many with their struggles—and faced her own as well.

Born to a family of "intuitive" women, MaryRose Occhino has used her "celestial whispers" to open the minds and hearts of people seeking a connection with those who have passed on. Then, at the age of thirty-nine, she was diagnosed with multiple sclerosis and forced to face her own hard times. Now she tells her fascinating story—of learning to see beyond the walls of this world, while making the most of life in the here and now.

"SENSITIVE, CARING, HUMOROUS AND ACCURATE, SHE IS AMONG THE VERY BEST MEDIUMS IN THE WORLD."
—GARY E. SCHWARTZ, PH.D.,
AUTHOR OF THE AFTERLIFE EXPERIMENTS

0-425-20021-3

Available wherever books are sold or at penguin.com

FREE LOVE READING

3 Minutes Free!
1-800-710-3511

Powerful Love Psychics. Gifted & caring, waiting to provide you with FREE answers for love, relationships, lost love, passions, romance, fortune, destiny & more!

CALL NOW OR VISIT:
www.AskNow.com

18+ ENT. PURPOSES ONLY. CALL FOR DETAILS.

MOTHER MYRIAM

Are you a good match?

Authentic Psychic Readings by Phone

PSYCHIC SOURCE®
insights for life

PsychicSource.com

Call Now 1.866.296.7215

MC4204

FOR ENTERTAINMENT ONLY. 18+

As seen on CBS's "Crossing Over"
John Edward
One Last Time

A Psychic Medium Speaks to Those We Have Loved and Lost

His television appearances have made millions of people believe in the afterlife—and in his ability to reach it.

Now Edward's many fans can read his remarkable true story and compelling accounts of his most important readings.

Edward empowers readers to tune in to their own psychic abilities, to read and understand signs of spiritual contact they may be experiencing every day without even knowing it.

"Compelling...poignant."
—Publishers Weekly

0-425-16692-9

Available wherever books are sold or at penguin.com

Cell Phone Psychics

Horoscopes to Your Cell Phone

Send a text message with your date of birth and get your personalized daily horoscope via text message to your cell phone every day for only $1.99 for a week!
Just Text SUPER and your birthdate to 82020
If your birthdate is Feb. 15 1968
your message should look like this
SUPER02.15.68 and be sent to **82020**

Text YOUR Message to a LIVE PSYCHIC

Send a Text message to one of our LIVE Psychics from your cell phone any time, anywhere Just text the word ISEE to 82020 and get the answer to that important question!

Dating - Just Text DATE to 82020
to find that "Special Someone" right on your cell phone!

Chat - Just Text CHAT to 82020
Make new friends, have fun stay connected!

Live Text services are billed to your cell phone account at a rate of $1.99 per answer message and .99c per request message. Horoscope service is billed at $1.99 for a weekly subscription with daily message delivery
Chat and Dating Svces are billed at .99c per message.
All services do not include your normal messaging or bandwidth fees from your carrier
Compatable with AT&T, Cingular, Sprint, Verizon & Nextel

CelebrityPsychic.com

IRENE HUGHES
America's Most Accurate Psychic
AS SEEN ON TV

1-800-279-2775
as low as $2.79/min

Sister LOVE LOVE PSYCHICS

1-800-611-4197
as low as $2.79/min

Sakki Tarot.com
Discover. Illuminate. Create.

1-800-736-1768
as low as $2.79/min

Kabbalah Now
Learn the secrets of the world's oldest & most powerful wisdom

1-800-627-0879
as low as $2.79/min

LINDA GEORGIAN
AS SEEN ON TV

Hosted the Psychic Friends Network* with Dionne Warwick*

★ ★ ★ ★

Voted Americas Top Psychic

1-800-251-1256
as low as $2.79/min

*MS. GEORGIAN IS NO LONGER AFFILIATED OR ASSOCIATED WITH PSYCHIC FRIENDS NETWORK OR DIONNE WARWICK

BARBARA NORCROSS ♥
THE PALM BEACH PSYCHIC

Psychic Advisor to the Rich & Famous

1-800-424-8007
as low as $2.79/min

US PAT. 5,802,156 • THE ZODIAC GROUP, INC. • MUST BE 18 YEARS + • FOR ENTERTAINMENT ONLY